Introduction to SPSS® in Psychology

Visit the *Introduction to SPSS in Psychology, Fourth Edition* Companion Website at **www.pearsoned.co.uk/howitt** to find valuable **student** learning material including:

- Chapter overviews to introduce and give a feel for topics covered in the chapter
- Additional data sets with exercises for further practice and self testing
- An online glossary to explain key terms
- Interactive online flashcards that allow you to check definitions against the key terms during revision

- A guide to using Microsoft Excel for doing statistical analyses
- A guide to statistical computations on the web
- Roadmaps to help students select a test for analysis of data

PEARSON
Education

We work with leading authors to develop the
strongest educational materials in psychology,
bringing cutting-edge thinking and best
learning practice to a global market.

Under a range of well-known imprints, including
Prentice Hall, we craft high quality print and
electronic publications which help readers to understand
and apply their content, whether studying or at work.

To find out about the complete range of our
publishing please visit us on the World Wide Web at:
www.pearsoned.co.uk

Introduction to
SPSS® in Psychology
For Version 16 and earlier
Fourth Edition

Dennis Howitt   Loughborough University
Duncan Cramer   Loughborough University

PEARSON

Prentice
Hall

Harlow, England • London • New York • Boston • San Francisco • Toronto • Sydney • Singapore • Hong Kong
Tokyo • Seoul • Taipei • New Delhi • Cape Town • Madrid • Mexico City • Amsterdam • Munich • Paris • Milan

Pearson Education Limited
Edinburgh Gate
Harlow
Essex CM20 2JE
England

and Associated Companies throughout the world

Visit us on the World Wide Web at:
www.pearsoned.co.uk

First published 1997
Second edition published 2000
Revised second edition published 2002
Third edition published 2005
Fourth edition published 2008

ISBN: 978-0-13-205164-4

British Library Cataloguing-in-Publication Data
A catalogue record for this book is available from the British Library

Library of Congress Cataloging-in-Publication Data
Howitt, Dennis.
  Introduction to SPSS(r) in psychology : for version 16 and earlier / Dennis Howitt, Duncan Cramer. — 4th ed.
    p. cm.
  ISBN 978-0-13-205164-4
  1. Psychometrics. 2. SPSS for Windows. 3. Psychometrics—Computer programs. I. Cramer, Duncan, 1948– II. Title.
  BF39.H72 2008
  150.1′5195—dc22

                    2007041688

10 9 8 7 6 5 4 3 2 1
12 11 10 09 08

Typeset in 10/12pt Times Roman by 35
Printed by Ashford Colour Press Ltd., Gosport

The publisher's policy is to use paper manufactured from sustainable forests.

Brief contents

Part 1 Introduction to SPSS   1

Part 2 Descriptive statistics   21

Part 3 Significance testing and basic inferential tests   97

Contents

Part 4   Analysis of variance   157

16   The variance ratio test: Using the *F*-ratio to compare two variances   159

17   Analysis of variance (ANOVA): Introduction to the one-way unrelated or uncorrelated ANOVA   164

18   Analysis of variance for correlated scores or repeated measures   171

Part 5 More advanced correlational statistics — 231

Supporting resources

Visit **www.pearsoned.co.uk/howitt** to find valuable online resources

Companion Website for students

- Chapter overviews to introduce and give a feel for topics covered in the chapter
- Additional data sets with exercises for further practice and self testing
- An online glossary to explain key terms
- Interactive online flashcards that allow you to check definitions against the key terms during revision
- A guide to using Microsoft Excel for doing statistical analyses
- A guide to statistical computations on the web
- Roadmaps to help students select a test for analysis of data

For instructors

- Testbank of testing material

Also: The Companion Website provides the following features:

- Search tool to help locate specific items of content
- E-mail results and profile tools to send results of quizzes to instructors
- Online help and support to assist with website usage and troubleshooting

For more information please contact your local Pearson Education sales representative or visit **www.pearsoned.co.uk/howitt**

Guided tour of the book

Clear overview

Introduces the chapter to give students a feel for the topics covered.

Background details

Outlines the background to each technique discussed in each chapter to encourage a deeper understanding. This includes details of:

- What the technique is;
- When you should and should not use it;
- The data required for the analysis;
- Typical problems to be aware of.

Example

An illustrative example is given of the appropriate sorts of data for each statistical technique. This allows you to work through an example computation before moving on to your own data.

Statistics book link

Refers to coverage of a topic offered within companion volume, *Introduction to Statistics in Psychology*, fourth edition, by the same authors.

Step by step illustrations and screenshots of SPSS

This visually presents the stages of data entry and data analysis to help you gain confidence in the processes and procedures of SPSS.

Interpreting the output

Offers a simple explanation of what the important parts of the output mean. SPSS statistical output is presented exactly as it appears on screen to help you become familiar with it.

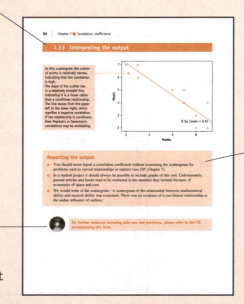

Reporting the output

Explains how you should present output from SPSS.

CD accompanying the book

The CD accompanying the book includes data sets relating to the book, additional data sets, self-test exercises and MCQs.

Guided tour of the accompanying CD

The CD accompanying this book contains a range of resources to help you consolidate and check your understanding of concepts, tests and procedures.

Homepage

When you load your CD into your computer, you will see this homepage. It lists and links to the resources featured on your CD.

Overview

Overview to introduce and give a feel for topics covered in the chapter.

Extra data sets and questions

Extra data sets and questions based on research completed within areas such as Forensic, Health, Clinical and Developmental Psychology. For each data set, you will find questions at three levels of difficulty to allow you to apply your understanding of data analysis.

Roadmaps

Roadmaps to help guide you to the right test to use to analyse a set of data.

Introduction

Statistical Package for the Social Sciences (SPSS) was initially developed in 1965 at Stanford University in California. Since then it has become the leading data analysis package in the field and is available all over the world in universities and elsewhere. It dominates the field. Modern computing developments have allowed it to be used on home computers. Because of its popularity and universality, using SPSS is one of the most readily transferable of all research skills. Once learnt, it can be used virtually anywhere in the world. SPSS is constantly being updated both in terms of the range of statistical techniques covered and the detail of the output.

This book is a stand-alone step-by-step approach to statistical analysis using SPSS for Windows and is applicable to Releases 10 to 16. It is suitable for students and researchers wishing to analyse psychological, sociological, criminological, health and similar data. SPSS does change with time but this book will be helpful to those using earlier releases.

This book updates the third edition of *Introduction to SPSS in Psychology* to cover recent changes in SPSS. Nevertheless, the structure provides the fastest possible access to computerised data analysis using SPSS even when using the most advanced techniques. Each statistical technique is carefully described step-by-step using screenshots of SPSS data analysis and output. The user's attention is focused directly on the screenshots, what each of them signifies, and why they are important. In other words, it is as close as is possible in a textbook to face-to-face individual instruction. Users with little or no previous computer skills will be able to quickly analyse quite complex data and appreciate what the output means.

The chapters have a common pattern. The computer steps (which keys to press) are given in exact sequence. However, this is not the end of any data analysis, and so there are also explanations of how to interpret and report the SPSS output. However, for this new edition we have moved the book forward by providing additional sections that give more extended background on the statistical procedures described. These sections are an extended compact discussion of what the statistical technique is, when it is used, when it is not used, the data requirements for the statistical technique and common problems experienced when using the technique.

The basic structure of the major chapters is:

- A brief bulleted overview of the use of the statistical technique. This will often be sufficient to get a clear idea of where and when to use the techniques.

- A need-to-know account of what the technique is for and what needs to be known in preparation to doing the SPSS analysis. This also gives information about when the technique is used, when it should not be used, the data required for the analysis and typical problems that we know from long experience cause users difficulties.

- An illustrative example is given of the appropriate sorts of data for each statistical technique. These examples allow the user to work through our computations and to gain confidence before moving on to their own data.

- Data entry for a particular statistical analysis is presented visually and explained in adjacent text.

- This is followed by a step-by-step, screenshot-by-screenshot, description of how a particular statistical analysis is done using SPSS for Windows.

- The SPSS statistical output is included exactly as it appears on the monitor screen and in printouts of the analysis. This is crucial – SPSS output can be confusing and unclear at first.

- The key features of the statistical output are highlighted on the output itself together with simple explanations of what the important parts of the output mean – SPSS output is infamous for its overinclusiveness.

- Suggestions are made on reporting the statistical findings in reports, theses and publications. These includes samples of how to describe research findings and present tables clearly.

This book is based on the latest version of SPSS for Windows (that is, Release 16); but remains suitable for Releases 10 to 15 because of its similarity. Notes after this Introduction describe the main differences between these releases. Although SPSS is updated every year or so, usually there is little difficulty in adapting knowledge gained on the older versions to the new version.

Introduction to SPSS in Psychology is an excellent single source for data analysis. It is complete in itself and contains many features not available elsewhere. Unlike other SPSS books, it meets the needs of students and researchers at all levels. However, it is also part of a package of methodology books by the same authors designed to be comprehensive, authoritative and exhaustive. The three volumes in this series are closely tied to each other. The other two are:

- *Introduction to Statistics in Psychology* (2008) (4th edition) (Pearson Education: Harlow): This is a thorough introduction to statistics for all students. It consists of a basic introduction to key psychological statistics and, although maintaining its accessibility to students, it also covers many intermediate and advanced techniques in detail. It contains chapters on topics, such as meta-analysis, which are seldom covered in other statistics texts. Importantly, the structure of the statistics textbook is closely linked to this book. Thus, anyone following a chapter in the statistics book will, where appropriate, find an equivalent chapter in this book with details of how to do the analysis using SPSS. Similarly, anyone using this book will be able to find a detailed account of the technique in the statistics textbook.

- *Introduction to Research Methods in Psychology* (2008) (2nd edition) (Pearson Education: Harlow): This is a major textbook on research methods in psychology. It covers both quantitative and qualitative methods. There are major chapters on report writing, ethics in psychology and searching the literature. All aspects of experimental, field study, survey and questionnaire construction are covered, and guidance is given on qualitative data collection and analysis. There are numerous cross-references to this book and *Introduction to Statistics in Psychology*.

In other words, the three books offer a comprehensive introduction to conducting research in psychology. They may be used independently or in any combination.

Introduction to SPSS in Psychology can be used alongside virtually any statistics text-book to support a wide variety of statistics and practical courses. The range of statistical techniques covered is large and includes the simplest as well as the most important advanced statistical techniques. The variety of techniques described and the relative ease of using SPSS for Windows ensure that this guide can be used at introductory, intermediate and advanced levels of statistics teaching. The structure of the book is such that statistical procedures are described more or less in order of conceptual difficulty. Generally speaking, computing with SPSS is as easy for advanced statistical techniques as it is for simple ones.

Chapter 1 is essential reading, as it explains data entry and basic computer operating. However, the remaining chapters can be used on a stand-alone basis if desired. Users with insufficient time to work chapter-by-chapter through the guide should find enough detail in the relevant chapters to complete an SPSS analysis successfully. Table 1.1, at the end of Chapter 1, states which chapter is most appropriate for which purpose, thereby enabling the reader to move directly to that part of the book.

Those who work steadily through the book will profit by doing so. They will have a much better overview of SPSS computing procedures. For most readers, this is possible in a matter of hours, especially if they have prior knowledge of statistics.

SPSS has an extensive catalogue of statistical procedures – far more than could be included. We have selected those suitable for most purposes when the range of possibilities is likely to confuse the average reader. The quickness and ease of SPSS mean that more advanced users can explore the alternatives by using the menus and dialog boxes. Most users will find our coverage more than sufficient.

The data and statistical analyses carried out in this book correspond almost always to those in the authors' accompanying statistics text, *Introduction to Statistics in Psychology* (2008) (4th edition) (Pearson Education: Harlow). This book is referred to as *ISP*, followed by the corresponding chapter or table number.

Acknowledgements

Authors' acknowledgements

A book is much more than a manuscript thanks to the hard work of numerous talented behind-the-scenes staff. Their work should be credited much more than it ever is. While we cannot mention everyone involved in the production of this book, some are especially significant to us. We will mention these by name though we are more than aware of the contribution of many others in so many different ways.

The design of any book does not simply make a tatty manuscript look good. Andrea Bannuscher did the tasty cover design and Kevin Ancient devised the text design which not only makes the words look good but adds enormously to the organisation of the material and the book's ease of use.

Anyone who has worked with a first-class copy editor will know how much they add and the confidence that authors can feel to be in such good hands. Linda Dhondy lived the nightmare of checking what is a particularly complex manuscript and sorted out the problems efficiently.

Emma Easy and Anita Atkinson were the masterminds overseeing the production process. While their jobs are far too complex for us to understand in detail, whatever we needed them to do they could and whatever they said would happen did with remarkable precision.

Janey Webb, the editor for Psychology, gently and effortlessly cajoled us into developments which greatly benefit the book and was a constant source of ideas. Our vague promises were quickly and seamlessly consolidated into firm commitments. And we fell for it every time! Sarah Busby the editorial assistant, ever bright and breezy, kept us on our toes throughout. Once you load the cover CD on to your computer, you will not fail to be impressed. All of this is done due to the amazing creation and IT skills of Melanie Beard.

We also would like to put on record the debt that we owe Morten Fuglevand and Emma Travis from the previous edition of the book. Not only were they great people to work with but they introduced us to many modern ideas. Morten, deservedly, remains a legend in British publishing.

Finally, the academic community has helped us a great deal by commenting on our material and freely contributing ideas. This was always positive, insightful and well-received. Their involvement is another example of the importance of cooperation in book production. They are:

Dr Liz Connors, Department of Psychology, University of Central Lancashire

Paul Gardner, The School of Psychology, University of St Andrews

Professor Koen Lamberts, Department of Psychology, The University of Warwick

Dr James Smith-Spark, Department of Psychology, London South Bank University

Dr Andrew Stewart, School of Psychological Sciences, The University of Manchester

Dr Richard Trigg, Division of Psychology, Nottingham Trent University

Professor James A. Hampton, Department of Psychology, City University London

Equally valuable were the contributions of the student reviewers:

Chad Shepherd, a psychology student at London South Bank University

Mary Low, a psychology student at University of St Andrews

Our thanks to everyone.

Dennis Howitt and Duncan Cramer

Publisher's acknowledgements

The screenshots in this book and reprinted by permission of SPSS Inc. Screenshots in this book are copyright SPSS Inc. SPSS is a registered trademark and the other product names are registered trademarks of SPSS Inc.

Key differences between SPSS 16 and earlier versions

SPSS 15

There seem to be very few differences between 16 and 15 for the procedures described in this book. Basic tables are no longer available in the Tables procedure so the tables in Chapter 6 are produced with Custom Tables. In the dialog boxes, the OK, Paste, Reset, Cancel and Help options are at the bottom of the box rather than on the right hand side, while the analyses options are on the right hand side rather than the bottom of the box.

SPSS 14

There also seem to be very few differences between 15 and 14. The Graph menu in 14 displays all available options. The procedure for Chart Builder is described in Chapter 2 of this book as it was not available in releases before 14. A slightly alternative procedure is shown in Chapter 4.

SPSS 13

Similarly there seem to be very few differences between 14 and 13. Release 13 does not have Chart Builder which was introduced in 14. In 14 the Properties dialog box of the Chart Editor has separate boxes for Text Style and Text Layout.

SPSS 12

The major differences between 12 and 13 are to 'Compute Variable ...', 'Scatter/Dot ...' and the 'Chart Editor'. Also the plots in the output of 13 are shaded.

In 12 the 'Compute Variable' dialog box has a single 'Functions' box from which options can be chosen. 'Scatter/Dot ...' is called 'Scatter ...', the 'Scatter/Dot' dialog box is called 'Scatterplot' and there is no 'Dot' option.

In 12, to label the slices of a pie diagram and add the percentages of cases in each, double click anywhere in the 'Chart Editor', double click on the pie diagram (to open the 'Properties' dialog box), select 'Data Value Labels' (in the 'Properties' dialog box), select 'Count' in the 'Contents' box, select the red '×' (to put 'Count' in the 'Available' box), select the variable name (e.g. 'Occupation'), select the curved upward arrow (to put 'Occupation' in the 'Contents' box), select 'Percent' and the curved upward arrow (to put 'Percent' in the 'Contents' box), select 'Apply' and then 'Close'.

To fit a regression line to a scatterplot, click on a dot in the chart of the 'Chart Editor' so that the circles in the plot become highlighted, select 'Chart', select 'Add Chart Element', and select 'Fit Line at Total' (which opens the 'Properties' dialog box). Assuming that the 'Fit Line' tab is active, select 'Linear' (this is usually the default) and then 'Close'.

SPSS 11

The major differences between 12 and 11 also apply to 10. They are relatively few. In 11 and 10 variable names cannot begin with a capital letter and are restricted to eight characters. The 'Data' and 'Transform' options are not available in the 'Viewer' or 'Output' window. Some output, such as partial correlation and reliability, is not organised into tables. The 'Chart Editor' works differently. To fit a regression line to a scatterplot, double click anywhere in the scatterplot to open the 'Chart Editor', select 'Chart', select 'Options ...' (which opens the 'Scatterplot Options' dialog box), select 'Total' under 'Fit Line' and then 'OK'.

SPSS 10

Differences between SPSS 10 and SPSS 11 are very minor and hardly noticeable.

Part 1 Introduction to SPSS

1 Basics of SPSS data entry and statistical analysis

Overview

- This chapter gives the basics of operating SPSS on a personal computer. It includes data entry as well as saving files. There will be small variations in how SPSS is accessed from location to location. The basics are fairly obvious and quickly learnt. By following our instructions, you will quickly become familiar with the essential steps in conducting a statistical analysis.

- Unfortunately, there is no gain without some effort in statistics. There are a number of statistical concepts that need to be understood in order to carry out a decent statistical analysis. Each of these is discussed and explained in this chapter. They include score variables versus nominal (category) variables, unrelated versus related designs, descriptive versus inferential statistics and significance testing.

- The chapter provides detailed advice on how to select a statistical technique for the analysis of psychological data.

1.1 What is SPSS?

SPSS Releases 16, 15, 14, 13 and 12 are commonly available on university and college computers. Individuals may still be using earlier versions such as Releases 11 and 10. SPSS is by far the most widely used computer package for statistical analysis throughout the world. As such, learning to use SPSS is a transferable skill which is often a valuable asset in the job market. The program is used at all levels from students to specialist researchers, and in a great many academic fields and practical settings. One big advantage is that once the basics are learnt, SPSS is just as easy to use for simple analyses as for complex ones. The purpose of this introductory chapter is to enable beginners quickly to take advantage of the facilities of SPSS.

Most people nowadays are familiar with the basic operation of personal computers (PCs). The total novice though will not be at too much of a disadvantage since the elements of SPSS are quickly learnt. Users who have familiarity with, say, word processing will find much of this relevant to using SPSS – opening programs, opening files and saving files, for instance. Do not be afraid to experiment.

Since SPSS is commonly used in universities and colleges, many users will require a user name and a password that is obtained from their institution. Documentation is often available on registration at the college or university. If not, such documentation is usually easily available.

SPSS may be found as a shortcut among the on-screen icons or it may be found in the list of programs on Windows. Each institution has its own idiosyncracies as to where SPSS can be found.

This book is based on Release 16 of SPSS. Although it is slightly different from earlier releases, the users of earlier releases will probably not notice the differences as they follow the instructions given in this book.

1.2 To access SPSS

SPSS for Windows is generally accessed using buttons and menus in conjunction with clicks of the mouse. Consequently the quickest way of learning is simply to follow our steps and screenshots on a computer. The following sequence of screenshots is annotated with instructions labelled Step 1, Step 2, etc.

Step 1:

Double left click on the SPSS icon with the mouse if it appears anywhere in the window – otherwise click the Start button to find the list of programs, open the list of programs, and click on SPSS.

Step 2:

This screen eventually appears after a few moments. You could choose any of the options in the window. However, it is best to close down the superimposed menu by clicking on the close-down button. The superimposed menu may not appear as it can be permanently closed down.

1.3 To enter data

Step 1:

The SPSS Data Editor can now be seen unobstructed by the menu. The Data Editor is a spreadsheet into which data are entered. The columns are used to represent different variables, the rows are the different cases (participants) for which you have data.

The columns are variables.

The rows are cases or individuals.

Step 2:

To enter data into SPSS simply highlight one of the cells by clicking on that cell – SPSS always has one cell highlighted.

Step 3:

Then type a number using the computer keyboard. On pressing return on the keyboard or selecting another cell with the mouse this number will be entered into the spreadsheet as shown here. The value 6.00 is the entry for the first row (first case) of the variable VAR00001.

Notice that the variable has been given a standard name automatically. It can be changed – just click on variable name which brings up 'Variable View' (see section 1.8) and make the change.

Step 4:

Correcting errors – simply highlight the cell where the error is using your mouse and type in the correction. On pressing return or moving to another cell, the correction will be entered.

1.4 Moving within a window with the mouse

One can move a row or column at a time by clicking on the arrow-headed buttons near the vertical and horizontal scroll bars.

For major movements, drag the vertical and horizontal scroll bars to move around the page.

The relative position of the scroll bar indicates the relative position in the file.

1.5 Moving within a window using the keyboard keys with the mouse

One can move one page up or down on the screen by pressing the Pg Up and Pg Dn keyboard keys.

The cursor keys on the keyboard move the cursor one space or character according to the direction of the arrow.

1.6 Saving data to disc

Step 1:

By selecting 'File' then 'Save As ...' it is possible to save the data as a file. The saved data file is automatically given the extension '.sav' by SPSS. A distinctive file name is helpful such as 'eg1' so that its contents will be clear.

Step 2:

To choose the place where the data file will be saved, indicate this place in the 'Save in:' box. Use the arrow to browse to the selected location.

1.7 Opening up a data file

Step 1:

To open an existing file, click on 'File', 'Open', 'Data', 'Look in:' if the file is not in the 'Open File' box (which it will be if you have just saved it), type in the file name ('eg1') and then 'Open'.

Step 2:

To open a new file click on 'File', 'New' and then 'Data'. This file can be saved as in Step 1 in section 1.6.

1.8 Using Variable View to create and label variables

Step 1:

Clicking on the 'Variable View' tab at the bottom changes the 'Data View' (the data spreadsheet) screen to one in which information about your variables may be entered conveniently.

Step 2:

This is the 'Variable View' spreadsheet. In this case one variable is already listed. We entered it in Step 3 in section 1.3. But we can rename it and add extra variables quite simply by highlighting the appropriate cell and typing in a new or further variable names.

Change the number of decimals here.

Change the width of the data column here.

Step 3:

There is no practical limit to the length of variable names in Release 12 and later. Earlier releases were limited to 8 characters. Highlight one of the cells under 'Name' and type in a distinct variable name. The rest of the columns are given default values but may be changed. These renamed and newly defined variables will appear on the 'Data View' screen when this is selected. That is, new variables have been created and specified.

This is the number of decimals that will appear on screen – the calculation uses the actual decimal value.

Step 4:

It is important to note that other columns are easily changed too.

Missing values are dealt with in Chapter 34.

Label allows one to give the variable a longer name than is possible using the Variable name column. Simply type in a longer name in the cells. This is no longer so important now that Variable names can be much longer in Release 12 and later.

Values allows one to name the different categories or values of a nominal (category or categorical) variable such as gender. See Step 5 for details. It is recommended that 'Values' are given for all nominal variables.

Step 5:

This 'button' appears. Click on it.

Step 6:

This small window appears. Follow the next few steps. They show how male and female would be entered using the codes 1 for male and 2 for female.

Step 7:

Type in 1 next to 'Value:' and male next to 'Value Label:'.

Then click 'Add'.

Step 8:

This transfers the information into the large box.

Step 9:

Now type in 2 next to 'Value:' and female next to 'Value Label:'.

Then click 'Add'.

Step 10:

This transfers the information into the large box.

Click OK to close the window.

Note: It is bad practice NOT to label values in this way.

1.9 More on Data View

Step 1:

To return to 'Data View' click on this tab at the bottom left of the screen.

Step 2:

This is how 'Data View' looks now. The data can be entered for all of the variables and cases. Remember that the value 5.00 was entered earlier along with the variable names. We can start entering the data in full now.

To enter data, simply highlight a cell, enter the number, then press return. You will be in the next cell down which will be highlighted.

Step 3:

This shows how a typical data spreadsheet appears. Notice how the values for gender are coded as 1.00 and 2.00. It is possible to reveal their value labels instead. Click on 'View' on the task bar at the top.

Step 4:

Then click on 'Value Labels'.

Step 5:

Now the values are given as male and female – just as we coded them in Steps 7 to 8 in section 1.8.

Step 6:

There are many options available to you – including statistical analyses. Some of these options are shown here.

Select 'Data' to insert extra variables, extra cases, select cases and other data manipulations.

Select 'Window' to switch between the data spreadsheet and any output calculated on the data.

Select 'Transform' for a range of things that can be done with the data – such as recoding the values and computing combinations of variables.

Select 'Analyze' to access the full range of statistical calculations that SPSS calculates.

Select 'Graphs' for bar charts, scatterplots and many other graphical representation methods.

1.10   A simple statistical calculation

Step 1:

To calculate the average (i.e. mean) age follow the following stages:

Click 'Analyze'.

Select 'Descriptive Statistics'.

Select 'Descriptives'.

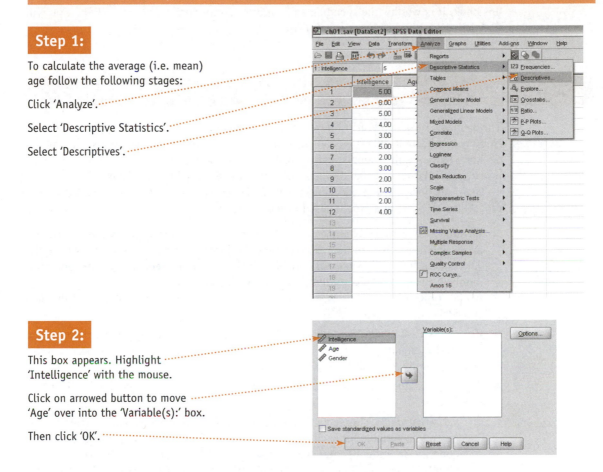

Step 2:

This box appears. Highlight 'Intelligence' with the mouse.

Click on arrowed button to move 'Age' over into the 'Variable(s):' box.

Then click 'OK'.

1.11   The SPSS output

The Data Editor window is replaced in view by the SPSS output.

The first part of output is a list of commands that can be used to run this procedure. These kinds of commands are discussed in Chapters 35–37.

The second part is a table of statistics.

The average (mean) intelligence score is circled here for clarity.

The good news is that anyone who can follow the above steps should have no difficulty in carrying out the vast majority of statistical analyses available on SPSS with the help of this book. It is worthwhile spending an hour or so simply practising with SPSS. You will find that this is the quickest way to learn.

1.12 Basic statistical concepts essential in SPSS analyses

The elements of statistics are quite simple. The problem is in putting the elements together. Nobody can become expert in statistical analysis overnight but, with a very small amount of knowledge, quite sophisticated analyses can be carried out by inexperienced researchers. Mathematical ability has very little role to play in data analysis.

There are just a few basic concepts that the researcher needs to understand before proceeding to SPSS analyses. These include:

- *Variable*   A variable is any concept that can be measured and that varies. Variables are largely inventions of the researcher and they vary enormously from study to study. There are a few fairly standard variables, such as age and gender, that are very commonly measured. Typically, however, the variables used tend to be specific to particular topics of study. Variables appear in SPSS analyses as the columns of the data spreadsheet.

- *Cases*   A case is simply a member of the sample. In psychology a case is usually a person (i.e. an individual participant in the research). Cases (normally) appear in SPSS analyses as the rows of the data spreadsheet.

- *Types of variable*   For all practical purposes, variables can be classified as being of *two* types:

  1. *Score variables*   Some variables are scores. A score is when a numerical value is given to a variable for each case in the sample. This numerical value indicates the quantity or amount of the characteristic (variable) in question. So age is a score variable since the numerical value indicates an increasing amount of the variable age. One could also describe this as quantitative.

  2. *Nominal or category variables*   Some variables are measured by classifying cases into one of several named categories. These are also known as nominal, categorical or category variables. For example, gender has two named categories – male and female. Nationality is another example: English, Welsh, Irish and Scottish are the traditional nationalities of people of Britain. They have *no* numerical implications as such. To say that a person is Scottish is simply to put them into that named category. One could also describe this as qualitative. There is one risk of confusion – categories such as gender are entered into SPSS using different numbers to represent the different categories. For example, the variable gender has two categories – males could be represented by the number 1 and females by the number 2 (or vice versa). The numbers used are arbitrary. It is vital not to confuse these numbers, which merely represent different coding categories with scores. For this reason, it is important to label the different values of nominal variables in full in the SPSS data spreadsheet. This is easily done as was shown on pages 9–10.

- *An alternative classification system:* Sometimes variables are classified as nominal, ordinal, interval and ratio. This is mainly of conceptual interest and of little practical significance in selecting appropriate statistics. Generally speaking, we would advise that this system is ignored because it does not correspond with modern practice. *Nominal* is exactly the same as our classification of nominal (category) data and is important. Of the other three, interval measurement is the most important. Interval measurement is where the steps on the scale of measurement are equal (just as centimetre steps on a rule are equal). Some psychologists are inclined to the view that this scale of measurement should reflect the underlying psychological variable being measured. Unfortunately, it is very difficult (near impossible) to identify whether a psychological measure has equal intervals but, nevertheless, it is a sort of holy grail to them. Others, us included, take the view that so long as the numerical scale on which variables are measured has equal intervals (which is always the case except for nominal (category) data, of course, from this perspective) then there is no problem as it is these numbers on which the statistical calculation is based. However, as a concession, we have mentioned equality of intervals as being desirable from time to time in the text though we (and no one else) can tell you how to establish this. *Ratio* measures have equal intervals and a zero point which means one can calculate ratios and make statements such as one score is twice as big as another score. Unfortunately, yet again, it is impossible to identify any psychological variables which are definitely measured on a ratio measurement scale. Finally, *ordinal* data are data that do not have equal intervals so that they only give the rank order of scores. Since the size of the intervals does not matter for ordinal data, then it is assumed that any psychological score data correspond to the ordinal measurement scale at a minimum. For this reason, some psychologists have advocated the use of non-parametric (distribution-free) statistics for the analysis of much psychological data. The problem is that these techniques are not so powerful or flexible as most statistics.

You will find an extended discussion of ordinal, interval and ratio scales of measurement in Howitt, D. and Cramer, D. (2008) *Introduction to Research Methods in Psychology*. Harlow: Pearson.

- *Importance of deciding the types of variable involved:* It is crucially important to decide for each of your variables whether it is a nominal (category) variable or a score variable. Write a list of your variables and classify each of them if you are a beginner. Eventually you will do it without much thought. The statistical techniques which are appropriate for score variables are often inappropriate for qualitative variables (and vice versa). So, for example, it is appropriate to calculate the mean (numerical average) of any variable which is a score (e.g. average age). On the other hand, it is totally inappropriate to calculate the mean (average) for variables which consist of categories. It would be nonsense to say that the average nationality is 1.7 since nationality is not a score. The problem is that SPSS works with the numbers in the data spreadsheet and does not know whether they are scores or numerical codes for different categories.

- *The difference between descriptive and inferential statistics:* There are two main types of statistical techniques – *descriptive* and *inferential* statistics:

  1. Descriptive statistics chiefly describe the main features of individual variables. So to calculate the average age of a sample of people is an example of descriptive statistics. Counting the number of English people would be another example of descriptive statistics. If one variable is considered at a time this is known as univariate statistics. Bivariate statistics are used when the relationship between two (or more) variables is being described.

2. Inferential statistics is a totally distinct aspect of statistics. It only addresses the question of whether one can rely on the findings based on a *sample* of cases rather than *all* cases. The use of samples is characteristic of nearly all modern research. The problem with samples is that some of them are not similar to the populations from which they are taken. The phrases 'statistically significant' and 'not statistically significant' simply indicate that any trends in the data can be accepted as substantial (i.e. statistically significant) or not substantial enough to rely on (i.e. not statistically significant). A statistically significant finding is one which is unlikely to be the result of chance factors determining the results in a particular sample.

 See Box 1.1 or the authors' accompanying statistics text, *Introduction to Statistics in Psychology* (4th edition, 2008: Pearson Education), for a detailed discussion of the meaning of statistical significance since it is difficult to explain accurately in a few words.

Every descriptive statistic has a corresponding inferential statistic. For example, the correlation coefficient is a descriptive statistic indicating the direction and the strength of the relationship between two variables. Associated with it is the inferential statistic – the significance of the correlation coefficient. The descriptive statistic is important for understanding the trends in the data – the inferential statistic simply deals with the reliance that can be placed on the finding.

■ *Related versus unrelated designs:* Researchers should be aware also of *two* different types of research design – that which uses *related measures* and that which uses *unrelated measures*. Related measures may also be called correlated measures or paired measures. Unrelated measures may also be called uncorrelated measures or unpaired measures. The terms are mostly used when the mean or averages of scores are being compared for two or more samples of data:

– Where the means of a single sample of individuals are compared on two (or more) measures of the same variable (e.g. taken at different points in time) then this is a related measures design.

– Where the means of two quite different samples of participants are compared on a variable, this is an unrelated design.

– Where two (or more) groups of participants have been carefully matched so that *sets* of participants in the two (or more) conditions are similar in some respects, then this is a related design too. In this case, members of each set are treated as if they were the same person. Normally, a researcher would know if the participants were matched in sets because it requires effort on the part of the researcher. For example, the researcher has to decide on what characteristics to match sets, then choose individuals for the sets on the basis of their similarity to these characteristics, and (often) has to allocate participants to the different samples (conditions), especially in experimental research.

The main point of using related designs is that variability due to sampling is reduced.

Almost without exception, the researcher will be using a variety of these techniques with the same data. Fortunately, once the data are entered, in many cases, data analysis may take just a minute or so.

| Box 1.1 | **STATISTICAL SIGNIFICANCE** |

A crucial fact about research is that it is invariably carried out on samples of cases rather than all possible cases. The reasons for this are obvious – economies of time and money. Sometimes it is very difficult to specify what the population is in words (e.g. when one collects a sample of participants from a university restaurant). The realisation that research could be done on relatively small samples was the initial stimulus for many of the statistical techniques described in this book.

For many, statistics = tests of significance. This is a mistaken emphasis since, in terms of importance in any analysis, basic descriptive statistics are the key to understanding one's data. Statistical significance is about a very limited question – is it reasonably safe to generalise from my sample?

In order to do this, in statistics usually we take the information based on the sample(s) of data that we have collected and generalise to the population from which we might assume the sample is drawn. Sometimes one simply takes the sample characteristics and assumes that the population characteristics are the same. On other occasions the sample characteristics have to be slightly modified to obtain the best estimate of the population characteristics. Whichever applies, one then uses these estimated population characteristics to plot the distribution of the characteristics of random samples taken from the estimated population. The most important characteristic that is estimated from samples is the variation of scores in the data.

The distribution of these random samples forms a baseline against which the characteristic of our sample obtained in our research can be compared with what happens under conditions of randomness. If our actual sample characteristic is unlikely to have occurred as a consequence of randomness then we say that it is *statistically significant*. All that we mean is that it is at the extremes of the distribution of random samples. If our sample is very typical of what happens by random sampling, then we say that our sample characteristic is *not statistically significant*.

Often in psychology this is put in terms of accepting the null hypothesis or rejecting the null hypothesis. The null hypothesis is basically that there is no relationship or no difference in our data. Usually the population is specified in terms of the null hypothesis. That is, in our population there is no correlation or in our population there is no difference.

Statistical significance is often set at the 0.05 or 5% significance level. This is purely arbitrary and is not actually set in stone. Sometimes one would require a more stringent significance level (say 0.01 or 1%) and in some circumstances one could relax the criterion a little. However, unless you are very experienced you perhaps ought to stick with the 0.05 or 5% level of statistical significance. This level of significance simply means that there is a 1 in 20 chance of getting a result as extreme as ours by random sampling from the estimated population.

One-tailed significance testing is used when the direction of the trend in the data is predicted on the basis of strong theory or consistent previous research. The prediction is made prior to collecting the data. Such conditions are rarely met in student research and it is recommended that you stick to two-tailed testing.

Finally, notice that the precision of this approach is affected by how representative the sample characteristics are of the population characteristics. One cannot know this, of course. This may help you understand that despite the mathematical sophistication of statistics, in fact it should be used as a guide rather than a seal of approval.

■ *Succinct methods of reporting statistics:* You will probably be aware of the short (succinct) methods used to report statistical findings throughout psychological research reports. We have, of course, used these in this book where we describe how to report research findings. The system is quite simple though there is no universal standard and there will be some variation. Typical of the methods used would be the following:

The hypothesis that students who just work and have no play was supported ($t = 2.10$, $df = 22$, $p < .05$)

What the stuff in brackets says is that the statistical test used was the *t*-test, that the degrees of freedom are 22, and that the significance level is less than .05. In other words, our findings are statistically significant.

■ *Confidence intervals versus point statistics:* Traditionally, psychological statistics use point statistics. These are where the characteristics of the data are defined by a single measure such as the average (mean) score. It is often recommended that confidence intervals should be used instead. Usually in statistics we are trying to estimate the characteristics of the population of scores from a sample of scores. Obviously samples tend to vary from the population characteristics so there is some uncertainty about what the population characteristic will be. Confidence intervals give the most likely range of values in the population and not simply a single value. In this way, the variability of the data is better represented. Chapter 12 discusses confidence intervals in more detail.

1.13 Which test to use

One common heartfelt plea is the demand to know how to choose appropriate statistical techniques for data. Over the years, writers of statistics textbooks have laboured to simplify the process of choosing. This is done largely by producing spreadsheets or tables that indicate what sorts of statistics are appropriate for different sorts of data. If you want that sort of approach then there are a number of web sites that take you through the decision-making process:

http://www.wtc.edu/online/bcanada/choose2.htm
http://www.members.aol.com/statware/pubpage.htm
http://www.socialresearchmethods.net/selstat/ssstart.htm
http://www.graphpad.com/www/Book/Choose.htm
http://www.whichtest.info/

For basic statistics this is probably a useful approach. The difficulty increasingly is that research designs, even for student projects, are very varied and quite complex. Once psychology was almost a purely laboratory-based subject that concentrated on randomised experiments. Psychologists still use this sort of experimentation, but their methods have extended greatly, so extending the demands on their statistical knowledge. Therefore, there is a distinct limit to the extent to which a simple spreadsheet or flow diagram can help the researcher select appropriate statistical analyses.

One fundamental mistake that novice researchers make is to assume that data analysis is primarily driven by statistics. It is more accurate to regard statistics as being largely a tool that adds a little finesse to the basic task of research – to answer the researcher's research questions. Only the researcher can fully know what they want their research to achieve – what issues they want resolving through collecting research data and analysing it. Unless the researcher clearly understands what they want the research to achieve, statistics can be

Table 1.1 Major types of analysis and suggested SPSS procedures

Type/purpose of analysis	Suggested procedures	Chapter
All types of study	Descriptive statistics, tables and diagrams	2–6
Assessing the relationship between two variables	Correlation coefficient	7
	Regression	8
Comparing two sets of scores for differences	Unrelated *t*-test	11
	F-ratio test	16
	Related *t*-test	10
	Unrelated ANOVA	17
	Related ANOVA	18
	Mann–Whitney	14
	Wilcoxon matched pairs	14
Comparing the means of two or more sets of scores	Unrelated ANOVA	17
	Related ANOVA	18
	Multiple comparisons	20
Comparing the means of two or more sets of scores (ANOVAs) while controlling for spurious variables influencing the data	ANCOVA	22
Complex experiments, etc. with *two* or more unrelated independent variables and *one* dependent variable	Two (or more)-way ANOVA	19
■ if you have related *and* unrelated measures	Mixed-design ANOVA	21
■ if other variables may be affecting scores on dependent variable	Analysis of covariance	22
ANOVA designs with several conceptually-relevant dependent variables	MANOVA	23, 24
Eliminating third variables which may be affecting a correlation coefficient	Partial correlation	25
Finding predictors for a score variable	Simple regression	8
	Stepwise multiple regression	28
	Hierarchical multiple regression	29
	Log-linear analysis	30
Finding predictors for a category variable	Multinomial logistic regression	31
	Binomial logistic regression	32
Analysing a questionnaire	Factor analysis	26
	Alpha reliability	27
	Split-half reliability	27
	Recoding	35
	Computing new variables	35–37
Comparing frequency data	Chi-square	13
	Fisher exact test	13
	McNemar test	13
	Kruskal–Wallis	15
	Friedman	15
	Log-linear analysis	30
Coding open-ended data using raters	Kappa coefficient	27

of little help. Very often, when approached for statistical advice, we find that we have to clarify the objectives of the research first of all – and then try to unravel how the researcher thought that the data collected would help them. These are *not* statistical matters but issues to do with developing research ideas and planning appropriate data collection. So the first thing is to list the questions that the data were intended to answer. Too often sight of the purpose of the research is lost in the forest of the research practicalities. The following may help clarify the role of statistics in research:

■ Many of the most important aspects of data analysis need little other than an understanding of averages and frequency counts. These are common in SPSS output. Many research questions may be answered simply by examining differences in means between samples, cross-tabulation tables or scattergrams. It is useful to ask oneself how one could answer the research questions just using such basic approaches. Too often, the complexities of statistical output become the focus of attention, which can lead to confusion about how the data relate to the research question. It is not easy to focus on the research issues and avoid being drawn in unhelpful directions.

■ Statistical analyses are actively constructed by the researcher. There is usually no single correct statistical analysis for any data but probably a range of equally acceptable alternatives. The researcher may need to make many decisions in the process of carrying out data analysis – some of these may have to be carefully justified but others are fairly arbitrary. The researcher is in charge of the data analysis – statistics is the researcher's tool. The analysis should not be a statistical *tour de force*, but led by the questions that necessitated data collection in the first place. There is no excuse – if you collected the data then you ought to know why you collected them.

■ The more research you read in its entirety the better you will understand how statistics can be used in a particular field of research. Very little research is carried out which is not related to other research. What are the typical statistical methods used by researchers in your chosen field? Knowing what techniques are generally used is often the best guide to what ought to be considered.

Table 1.1 gives some insight into the styles of analysis that researchers may wish to apply to their data and what sections of this book describe these statistical techniques in detail.

For further resources including data sets and questions, please refer to the CD accompanying this book.

Part 2 Descriptive statistics

2 Describing variables
Tables and diagrams

Overview

- Tables and diagrams should quickly and effectively communicate important features of one's data. Complexity, for its own sake, is not a helpful characteristic of good tables and diagrams.

- Clear and meaningful tables and diagrams are crucial in statistical analysis and report writing. Virtually every analysis of data uses them in order to allow the distributions of variables to be examined. In this chapter we provide the basic computer techniques to allow the construction of tables and diagrams to describe the distributions of individual variables presented one at a time.

- All tables and diagrams should be clearly titled and labelled. Depending on the table or diagram in question, horizontal and vertical axes should be labelled, bars identified, scales marked and so forth. Great care should be taken with this. Generally speaking, SPSS tables and diagrams require considerable work to make them optimally effective.

- Frequency tables merely count the number of times the different values of the variable appear in the data. A simple example would be a count of the number of males and the number of females in the research. Tables need to be relatively simple and this usually requires that the variable only has a small number of values or, if not, that a number of different values of the variable are grouped together.

- Pie diagrams are effective and simple ways of presenting frequency counts. However, they are only useful when the variable being illustrated has a small number of different values. Pie diagrams are relatively uncommon in publications because they consume space, although they are good for conference presentations and lectures.

- A bar chart can be used in similar circumstances to a pie chart but can cope with a larger number of values of variables before becoming too cluttered. Frequencies of the different values of the variable are represented as physically separated bars of heights that vary according to the frequency in that category.

■ A histogram looks similar to a bar chart but is used for numerical scores rather than categories. Thus the bars in a histogram are presented in size order of the scores that they represent. The bars in histograms are *not* separated by spaces. Often a histogram will need the ranges of scores covered by each bar to be changed in order to maximise the usefulness and clarity of the diagram. This can be done by recoding variables (Chapter 35) but SPSS also allows this to be done in the 'Chart Editor'. Producing charts like these is one of the harder tasks on SPSS.

2.1 What are tables and diagrams?

Now this sounds like a really silly question because we all know what tables and diagrams are, don't we? But simply because we know about these things does not mean that we understand their importance in a good statistical analysis or what makes a good table or diagram. The bottom line is that unless you very carefully study each of your variables using the methods described in this and the next few chapter then you risk failing to identify problems that may undermine the validity of your analysis.

Tables in data analysis are almost always summary tables of key aspects of the data since rarely are the actual data tabulated and reported in statistical analyses – usually because this would be very cumbersome. Tables then report important features of the data such as: (1) frequencies (counts) or the number of participants in the research having a particular characteristic such as the number of males and the number of females in the study; and (2) the average score on a variable in different groups of participants such as the average (known as the mean in statistics) age of the male participants and the female participants in the research.

Diagrams in statistics do much the same sort of job as tables but, of course, they are intended to have greater visual impact. So you are almost certain to be familiar with diagrams that illustrate frequencies of things in data. Pie charts represent the proportion of cases in each category of a variable using proportionate slices of a circle (the pie) (see the examples on pages 32–35). Very much the same sort of thing can be illustrated using bar charts in which each category of a variable is represented by a bar and the frequencies by the heights of the relevant bar (see the examples on page 36). Neither is better than the other except a pie chart shows more quickly the proportions of each category compared to the total number of participants. Histograms are very similar in appearance to bar charts but are used when the categories are actually scores on a particular measure which are ordered from smallest to the largest. Examples of histograms are to be found on pages 37– 38. Technically, a bar chart should have a gap between the bars but a histogram should not since it represents a dimension rather than a number of distinct categories.

Tables do much the same task as diagrams but usually in a more compact form so that more information can be put into the same physical space. They are much more common in professional publications than diagrams. There is probably an infinite variety of possible tables. Table 2.1 on page 26 is quite a simple example of a table. It gives a number of occupations together with the frequencies and percentage frequencies of participants in a study who have a particular type of job.

Although it may be tempting to think that diagrams are preferential to tables this is not the case. Complex data are often difficult to report in a simple diagram and possibly much easier to put into a table. Diagrams tend to be reserved for circumstances where the researcher is trying to communicate the findings of a study quickly and with impact. This is more likely to be the case with spoken presentations of research findings rather than written ones. So diagrams are often better as part of lectures than tables so long as the diagram does not get too complicated.

2.2 When to use tables and diagrams

Tables and diagrams are a vital part of the analysis of data as well as being used to present data. The examination of basic tables and diagrams that describe the data is an important aspect of understanding one's data and familiarising oneself with it. There is nothing unsophisticated in using them – quite the contrary since it is poor statisticians who fail to make good use of them. We will look at a number of circumstances where tables and diagrams can prevent us making basic mistakes.

In terms of practical reports and dissertations, you may well find that tables are generally more useful than diagrams because they can handle complexity better.

2.3 When not to use tables and diagrams

Never use tables and diagrams as a substitute for reporting your research findings in words in the body of a report. To do so is not good because it leaves the reader with the job of interpreting the tables and diagrams, which is really the task of the researcher.

2.4 Data requirements for tables and diagrams

Different sorts of tables and diagrams have different requirements in terms of the variables measured. Bar charts and pie charts are largely used for nominal (category) data that consist of named categories. Histograms are used for score data in which the scores are ordered from the smallest values to the largest on the horizontal axis of the chart.

2.5 Problems in using tables and diagrams

There are many problems, including the following:

- Remember to label clearly all of the important components of tables and diagrams. Not to do so is counterproductive.
- Problems can occur because of rounding errors for percentages such that the total of the percentages for parts of the table or diagram do not add up to 100%. Keep an eye open for this and make reference to it in your report if it risks confusing the reader.

- Technically, the bars of histograms should each have a width proportionate to the range of numbers covered by that bar. SPSS does not do this so the output can be misleading.

- You need to be very careful when a scale of frequencies on a bar chart or histogram does not start at zero. This is because if part of the scale is missing then the reader can get a very wrong impression of the relative frequencies as some bars can look several times taller than others whereas there is little difference in absolute terms. This is one of the 'mistakes' which has led to the suggestion that one can lie using statistics.

- We would recommend that you *never* use tables and diagrams directly copied and pasted from SPSS. For one thing, SPSS tables tend to contain more information than is appropriate to report. But the main reason is that often SPSS tables and diagrams are simply confusing and could be made much better with a little work and thought. Many SPSS diagrams can be modified on SPSS to improve their impact and clarity. For example, there is no point in using coloured slices in a pie chart if it is to be photo-copied in black and white. Such a chart may be very confusing because the shades of gray cannot be deciphered easily.

 You can find out more about tables and diagrams in Chapter 2 of Howitt, D. and Cramer, D. (2008) *Introduction to Statistics in Psychology*. Harlow: Pearson.

2.6 The data to be analysed

SPSS is generally used to summarise raw data but it can use data that have already been summarised such as those shown in Table 2.1 (*ISP*, Table 2.1).

In other words, since the data in Table 2.1 are based on 80 people, the data would occupy 80 cells of one column in the 'Data Editor' window and each occupation would be coded with a separate number, so that nuns might be coded 1, nursery teachers 2 and so on. Thus, one would need 17 rows containing 1 to represent nuns, 3 rows containing 2 to represent nursery teachers and so on. However, it is possible to carry out certain analyses on summarised data provided that we appropriately weight the categories by the number or frequency of cases in them.

Table 2.1   Occupational status of participants in the research expressed as frequencies and percentage frequencies

Occupation	Frequency	Percentage frequency
Nuns	17	21.25
Nursery teachers	3	3.75
Television presenters	23	28.75
Students	20	25.00
Other	17	21.25

2.7 Entering summarised categorical or frequency data by weighting

It seems better practice to define your variables in 'Variable View' of the 'Data Editor' before entering the data in 'Data View' because we can remove the decimal places where they are not necessary. So we always do this first. If you prefer to enter the data first then do so.

For this table we need two columns in 'Data View': one to say what the categories are; the other to give the frequencies for these categories. In 'Variable View' variables are presented as rows.

Step 1:

Select 'Variable View' in 'Data Editor'. Name the first 2 variables 'Occupation' and 'Freq'. Remove the 2 decimal places. Select the right side of the cell for the 'Values' of 'Occupation'.

Step 2:

Label the 5 'Values' of 'Occupation' as shown and as described in Steps 6–10 in section 1.8 in Chapter 1.

Select 'OK'.

Step 3:

Select 'Scale' for this variable and the downward arrow to give the drop-down menu.

Select 'Nominal'.

Step 4:

Select 'Data View'. Enter the data as shown.

Step 5:

Select 'Data' and 'Weight Cases ... '.

Step 6:

Select 'Freq', 'Weight cases by' and the ▶ button to put it in the 'Frequency Variable:' box.

Select 'OK'.

Step 7:

The cases, which are the occupations, are now weighted by the frequencies as shown by the 'Weight On' message in the lower right corner of the Data Editor.

2.8 Percentage frequencies

Step 1:

Select 'Analyze', 'Descriptive Statistics' and 'Frequencies ...'.

Step 2:

Select 'Occupation' and the ▶ button to put 'Occupation' in the 'Variables(s):' box.

Select 'OK'.

2.9   Interpreting the output

Occupation

The first column of this table gives the value of the 5 categories. To change these to labels, which is more meaningful, carry out the following 3 steps and rerun the analysis as in the next section.

		Frequency	Percent	Valid Percent	Cumulative Percent
Valid	1	17	21.3	21.3	21.3
	2	3	3.8	3.8	25.0
	3	23	28.8	28.8	53.8
	4	20	25.0	25.0	78.8
	5	17	21.3	21.3	100.0
	Total	80	100.0	100.0	

2.10   Labelling the values

Step 1:

Select 'Edit' and then 'Options ...'.

Step 2:

Select 'Output Labels'.

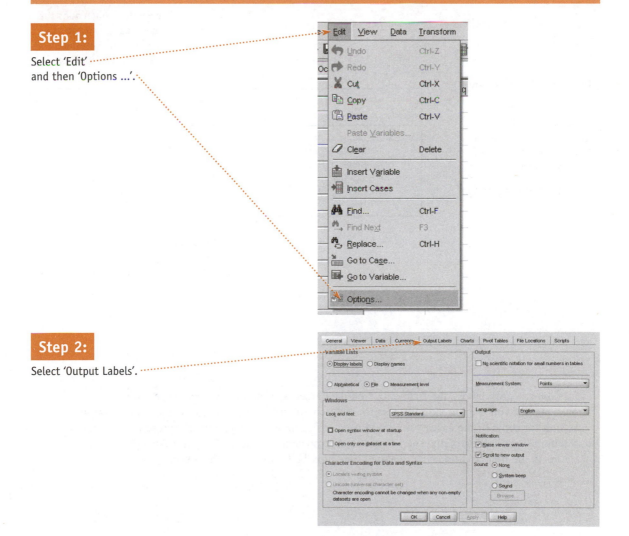

Step 3:

Select the ▼ button below 'Variable values in labels shown as:' and 'Labels' from the drop-down menu.

Select 'OK'.

The fourth column adds the percentages down the table so 25.0 of the cases are nuns or nursery teachers.

The labels are now given.

The second column gives the percentage frequency for each category, including any missing values of which there are none.

So 17 is 21.3% of a total of 80.

Occupation

		Frequency	Percent	Valid Percent	Cumulative Percent
Valid	Nuns	17	21.3	21.3	21.3
	Nursery Teachers	3	3.8	3.8	25.0
	Television Presenters	23	28.8	28.8	53.8
	Students	20	25.0	25.0	78.8
	Other	17	21.3	21.3	100.0
	Total	80	100.0	100.0	

The third column gives the percentage frequency, excluding any missing values. As there are none, these percentages are the same as those in the second column.

Reporting the output

Only the category labels, the frequency and the percentage frequency need be reported, consequently you need to simplify this table if you are going to present it. If the occupation was missing for some of the cases you would need to decide whether you would present percentages including or excluding them. There is no need to present both sets of figures. Also omit the term 'Valid' in the first column as its meaning may only be familiar to SPSS users.

2.11 Pie diagram of category data

Step 1:

Select 'Graphs'
and 'Chart Builder ...'.

Step 2:

Select 'OK'.

If you have not defined 'Occupation'
as a nominal variable select 'Define
Variable Properties ...'.

Before you use this dialog, measurement level should be set
properly for each variable in your chart. In addition, if your chart
contains categorical variables, value labels should be defined for
each category.

Press OK to define your chart.

Press Define Variable Properties to set measurement level or
define value labels for chart variables.

☐ Don't show this dialog again

OK   Define Variable Properties...

Step 3:

Drag the pie diagram into the box
above it.

Select 'OK'.

Step 4:

Drag 'Occupation' into 'Slice by?'.

Select 'OK'.

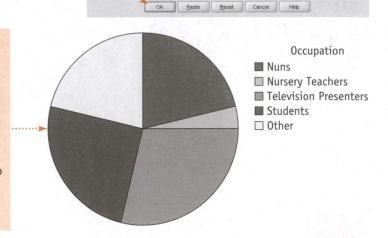

This is the way the pie diagram appears if the default options in SPSS have not been altered.

The slices are colour coded. The colours have not been reproduced here.

Features in this diagram may be altered with the 'Chart Editor'.

We will show how to label each slice (so that the reader does not have to refer to the colour code) and how to change the colours to monochrome patterns.

Occupation
■ Nuns
□ Nursery Teachers
■ Television Presenters
■ Students
□ Other

2.12 Adding labels to the pie diagram and removing the legend and label

Step 1:

Double click anywhere in the rectangle containing the diagram to select the 'Chart Editor'.

Select 'Elements' and 'Show Data Labels'.

Step 2:

Select 'Percent' and the red 'X' to put it in the box below.

Select 'Occupation' and the curved upward green arrow to display the names of the occupations.

Do the same for 'Percent' to display the percentage of each occupation.

Select 'Apply' and 'Close' if you do not want to make further changes to the properties of the pie diagram.

Step 3:

Select 'Text Style' if you want to change aspects of the text such as making it bold and increasing its font size.

To make it bold, select the ▼ button next to 'Style' and 'Bold' from the dropdown menu.

To increase the font size to 14, select the ▼ button next to 'Size' and '14' from the dropdown menu.

Note: Because of the small size of this slice, the font for Nursery Teachers will not be 14. To change this you need to click on the box for this group. If you do not want to make further changes, select 'Apply' and 'Close' ('Cancel' changes to 'Close').

Step 4:

To remove the legend, select 'Options' and 'Hide Legend'.

This is the pie diagram with the slices named and the percentage frequency given.

2.13 Changing the colour of a pie diagram slice to a black and white pattern

Step 1:

In the 'Chart Editor', click on the slice you want to change and then click again when the border will have a double line.

Select 'Edit' and 'Properties'.

Select 'Fill' and the colour of white.

To add a black border, select
'Border' and the colour of black.

To add a pattern, select the ▼
button beside 'Pattern' and the
pattern you want.

Select 'Apply' and then 'Close'.
Apply this same procedure to the
other 4 slices.

This is a pie diagram with black
and white patterned slices.

2.14   Bar chart of category data

Follow the first two steps for the
pie diagram, selecting 'Graphs' and
'Chart Builder ...', and then 'OK' in
the dialog box.

Select 'Bar' and then drag the
'Simple Bar' icon into the box
above.

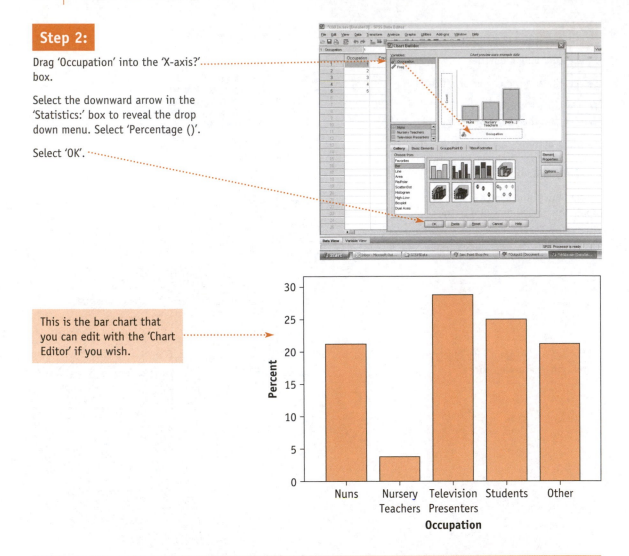

Step 2:

Drag 'Occupation' into the 'X-axis?' box.

Select the downward arrow in the 'Statistics:' box to reveal the drop down menu. Select 'Percentage ()'.

Select 'OK'.

This is the bar chart that you can edit with the 'Chart Editor' if you wish.

2.15 Histograms

We will illustrate the making of a histogram with the data in Table 2.2 which shows the distribution of students' attitudes towards statistics. We have labelled this variable 'Response'.

Table 2.2 Distribution of students' replies to the statement 'Statistics is my favourite university subject'

Response category	Value	Frequency
Strongly agree	1	17
Agree	2	14
Neither agree nor disagree	3	6
Disagree	4	2
Strongly disagree	5	1

Step 1:

In the 'Data Editor' enter the data, weight and label them as described at the beginning of this chapter.

	Response	Freq
1	1	17
2	2	14
3	3	6
4	4	2
5	5	1

Step 2:

Follow the first two steps for the pie diagram and bar chart, selecting 'Graphs' and 'Chart Builder ...', and then 'OK' in the dialog box.

Select 'Histogram' and then drag the 'Simple Histogram' icon into the box above.

Step 3:

Drag 'Response' into the 'X-axis?' box.

Select 'OK'.

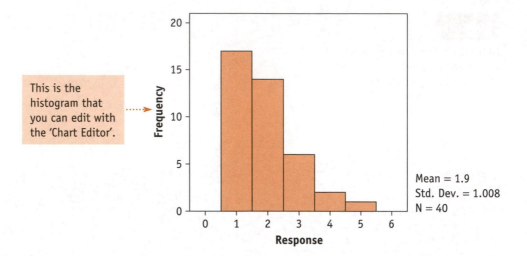

This is the histogram that you can edit with the 'Chart Editor'.

Mean = 1.9
Std. Dev. = 1.008
N = 40

For further resources including data sets and questions, please refer to the CD accompanying this book.

3 Describing variables numerically
Averages, variation and spread

Overview

- The computation of a number of statistics that summarise and describe the essential characteristics of each important variable in a study is explained. The techniques presented in this chapter involve individual variables taken one at a time. In other words they are single variable or univariate statistical techniques.

- Each technique generates a numerical index to describe an important characteristic of the data.

- With the exception of the mode, which can be used for any type of data, all of the techniques are for data in the form of numerical scores.

- The mean is the everyday or numerical average of a set of scores. It is obtained by summing the scores and dividing by the number of scores.

- The mode is simply the most frequently occurring score. A set of scores can have more than one mode if two or more scores occur equally frequently. The mode is the value of the score occurring most frequently – it is *not* the frequency with which that score occurs.

- The median is the score in the middle of the distribution if the scores are ordered in size from the smallest to the largest. For various reasons, sometimes the median is an estimate of the score in the middle – for example, where the number of scores is equal, and so that there is no exact middle.

- The procedures described in this chapter can readily be modified to produce measures of variance, kurtosis and other descriptive statistics.

3.1 What are averages, variation and spread?

Most of us when we think of averages imagine what statisticians call the *mean*. This is the sum of a number of scores divided by the number of scores. So the mean of 5, 7 and 10 is $22/3 = 7.33$. However, statisticians have other measures of the average or typical score or observation that are conceptually different from the mean. These include the median and mode. The *median* is obtained by ordering the scores from the smallest to the largest and the score that separates the first 50% of cases from the second 50% of cases is the median. If there is an even number of scores then there is no one score right in the middle and so a slight adjustment has to be made involving the mean of the score just below the middle and the score just above the middle. Sometimes even finer adjustments are made but SPSS will do the necessary calculation for you. The third measure of the average is called the *mode*. This is the most frequently occurring value in the data. This can be the most frequently occurring score if the data are score data or the most frequently occurring category if the data is nominal (category) data. The mode is the only measure of the average that can be used for nominal (category) data.

In statistics, rather than speak of average it is more usual to refer to measures of *central tendency*. The mean, median and mode are all measures of central tendency. They are all measures of the typical score in the set of scores.

If a frequency distribution of scores is symmetrical (such as in the case of the normal distribution discussed in Chapter 4), then the value of the mean, the median and the mode will be identical. But only in those circumstances. Where the frequency distribution of scores is not symmetrical then the mean, the median and the mode will have different values. Figure 3.1 contains an example of an asymmetrical frequency distribution – though it is only slightly so. There are a total of 151 participants. The mean in this case is 5.47, the median is 6.00, and the mode is also 6.00. It is easy to see that the mode is 6.00 as this is the most frequently appearing score (i.e. it has the highest bar). Since there are 151 cases then the median is the 76th score from the left-hand side of the bar chart.

The spread of the scores is another characteristic that can be seen in Figure 3.1. Quite clearly the scores vary: the largest is 10 and the smallest is 1. The difference between the largest score and the smallest score is known as the *range*, which in this case is 9. Sometimes the top and bottom quarter of scores are ignored to give the *interquartile range*,

Figure 3.1   A slightly asymmetrical frequency distribution

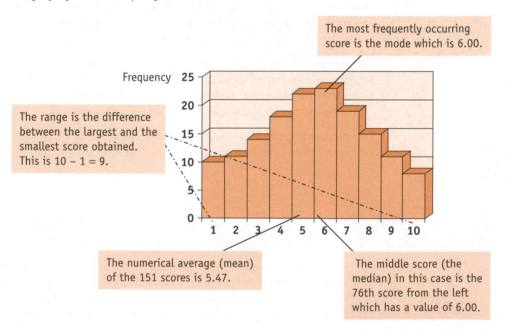

The most frequently occurring score is the mode which is 6.00.

The range is the difference between the largest and the smallest score obtained. This is 10 – 1 = 9.

The numerical average (mean) of the 151 scores is 5.47.

The middle score (the median) in this case is the 76th score from the left which has a value of 6.00.

which is less susceptible to the influence of unusual exceptionally large or small scores (outliers).

Variance is the most important measure of the spread of scores. It is based on the squared deviation (difference) between each score and the mean of the set of scores in the data. In fact it is the average squared deviation from the mean. SPSS calculates this to be 6.06 for these data. (Actually SPSS calculates the variance estimate and not the variance which is a little smaller than 6.06. This is no great problem as the variance estimate is generally more useful – it is an estimate of what the variance is in the population from which our sample came. The variance estimate is bigger than the variance since it is the sum of the squared deviations of each score from the mean score divided by the number of scores minus 1).

3.2   When to use averages, variation and spread

These should be routinely (always) calculated when dealing with score variables. However, many of these can be calculated using different analysis procedures on SPSS and there may be more convenient methods than the ones in this chapter in some circumstances. For example, you will find that SPSS will calculate means as part of many tests of significance such as the *t*-tests or ANOVA though they may have to be requested.

3.3   When not to use averages, variation and spread

Apart from when using nominal (category) data, all measures of average, variation and spread discussed in this chapter are useful when exploring one's data.

3.4   Data requirements for averages, variation and spread

All of the techniques described in this chapter require a variable which is in the form of scores. The only exception is the mode which can be calculated on any type of data.

3.5   Problems in the use of averages, variation and spread

The measures of central tendency (mean, median and mode) refer to quite different ideas and none of them is intrinsically better than the others. They each contain different information and each can be presented in any data analysis. There is, however, a tendency to ignore the median and mode, which is a mistake, for anything other than symmetrical distributions of scores (for which the three different measures of central tendency give the same value). Be careful when considering the mode since a distribution has more than one mode if it has more than one peak. SPSS will not warn you of this but a glance at the frequency distribution for the scores will also alert you to this 'bimodal' or 'multimodal' characteristic of the distribution.

The range is sometimes given in error as being from 1 to 10, for example. This is not the range as the range is a single number such as 9. The value 1 is the *lower bound* of the range and the value 10 is the *upper bound* of the range.

Initially when learning statistics, it is sometimes easy to understand a concept but difficult to see the importance or point of it. Variance is a good example of this since it is basically a very abstract notion (the average of the sum of squared differences between each score and the mean score). A particular value of variance is not intuitively meaningful since it does not refer to something that we regard as concrete such as, say, the mean score. Although variance is a fundamental statistical concept, it becomes meaningful only when we compare the variances of different variables or groups of participants. Nevertheless, it will rapidly become apparent that the concept of variance is involved in a great many different statistical techniques. Indeed, nearly all of the techniques in this book involve variance in some guise.

Be careful to note that variance as calculated by SPSS is really what is known technically as the variance estimate. It would be better to refer to it as the variance estimate but in this respect SPSS does not set a good example.

 You can find out more about describing data numerically in Chapter 4 of Howitt, D. and Cramer, D. (2008) *Introduction to Statistics in Psychology*. Harlow: Pearson.

3.6 The data to be analysed

We will illustrate the computation of the mean, median and mode on the ages of university students – see Table 3.1 (*ISP*, Table 3.7).

Table 3.1 Ages of 12 students

18	21	23	18	19	19	19	33	18	19	19	20

3.7 Entering the data

Step 1:

In 'Variable View' of the 'Data Editor' name the 1st variable 'Age'.

Remove the 2 decimal places.

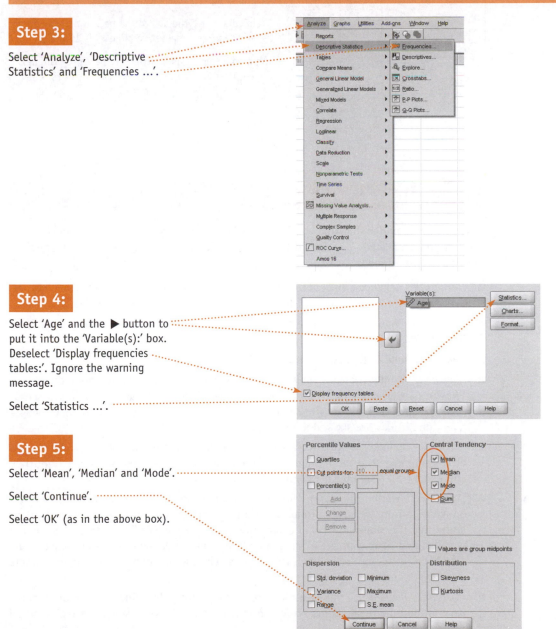

Step 2:

In 'Data View' of the 'Data Editor'
enter the ages in the 1st column.

3.8 Conducting the analysis

Step 3:

Select 'Analyze', 'Descriptive
Statistics' and 'Frequencies ...'.

Step 4:

Select 'Age' and the ▶ button to
put it into the 'Variable(s):' box.
Deselect 'Display frequencies
tables:'. Ignore the warning
message.

Select 'Statistics ...'.

Step 5:

Select 'Mean', 'Median' and 'Mode'.

Select 'Continue'.

Select 'OK' (as in the above box).

3.9 Interpreting the output

Statistics

Age

N	Valid	12
	Missing	0
Mean		20.50
Median		19.00
Mode		19

There are 12 cases with valid data on which the analysis is based.

There is no (0) missing data. See Chapter 34 on 'missing values' for a discussion.

The mean age (mathematical average) = 20.5 years.

The median age (the age of the person halfway up a list of ages from smallest to largest) is 19.00.

The modal (most common) age is 19. Check the next table on the output. This gives frequencies for each value. A variable may have more than one mode.

3.10 Other features

You will see from the dialogue box in Step 5 there are many additional statistical values that may be calculated. You should have little difficulty obtaining these by adapting the steps already described.

■ *Percentiles* – indicate the cutoff points for percentages of scores. Thus the 90th percentile is the score that cuts off the bottom 90% of scores in terms of size.

■ *Quartiles* – values of a distribution that indicate the cutoff points for the lowest 25%, lowest 50% and lowest 75% of scores.

■ *Sum* – the total of the scores on a variable.

■ *Skewness* – frequency distributions are not always symmetrical about the mean. Skewness is an index of the asymmetry or lop-sidedness of the distribution of scores on a variable. It takes a positive value if the values are skewed to the left and a negative value if they are skewed to the right.

■ *Kurtosis* – an index of how much steeper or flatter the distribution of scores on the variable is compared to the normal distribution. It takes a '+' sign for steep frequency curves and a '−' sign for flat curves.

■ *Standard deviation (estimate)* – this is a measure of the amount by which scores differ on average from the mean of the scores on a particular variable. Its method of calculation involves unusual ways of calculating the mean. In SPSS the standard deviation is calculated as an estimate of the population standard deviation. It is an index of the variability of scores around the mean of a variable. Some authors call this the sample standard deviation.

■ *Variance (estimate)* – this is a measure of the amount by which scores on average vary around the mean of the scores on that variable. It is the square of the standard deviation and is obviously therefore closely related to it. It is also always an estimate of the population variance in SPSS. Some authors call this the sample variance. Like standard deviation, it is an index of the variability of scores around the mean of a variable but also has other uses in statistics. In particular, it is the standard unit of measurement in statistics.

■ *Range* – the numerical difference between the largest and the smallest scores obtained on a variable. It is a single number.

■ *Minimum (score)* – the value of the lowest score in the data for a particular variable.

■ *Maximum (score)* – the value of the highest score in the data for a particular variable.

■ *Standard error (SE mean)* – the average amount by which the means of samples drawn from a population differ from the population mean. It is calculated in an unusual way. Standard error can be used much like standard deviation and variance as an index of how much variability there is in the scores on a variable.

Reporting the output

■ The mean, median and mode can be presented in tabular form such as Table 3.2.

■ Two decimal places are more than enough for most data. Most measurement is approximate, and the use of several decimal places tends to imply an unwarranted degree of precision.

■ For the median, it is probably less confusing if you do not report values as 19.00 but as 19. However, if the decimal places were anything other than .00 then this should be reported since it indicates that the median is estimated and does not correspond to any actual scores for these particular data.

Table 3.2   Mean, median and mode of age

	Ages of students ($N = 12$)
Mean	20.50 years
Median	19 years
Mode	19 years

For further resources including data sets and questions, please refer to the CD accompanying this book.

4 Shapes of distributions of scores

Overview

- It is important to study the shape of the distribution of scores for each variable. Ideally for most statistical techniques, a distribution should be symmetrical and normally distributed (bell-shaped).

- Some statistical techniques are at their most powerful when the distributions of the variables involved are normally distributed. Major deviations from normality should be avoided but, for relatively small sample sizes, visual inspection of frequency diagrams is the only practical way to assess this. The effects of failure to meet this criterion can be overstated. Sometimes it is possible to transform one's scores statistically to approximate a normal distribution but this is largely a matter of trial and error, using, for example, logarithmic scales.

- Nevertheless, researchers should be wary of very asymmetrical (skewed) distributions and distributions that contain a few unusually high or low scores (outliers). Histograms, for example, can be used to help detect asymmetry and outliers.

- Consider combining ranges of scores together (as opposed to tabulating each individual possible score) in order to clarify the distribution of the data. Small sample sizes, typical of much work in psychology and other social sciences, can lead to a sparse figure or diagram in which trends are not clear.

4.1 What are the different shapes of scores?

The initial stages of data analysis involve calculating and plotting statistics that describe the shape of the distribution of scores on each variable. Knowing how your data are distributed is obviously an intrinsic part of any study though it is frequently by-passed by those who see the primary aim of research as checking for statistical significance rather than understanding the characteristics of the things they are investigating. But there are other reasons for examining the distributions of scores. Statistical techniques are developed based on certain working assumptions – a common one is that that scores on the variables follow the pattern of the bell-shaped curve or normal distribution (Figure 4.1). Since

Figure 4.1   The normal distribution

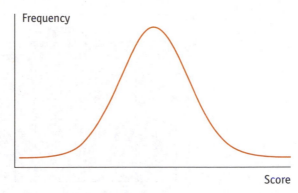

many statistical techniques are built on this assumption, if the data being analysed do not correspond to this ideal then one would expect, and it is the case, that the statistical techniques would work less than perfectly. Some departures from the 'ideal' bell-shaped curve can affect how powerful (capable of giving statistically significant results) the test is. Distributions which are heavily skewed to the left or to the right may have this effect. Figure 4.2 is an example of a distribution skewed to the left.

Apart from skewness in a distribution, some distributions depart from the ideal normal distribution by being relatively steep or relatively flat (Figures 4.3 and 4.4). The degree of flatness and steepness is known as kurtosis. Kurtosis compares the shape of a distribution with that of the normal distribution using a special formula but SPSS will calculate it for you (see Chapter 3). If the curve is steep then the kurtosis has a positive value, if the curve is flat then the kurtosis has a negative value.

We discussed histograms in Chapter 3. There is more to be said about them – in particular the concept of the frequency curve. A frequency curve is basically a smoothed-out line that joins the peaks of the various bars of the histogram. This smoothed-out line fits very uncomfortably if there are just a few different values of the scores obtained. It is not easy to fit a smooth curve to the histogram that appears at the end of Chapter 2 (p. 38). The more data points the better from this point of view. Figure 4.5 is a histogram with many

Figure 4.2   An example of a skewed distribution

Figure 4.3 A flat frequency distribution

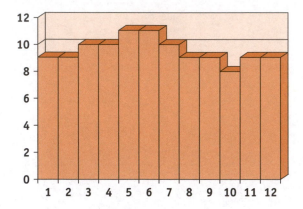

Figure 4.4 A steep frequency distribution

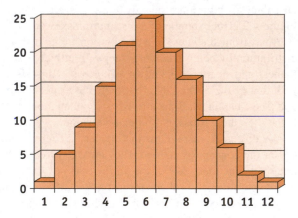

Figure 4.5 A histogram with more data points making frequency curve fitting a little easier

more data points – it is easier to fit a relatively smooth curve in this case as can be seen from the roughly drawn curve we have imposed on the figure.

As might be expected, and assuming that all other things are equal, the more data points the better the fit the data can be to the normal curve. For this reason, often continuous variables (those with an infinite variety of data points) are regarded as ideal. Few psychological measures meet this ideal. Most psychological measures yield relatively bumpy frequency curves. Again this means that the fit of the data to the normal distribution is not as good as it could be. The consequence is that the data depart somewhat from the assumptions on which many statistical tests are built. Again this will result in a degree of inaccuracy though psychologists happily tolerate this. Generally speaking, these inaccuracies will tend to make the statistical test less powerful (i.e. less capable of giving statistical significant outcomes). This is illustrated in Figure 4.6.

Of course, sometimes it may be preferable to use frequency tables to look at the way in which the scores on a variable are distributed. Naturally, this makes it more difficult to identify a normal distribution but it does make it easier to spot errors in data entry (e.g. scores out of the range).

Figure 4.6   The influence of distribution shapes on tests of significance

4.2 When to use histograms and frequency tables of scores

It is always highly desirable to obtain histograms and/or tables of frequencies of scores. This is an essential part of data analysis as conducted by a good researcher. Not to do so is basically incompetent as many important items of information are contained within these simple statistics. Authorities on statistics have often complained that psychologists fail to use simple statistical techniques to explore their data prior to more complex analyses. Too often this failing is encouraged by SPSS instruction manuals that hardly mention descriptive statistics.

4.3   When not to use histograms and frequency tables of scores

Use a histogram in favour of a frequency table when the frequency table would contain so many categories of scores that it would be unwieldy. Too large frequency tables can be problematic.

4.4   Data requirements for histograms and frequency tables of scores

Histograms require score variables. But frequency tables can also be computed for nominal (category) data.

4.5   Problems in using histograms and frequency tables of scores

The major problem occurs when frequency tables are computed without consideration of the number of scores or categories that it will produce. Any variable can be used to generate a frequency table on SPSS but it needs to be remembered that for every different score then a new category will be created in the table. So if you measured people's heights in millimetres the resulting frequency table would be horrendous. This is a common problem with SPSS – that it readily generates output whether or not the requested output is sensible. The adage 'junk in – junk out' is true but it is also true that thoughtless button pressing on SPSS means that a wheelbarrow may be needed to carry the printout home. Of course, it is possible to use SPSS procedures such as recode (see Chapter 35) to get output in a manageable and understandable form.

Be wary of the first charts and diagrams that SPSS produces. Often these need to be edited to produce something optimal.

Finally, it is common to find that student research is based on relatively few cases. This can result in somewhat difficult tables and diagrams unless some care is taken. It is very difficult to spot shapes of distributions if there are too many data points in the table or diagram. Consequently, sometimes it is better to use score ranges rather than the actual scores in order to generate good tables and diagrams. This will involve recoding your values (Chapter 35). Remember that in the worst cases SPSS will generate a different category for each different score to be found in your data. Recoding data would involve, for example, expressing age in ranges such as 15–19 years, 20–24 years, 25–39 years and so so. Some experimentation may be necessary to achieve the best tables and diagrams.

You can find out more about distributions of scores in Chapter 4 of Howitt, D. and Cramer, D. (2008) *Introduction to Statistics in Psychology*. Harlow: Pearson.

4.6 The data to be analysed

We will compute a frequency table and histogram of the extraversion scores of the 50 airline pilots shown in Table 4.1 (*ISP*, Table 4.1).

Table 4.1 Extraversion scores of 50 airline pilots

3	5	5	4	4	5	5	3	5	2
1	2	5	3	2	1	2	3	3	3
4	2	5	5	4	2	4	5	1	5
5	3	3	4	1	4	2	5	1	2
3	2	5	4	2	1	2	3	4	1

4.7 Entering the data

Step 1:

In 'Variable View' of the 'Data Editor',
name the 1st variable 'Extrav'.
Remove the 2 decimal places.
Save this data as a file to use for
Chapter 9.

Step 2:

In 'Data View' of the 'Data Editor'
enter the extraversion scores in the
1st column.

4.8 Frequency tables

Step 1:

Select 'Analyze',
'Descriptive Statistics' and
'Frequencies ...'.

Step 2:

Select 'Extrav' and the ▶ button to put it in the 'Variable(s):' box.

Select 'OK'.

4.9 Interpreting the output

The 1st column shows the 5 values of extraversion which are 1 to 5. The 2nd column shows the frequency of these values. There are 7 cases with a value of 1. The 3rd column expresses these frequencies as a percentage of the total number including missing data. Of all cases, 14% have a value of 1.

Extrav

		Frequency	Percent	Valid Percent	Cumulative Percent
Valid	1	7	14.0	14.0	14.0
	2	11	22.0	22.0	36.0
	3	10	20.0	20.0	56.0
	4	9	18.0	18.0	74.0
	5	13	26.0	26.0	100.0
	Total	50	100.0	100.0	

The 4th column expresses these frequencies as a percentage of the total number excluding missing data. As there are no missing cases the percentages are the same as in the 3rd column.

The 5th column adds these percentages together cumulatively down the table. So 56% of the cases have values of 3 or less.

Reporting the output

Notice that we omitted some of the confusion of detail in Table 4.2. Tables and diagrams need to clarify the results.

Table 4.2 One style of reporting output in Table 4.2

Extraversion score	Frequency	Percentage frequency	Cumulative percentage frequency
1	7	14.0	14.0
2	11	22.0	36.0
3	10	20.0	56.0
4	9	18.0	74.0
5	13	26.0	100.0

4.10 Histograms

Step 1:

Select 'Graphs', 'Legacy Dialogs' and 'Histogram ...'.

Step 2:

Select 'Extrav' and the ▶ button to put it in the 'Variable:' box.

Select 'OK'.

4.11 Interpreting the output

The vertical axis shows the frequency of cases from 0 to 12.5 in steps of 2.5.

The heights of the bars tells you how frequent each extraversion score is.

The horizontal axis gives the 5 different values of 'Extrav' from 1 to 5.

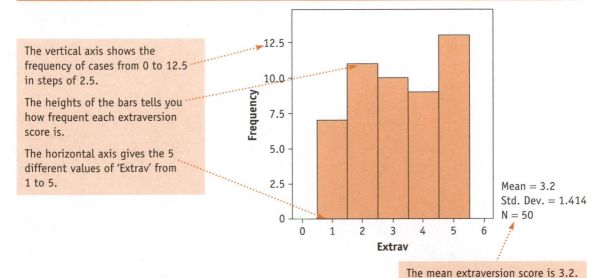

Mean = 3.2
Std. Dev. = 1.414
N = 50

The mean extraversion score is 3.2.
The standard deviation is 1.414.
The number of cases is 50.

Reporting the output

You should edit the histogram before reporting it.

Change 'Frequency' to 'Frequencies' and 'Extrav' to 'Extraversion scores' by clicking on these boxes and making these changes as shown.

 For further resources including data sets and questions, please refer to the CD accompanying this book.

5 Standard deviation
The standard unit of measurement in statistics

Overview

- Basically, standard deviation is an index of how much scores deviate (differ) 'on average' from the average of the set of scores of which they are members. In other words, standard deviation is an index of the amount of variability of scores around the mean of the scores.

- Standard deviation can also be used in order to turn scores on very different variables into z or 'standard scores' that are easily compared and summed since they are on the same scale of measurement. This standard scale always has a mean of zero and a standard deviation of 1.0 irrespective of the variable in question.

- Standard scores occur in a variety of ways in statistics although not always in an obvious form. For example, Beta weights in multiple regression are based on standard scores. z-Scores are easily computed in SPSS but a conceptual understanding of them is helpful in many contexts.

- Standard deviation itself always takes a positive value, *but* researchers write of a number of standard deviations above the mean (i.e. '+' relative to the mean) or a number of standard deviations below the mean (i.e. '−' relative to the mean). That is, scores above the mean of the sample will always convert to a z-score or standard score with a positive prefix. Scores below the mean will always convert to a z-score or standard score with a negative prefix.

5.1 What is standard deviation?

Whoever invented the standard deviation did not have psychology students in mind. Like a lot of statistical concepts, it was not designed to be easily comprehended by mere mortals but for its very special mathematical properties. It is actually fairly easy to say what the standard deviation is but much harder to understand what it is. Standard deviation is no more or less than the square root of the variance of a set of scores. If you understood the concept of variance (Chapter 3) then the standard deviation is simply the square root of the value of the variance. Unfortunately, the concept of variance is not that easy either since it is calculated by taking each score in a set of scores and subtracting the mean from that score, squaring each of these 'deviations' or differences from the mean, summing them up to give the total, and finally dividing by the number of scores (or the number of scores − 1 to calculate the variance estimate). Easy enough computationally but it is a bit of a struggle to fix the concept in one's head.

Notice that the standard deviation is simply the square root of the variance. So it is the square root of something that involved squaring the deviation of each of the scores from the mean. So since it is the square root of squares the standard deviation gets us near to getting back to the original deviation anyway. And this is what conceptually the standard deviation is – just as the label says – it is a sort of average amount by which scores differ (deviate) from the mean. That's what it is but most of us mortals would simply have taken the average deviation from the mean in the first place without all of this squaring and square rooting. The gods who invented statistics had worked out that the commonsense measure of average deviation from the mean did not have the mathematical advantages that standard deviation had.

Standard deviation comes into its own when our data have a normal distribution (the bell-shaped distribution we discussed in Chapter 4). In these circumstances, it so happens that if one counts the number of standard deviations a score is from the mean then one can say exactly what proportion of scores lie between the mean and that number of standard deviations from the mean. So if a score is one standard deviation from the mean then 34.13% of scores lie between this score and the mean; if a score is two standard deviations from the mean then 47.72% of scores lie between this score and the mean. How do we know this? Simply because these figures are a property of the normal curve. Most importantly, these figures apply to every normal curve. There are tables which give the percentages for every number of standard deviations from the mean.

These precise figures only apply to the normal distribution. If one does not have data which correspond to the normal curve then these figures are not accurate. The greater the deviation from the normal curve the more inaccurate become these figures. Perhaps now it is easier to see the importance of the normal distribution and the degree to which the normal distribution describes the frequency curve for your data.

One application of the standard deviation is something known as z-scores. This is simply a score re-expressed in terms of the number of standard deviations it is away from the mean score. So the z-score is simply the score minus the mean score of the set of data then divided by the standard deviation. In other words, the z-score is the number of standard deviations a score is away from the mean score. This is important since no matter the precise nature of a set of scores, they can always be converted to z-scores which, then, serve as a standard unit of measurement in statistics. It also means that one can quickly convert this number of z-scores to the proportion of scores in which the score lies away from the mean of the set of scores.

You may not wish to do this for a particular set of data, but you need to know that many of the statistics described in this book can involve standardised measures that are very closely related to z-scores (e.g. multiple regression, log-linear analysis and factor analysis).

By the way, SPSS actually does not compute standard deviation but something called the estimated standard deviation. This is slightly larger than the standard deviation. Standard deviation applies when you simply wish to describe the characteristic of a set of scores whereas estimated standard deviation is used when one is using the characteristics of a sample to estimate the same characteristic in the population from which the sample came. It would be good to label estimated standard deviation as such despite what SPSS says in its output.

5.2 When to use standard deviation

Standard deviation is always valuable when considering any score variable. It is clearly much more informative when it is based on a normally distributed set of scores than where the distribution deviates substantially from that ideal. Variance, standard deviation and standard error (Chapter 3) are all used as measures of the variation in the scores on a variable. This is because there is such a close mathematical relation between each of them. The square root of variance is standard deviation and the variance divided by the square root of the sample size is the standard error. Of course, it is important to be consistent in terms of which one is used.

5.3 When not to use standard deviation

Do not use standard deviation when dealing with nominal (category variables). SPSS will do a calculation for you but the outcome is mathematically precise gibberish in this case.

5.4 Data requirements for standard deviation

Standard deviation can only be calculated on score data. Ideally, the variable in question should be normally distributed and, some would say, be measured on an equal-interval scale.

5.5 Problems in the use of standard deviation

Getting to understand standard deviation is a bit like a child trying to play a concerto on the piano before learning to play simple scales. That is, standard deviation, because of its abstract nature, is very difficult to grasp but invariably taught early in a statistics module.

Because of this, novices often stare blankly at SPSS output for standard deviation since it does not immediately tell a story to them. It's rather like finding out that the average length of a plank of wood is 1.6 metres long – it is something to be taken for granted. Standard deviation is simply a sort of average amount by which scores deviate from the mean.

Remember that what SPSS calls standard deviation should really be labelled estimated standard deviation if one wishes to be precise.

You can find out more about standard deviation and *z*-scores in Chapter 5 of Howitt, D. and Cramer, D. (2008) *Introduction to Statistics in Psychology*. Harlow: Pearson.

5.6 The data to be analysed

The computation of the standard deviation and *z*-scores is illustrated with the nine age scores shown in Table 5.1 (based on *ISP*, Table 5.1).

Table 5.1 Data for the calculation of standard deviation

Age	20	25	19	35	19	17	15	30	27

5.7 Entering the data

Step 1:

In 'Variable View' of the 'Data Editor' name the 1st variable 'Age'.

Remove the 2 decimal places.

	Name	Type	Width	Decimals
1	Age	Numeric	8	0

Step 2:

In 'Data View' of the 'Data Editor' enter age in the 1st column.

	Age
1	20
2	25
3	19
4	35
5	19
6	17
7	15
8	30
9	27

5.8 Standard deviation

Step 1:

Select 'Analyze', 'Descriptive Statistics' and 'Descriptives ...'.

Step 2:

Select 'Age' and the ▶ button to
put it in the 'Variable(s):' box.

Select 'Options ...'.

Step 3:

Deselect 'Mean',
'Minimum'
and 'Maximum'.

Select 'Continue'.

Select 'OK' (as in the previous box).

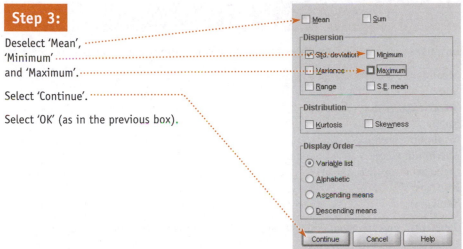

5.9 Interpreting the output

Descriptive Statistics

	N	Std. Deviation
Age	9	6.652
Valid N (listwise)	9	

The number of cases is 9.
The standard deviation of 'Age'
is 6.652.

5.10 *z*-Scores

Step 1:

Select 'Save standardized
values as variables'.

Select 'OK'.

The z or standardised scores are in
the 2nd column of 'Data View' in the
'Data Editor' and are called 'ZAge'.

	Age	ZAge
1	20	-0.45099
2	25	0.30066
3	19	-0.60132
4	35	1.80395
5	19	-0.60132
6	17	-0.90198
7	15	-1.20263
8	30	1.05230
9	27	0.60132

5.11   Other features

'Descriptives . . .' contains a number of statistical calculations that can easily be selected:

■ Mean
■ Sum
■ Standard deviation (estimate)
■ Range
■ Minimum (score)
■ Maximum (score)
■ Standard error (S.E. mean)
■ Kurtosis
■ Skewness.

These different statistical concepts are briefly explained at the end of Chapter 3.

Reporting the output

The standard deviation of just one variable can easily be mentioned in the text of your report: 'It was found that the standard deviation of age was 6.65 years ($N = 9$).'

However, it is more likely that you would wish to record the standard deviation alongside other statistics such as the mean and range, as illustrated in Table 5.2. You would probably wish to include these statistics for other numerical score variables that you have data on.

Table 5.2   The sample size, mean, range and standard deviations of age, IQ and verbal fluency

	N	**Mean**	**Range**	**Standard deviation**
Age	9	23.00	20.00	6.65
IQ	9	122.17	17.42	14.38
Verbal fluency	9	18.23	4.91	2.36

For further resources including data sets and questions, please refer to the CD accompanying this book.

6 Relationships between two or more variables

Diagrams and tables

Overview

- A great deal of research explores the relationship between two or more variables. The univariate (single-variable) statistical procedures described so far have their place in the analysis of practically any data. Nevertheless, most research questions also require the interrelationships or correlations between different variables to be addressed.

- As with univariate statistics, a thorough bivariate statistical analysis of data requires an exploration of the basic trends in the data using tables and diagrams. Methods of presenting bivariate relationships include cross-tabulation tables, compound histograms (clustered bar charts) and scattergrams. Most of these will be familiar to you already, but nevertheless can cause difficulties.

- Care has to be taken to make sure that the tables and diagrams you obtain are useful and communicate well. In particular, ensure that your data for cross-tabulation tables and compound histograms (clustered bar charts) only contain a small number of different data values. If they do not, SPSS will produce massive tables and dense unreadable graphs and diagrams.

- Labelling tables and diagrams in full is a basic essential, along with a clear title.

- Scattergrams, on the other hand, also work well when you have many different values for the scores on your variables.

- The type of table or diagram which is most effective at communicating relationships in your data depends very much on the types of data involved. Two score variables will generally be most effectively presented as a scattergram whereas two nominal variables are generally presented in terms of a cross-tabulation table.

- Remember that the effective presentation of basic descriptive statistics requires that researchers consider their tables and diagrams carefully. Often researchers will have to 'tweak' things to make the finished tables and graphs effective forms of communication. That this can be done quickly is one of the advantages of using SPSS. It is recommended that the temptation to simply cut and paste tables and diagrams from SPSS output into reports is avoided. There is virtually no SPSS output which cannot be improved upon and made clearer. The basic options of SPSS are not always ideal in this respect. Often the editing procedures available for SPSS charts can improve things enormously.

■ Producing charts like those discussed in this chapter is one of the harder tasks of SPSS.

6.1 What methods are used to show relationships between variables?

Relationships between variables are the foundation stone of most psychological research. The idea of relationships imbues many common psychological research questions. Is intelligence related to income? Does depression cause suicide? Is there a correlation between age and memory deterioration? Is there an association between childhood attachment difficulties and adult attachment difficulties? These are all examples of questions that imply an association or, in other words, a relationship. There are other research questions that superficially may not imply a relationship but nevertheless do when examined more carefully: for example, 'Is there a difference between men and women in terms of their emotional intelligence?' This is a research question that can be put another way: Is there a relationship between a person's gender and the strength of their emotional intelligence? In other words, the conventional psychological notion of tests of difference and tests of association found in many current, popular textbooks is fundamentally misleading.

There are many statistical techniques for showing that there are relationships between variables. But in this chapter we will concentrate on tables and graphs that do this. The appropriate graphical and tabular methods used to investigate relationships depend on the sorts of data in question:

1. If both variables are nominal (category) variables then the simplest graphical procedure is to produce a compound bar chart as in Figure 6.1 (or alternatively a stacked bar chart as in Figure 6.2). The tabular version is a cross-tabulation table. The value of analysis becomes problematic if there are too many categories in one or both of the variables. One thing that might be done is to combine categories together into one if that is a reasonable thing to do given the detail of your data.

2. If *both* variables are score variables then the appropriate graphical method is the scattergram or scatterplot. Tabular methods to deal with this case are usually inferior to the scattergram. The problem with tables is usually the large number of different values of scores on each variable. This can be dealt with by breaking each score variable into a small number of score ranges prior to producing the table using SPSS. How data can be recoded is described in Chapter 35. Apart from that, it is simply a matter of computing the cross-tabulation table of the two variables – or recoded variables. An example of a scatterplot is given in Figure 6.3. We explain how to do a scatterplot on SPSS in Chapter 7 where it is dealt with in conjunction with the correlation coefficient. It sometimes is not quite so apparent that a cross-tabulation table shows a relationship between two variables. Look at the table in Figure 6.4. There is a correlation indicated there since the frequencies near the diagonal from top left to bottom right tend to be larger than the frequencies found in other sections (cells) of the table.

Figure 6.1   A compound bar chart

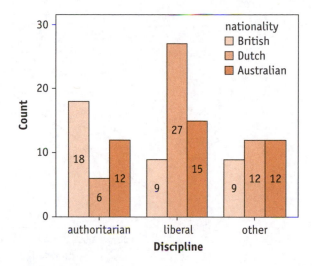

Figure 6.2   A stacked bar chart

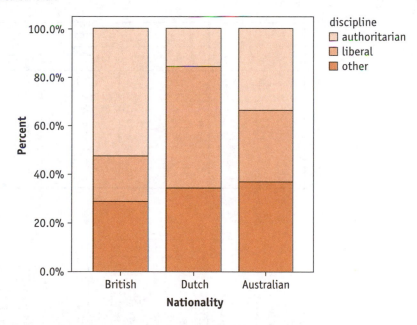

3. If one variable is a score variable and the other is a nominal (category) variable then it might be appropriate to produce the sort of bar chart that essentially displays the means for each nominal category (see Figure 6.5). However, there is not a great deal to be gained from the use of such a chart other than when giving, say, a PowerPoint presentation of some research to an audience. In this context the chart does add to the impact of the presentation. On the other hand, it is easier and often more convenient to use a simple table that names the category and then gives the mean (and possibly other statistics such as the standard deviation, maximum and minimum scores and so on). Tables such as Table 6.1 are quick and easy to interpret. Another advantage is that a lot of similar analyses can be presented in a single, compact table.

Figure 6.3 Example of a scatterplot

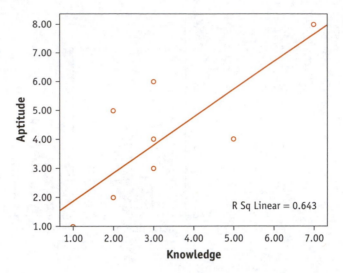

Figure 6.4 A cross-tabulation table

		Knowledge					
		1.00	2.00	3.00	5.00	7.00	Total
Aptitude	1.00	6	0	0	0	0	6
	2.00	0	3	0	0	0	3
	3.00	0	0	3	0	0	3
	4.00	0	0	6	3	0	9
	5.00	0	3	0	0	0	3
	6.00	0	0	3	0	0	3
	8.00	0	0	0	0	3	3
Total		6	6	12	3	3	30

Figure 6.5 A bar chart representing means

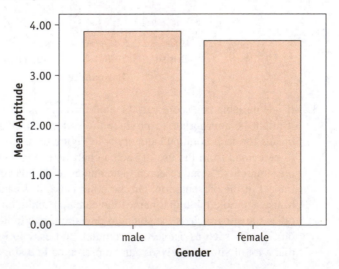

Table 6.1   Means presented as a table

	Mean aptitude score
Males	3.88
Females	3.69

 You can find out more about methods of relating variables in Chapter 6 of Howitt, D. and Cramer, D. (2008) *Introduction to Statistics in Psychology*. Harlow: Pearson.

6.2   When to use methods to show relationships between variables

It is hard to conceive of circumstances in which a researcher would not wish to use some of the graphical and tabular methods of showing relationships. Basic descriptive statistics are not kindergarten statistics, there to ease students into their studies. They are vital to truly understanding not just the characteristics of one's variables but also clarifying exactly what the findings of one's research are. Too often novice researchers fail to understand their statistical analysis simply because they have not studied the essential descriptive statistics as part of their data analysis. Likewise, often novice researchers leap to the stage of testing statistical significance that leaves them knowing that something is statistically significant but they don't quite know what that something is or what it means. SPSS speeds up the process of data analysis remarkably so there is little excuse for skipping vital stages such as checking scattergrams or computing means and standard deviations, for example. Put simply, descriptive statistics are the way in which you discover what your data have to say, whereas tests of significance simply tell you the extent to which what the data say is statistically reliable enough to have faith in the trends you discover.

6.3   When not to use methods to show relationships between variables

The key thing is to select a method of graphical or tabular analysis that suits the data in question. We have given advice that will help you find the appropriate method for the majority of cases but, of course, there is always an element of judgement to apply in certain instances. Furthermore, one has to consider what to do when one has many similar analyses to report. In these circumstances a different approach may be preferable. Simply do not generate too many separate diagrams or tables – try to keep them to an essential minimum otherwise your report will be too cluttered. Also remember that the primary purpose of descriptive statistics is to help you with your data analysis – it does not follow that you should stuff your reports with them. Again, it is a matter of judgement how many you use.

6.4 Data requirements for methods to show relationships between variables

There are different data requirements for the different methods. Two score variables are dealt with by scattergrams or more problematic ones by carefully planned cross-tabulation tables; two nominal variables are dealt with using stacked or clustered bar charts or cross-tabulation tables. Situations in which you have one score variable and one nominal variable can be most adequately dealt with by giving the means for each category of the nominal variable but it is also possible to create a bar chart to do much the same thing.

6.5 Problems in the use of methods to show relationships between variables

While the SPSS default versions of tables and charts are adequate for most aspects of data analysis, one should be very careful to consider what is needed for inclusion in research reports. Here the main criterion has to be how readily the table or chart actually communicates to the reader. Consequently you may need to adjust things such as the labelling of the table or diagram to make it readily interpretable and meaningful to the reader.

Errors in the selection of appropriate tables and charts can often be seen in their unusual look. In particular, scattergrams where a nominal variable has inadvertently been included as one of the variables tend to have the data points seemingly stacked vertically. Be on the look out for oddities like this. Figure 6.6 is a good example. Why does it look odd? Simply because gender has been included and this only has two categories. Hence the points on the plot pile up on top of each other.

Figure 6.6 There are problems with this scatterplot as explained in the text

6.6 The data to be analysed

We will illustrate the drawing up of a cross-tabulation table and compound bar chart using the data shown in Table 6.2 (*ISP*, Table 6.4). This shows the number of men and women in a study who have or have not been previously hospitalised. If your data are already entered into SPSS then Steps 1 to 5 may be ignored.

Table 6.2 Cross-tabulation table of sex against hospitalisation

	Male	Female
Previously hospitalised	F = 20	F = 25
Not previously hospitalised	F = 30	F = 14

6.7 Entering the data

Step 1:

The quickest way to enter the data in Table 6.2 is to create the 4 cells as 3 rows.

To do this we need 3 variables.

In 'Variable View' of the 'Data Editor' name the 1st variable 'Hospitalisation', the 2nd variable 'Gender' and the 3rd variable 'Freq'. Remove the 2 decimal places.

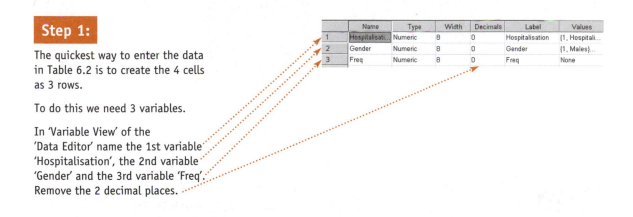

Step 2:

Label the 2 values of 'Hospitalisation' (1 = 'Hospitalised'; 2 = 'Not hospitalised') and 'Gender' (1 = 'Males'; 2 = 'Females'). How to do this was discussed in Chapter 1.

Step 3:

Enter these numbers in 'Data View' of
the 'Data Editor'.

The 1st variable refers to 'Hospitalised'
'Males' of whom there are 20.
The 2nd variable to 'Hospitalised'
'Females' of whom there are 25.
The 3rd variable to 'Not hospitalised'
'Males' of whom there are 30.
The 4th variable to 'Not hospitalised'
'Females' of whom there are 14.

	Hospitalisation	Gender	Freq
1	1	1	20
2	1	2	25
3	2	1	30
4	2	2	14

6.8 Weighting the data

Step 1:

To weight the data so that the
4 cells have the appropriate number
of cases in them, select 'Data' and
'Weight Cases ...'.

Step 2:

Select 'Freq', 'Weight cases by' and
the ▶ button to put it in the
'Frequency Variable:' box.

Select 'OK'.

Step 3:

The cases are now weighted as
shown by the 'Weight On' message
in the lower-right corner of the
'Data Editor'.

6.9 Cross-tabulation with frequencies

Step 1:

Select 'Analyze',
'Tables' and
'Custom Tables ...'.

Step 2:

If the variables have not been
defined then do so (see page 27).

Otherwise select 'OK'.

Step 3:

Select 'Hospitalisation' and drag it
to 'Rows'.

Select 'Gender' and drag it to
'Columns'.

Ensure 'nnnn' are in the cells. If
they are not, go to Section 6.10 to
see how to select them.

Select 'OK'.

The table in the output is laid
out like Table 6.3 except that
the two values for each variable
are not labelled. If necessary,
label these values using Steps 4
and 5 and rerun the analysis.

		Gender	
		1	2
Hospitalisation	1	20	25
	2	30	14

Step 4:

Select 'Edit' and 'Options'.

Step 5:

Select 'Output Labels'.

Select the ▼ button below 'Variable values in labels shown as:' and 'Labels' from the drop-down menu.

Select 'OK'.

This is the table with the values labelled.

		Gender	
		Males	Females
Hospitalisation	Hospitalised	20%	25%
	Not hospitalised	30%	14%

6.10 Displaying frequencies as a percentage of the total number

Step 1:

Double click on 'Hospitalisation' in the cell of the table.

Step 2:

Select 'Count' in 'Display:' and the ◄ button to put it back under 'Statistics:'

Select 'Table N%' and the ► button to put it under 'Display:'

Select 'Apply to Selection' to return to original dialog box.

Select 'OK'.

If you add the % in each of the 4 cells they total 100.

		Gender	
		Males	Females
		Table %	Table %
Hospitalisation	Hospitalised	22.5%	28.7%
	Not hospitalised	33.7%	15.7%

6.11 Displaying frequencies as a percentage of the column total

Select 'Col N%' and the ► button to put it under 'Display:'

Select 'Table N%' and the ◄ button to put it back under 'Statistics:'

Select 'Apply to Selection' to return to original dialog box.

Select 'OK'.

		Gender	
		Males	Females
		Col %	Col %
Hospitalisation	Hospitalised	40.0%	64.1%
	Not hospitalised	60.0%	35.9%

If you add the % in each column they total 100.

6.12   Compound (stacked) percentage bar chart

Step 1:

To obtain a compound (stacked) percentage bar chart in which the bars represent 100% you need to enter the percentage figures (called 'ColPerCent') for the two bars and weight them.

Step 2:

Select 'Graphs', 'Legacy Dialogs' and 'Bar ...'.

Step 3:

Select 'Stacked'.

Select 'Define'.

Step 4:

Select 'Hospitalisation' and the ▶ button next to 'Category Axis:'.

Select 'Gender' and the ▶ button next to 'Define Stacks by:'.

Select 'OK'.

'Count' refers to 'Per cent' which you could change with the Chart Editor (see Chapter 4).

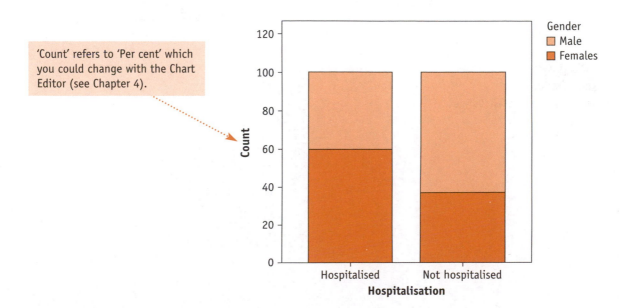

6.13 Compound histogram (clustered bar chart)

Step 1:

Weight cases by 'Freq' instead of 'ColPerCent' by selecting 'Data', 'Weight Cases ...', 'Freq', 'Weight cases by' and the ▶ button to put it in the 'Frequency Variable:' box.

Select 'OK'.

Step 2:

Select 'Graphs', 'Legacy Dialogs' and 'Bar ...'.

Step 3:

Select 'Clustered' then 'Define'.

Step 4:

Select 'Hospitalisation' and the ▶ button next to 'Category Axis:'.

Select 'Gender' and the ▶ button next to 'Define Clusters by:'.

Select '% of cases'.

Select 'OK'.

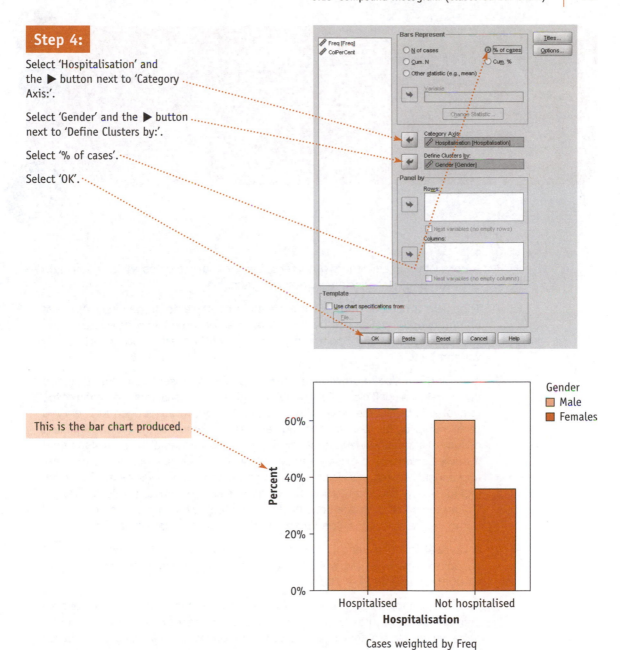

This is the bar chart produced.

Cases weighted by Freq

For further resources including data sets and questions, please refer to the CD accompanying this book.

7 Correlation coefficients
Pearson's correlation and Spearman's rho

Overview

- A correlation coefficient is a numerical index that indicates the strength and direction of a relationship between two variables.

- There are a number of different correlation coefficients. In general, the most common and most useful by far is the Pearson correlation coefficient. The phi, point biserial and Spearman's rho correlation coefficients are all merely variants of it.

- It is good practice to draw a scattergram as this represents the data included in a correlation coefficient. Not only will this give you a visual representation of the relationship but it also helps identify a number of problems such as a curved relationship or the presence of outliers. The Pearson correlation coefficient assumes a straight-line relationship between two variables. It is misleading if a curved relationship exists between the two variables. Outliers are extreme and unusual scores that distort the size of the correlation coefficient. Remedies include examining the relationship if the outliers are omitted. Alternatively, a Spearman correlation coefficient is less affected by outliers, and so one could compare the size of the Spearman correlation for the same data.

- A correlation coefficient is a numerical measure or index of the amount of association between two sets of scores. It ranges in size from a maximum of +1.00 through 0.00 to −1.00.

- The '+' sign indicates a positive correlation: that is, the scores on one variable increase as the scores on the other variable increase. A '−' sign indicates a negative correlation: that is, as the scores on one variable increase, the scores on the other variable decrease.

- A correlation of 1.00 indicates a perfect association between the two variables. In other words, a scattergram of the two variables will show that *all* of the points fit a straight line exactly. A value of 0.00 indicates that the points of the scattergram are essentially scattered randomly around any straight line drawn through the data or are arranged in a curvilinear manner. A correlation coefficient of −0.5 would indicate a moderate negative relationship between the two variables.

- Spearman's rho is the Pearson correlation coefficient applied to the scores after they have been ranked from the smallest to the largest on the two variables separately. It is used when the basic assumptions of the Pearson correlation coefficient have not been met by the data – that is especially when the scores are markedly asymmetrical (skewed) on a variable.

- Since correlation coefficients are usually based on samples of data, it is usual to include a statement of the statistical significance of the correlation coefficient. Statistical significance is a statement of the likelihood of obtaining a particular correlation coefficient for a sample of data *if* there is no correlation (i.e. a correlation of 0.00) in the population from which the sample was drawn. SPSS can give statistical significance as an exact value or as one of the conventional critical significance levels (e.g. 0.05 and 0.01).

7.1 What is a correlation coefficient?

The simplest way to understand correlation coefficients is to conceive of them as a single numerical index that summarises some of the vital information in a scattergram or scatterplot. Figure 7.1 shows a scatterplot of the information to be found in Table 7.1. We have included a line of best fit through the various points on the scatterplot and this is a straight line. You will notice that the data points on the scatterplot are spread around the straight line. This means that the data do not fit the straight line perfectly. The correlation coefficient is really just an index of the spread of the data points around that best-fitting straight line. Correlation coefficients range from absolute values of 1.00 at the most to 0.00 at the least. A correlation of 1.00 means that *all* the data points fit perfectly on the straight line whereas a correlation of 0.00 means that the data points fit the straight line very

Figure 7.1   A scattergram showing the relationship between maths ability and musical ability

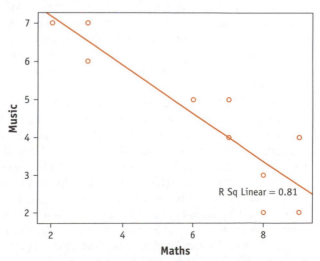

Table 7.1 Correlations and proportion and percentage of variance explained

Value of correlation coefficient r	Square of correlation coefficient	% of variance in relationship between two variables explained (by best-fitting straight line)
1.00	1.00	100.00%
0.70	0.49	49.00%
0.50	0.25	25.00%
0.25	0.0625	6.25%
0.10	0.01	1.00%
0.00	0.00	0.00%
−0.5	0.25	25.00%
−1.00	1.00	100.00%

poorly. Actually, a 0.00 correlation indicates that there is no straight line that fits the data points any better than on a chance basis. Values between 0.00 and 1.00 are indicative of increasingly strong relationships between the two variables – that is the fit of the data points to the straight line is getting closer and closer.

There is a little more to things than this. Some correlation coefficients have a negative sign in front of them such as −1.00 or −0.50. The negative sign simply indicates that the slope of the scatterplot between two variables is negative – that is, the straight line points downwards from left to right rather than upwards. This negative slope can be seen in Figure 7.1. In other words, a negative sign in a correlation coefficient indicates that as scores get bigger on one of the two variables then they begin to get smaller on the other variable.

A correlation coefficient can explain or account for a certain amout of the variance between two variables. A correlation coefficient of 1.00 explains all of the variance between two variables – that is there is no variation at any of the data points from the best-fitting straight line on the scatterplot so that all of the variation in data points is accounted for by the best-fitting straight line. A correlation coefficient of 0.00 means that there is no variance accounted for by the best-fitting straight line since the fit of the data points to the straight line is merely random. This idea of variance explained by a correlation coefficient is very important in psychology and needs to be understood in order to grasp the meaning of correlation coefficients adequately. The variance explained by a correlation coefficient is calculated by squaring its value and expressing this as a proportion or percentage of the maximum value of a correlation coefficient possible, i.e. 1.00. Some examples of such values are shown in Table 7.1.

This table tells us that there is no direct relationship between a correlation coefficient and the amount of variance that it accounts for. The relationship is curvilinear because it is based on squares. The percentage of variation explained is a better indicator of the strength of the relationship than the size of the correlation coefficient. So for example, although a correlation of 0.5 may seem to be half as good as a correlation of 1.00, this is not really the case. A correlation of 0.5 actually only explains 0.25 (25%) of the variance. So a correlation of 0.5 is really only a quarter as good as a correlation of 1.00.

The above comments apply directly to what is known as the Pearson product moment correlation coefficient – or Pearson correlation for short. This is a correlation coefficient based on variables measured as numerical scores. It is the parent of a range of other correlation coefficients such as the Spearman rho.

The Spearman rho correlation coefficient is based on the Pearson correlation coefficient. It only differs in that the scores on the two variables are ranked separately from the smallest to the largest values. (Ranking simply puts scores in order from the smallest to the largest values. The smallest score would be given the rank 1, the next biggest score is given the rank 2, and so on.) One has two sets of ranks to calculate the Spearman rho. Essentially if the Pearson correlation coefficient formula is applied to these ranks rather than the original scores, the resulting correlation coefficient is known as the Spearman correlation coefficient. It has traditionally been regarded as an alternative to the Pearson correlation coefficient when the variables involved are measured on a scale that does not have equal intervals. That is, the difference between 5 and 6 on the scale, say, is not the same quantity as the difference between 8 and 9 on the scale in terms of the 'psychological' units being measured. Modern psychologists tend to ignore this issue which once created fierce debates among researchers and statisticians. So the preference seems to be (although few would admit it) to use the Pearson correlation coefficient. There are advantages to this since more powerful statistical techniques are available which are based on the Pearson correlation rather than on the Spearman rho.

Correlation coefficients are usually based on samples of data. As a consequence, it is necessary to test the statistical significance of correlation coefficients (see Box 1.1 on page 17). The test of statistical significance assesses the possibility that the obtained correlation coefficient could come from a sample taken from a population in which the correlation is 0.00 (i.e. no correlation). SPSS displays significance levels routinely.

7.2 When to use Pearson and Spearman rho correlation coefficients

The Pearson correlation coefficient can be used in any circumstance in which it would be appropriate to draw a scattergram (scatterplot) between two score variables. In other words, the Pearson correlation coefficient can be used any time that the researcher wishes to know the extent to which one variable is related to another. It assesses the association between two variables – it is not a way of comparing means, for example. So many statistical techniques described later in this book are based on Pearson correlation in some form or another that it is impossible to avoid. Thus it is one of the key statistical ideas to understand before going on to study many advanced techniques.

The Spearman rho correlation coefficient, in comparison, is infrequently used. Its main function is to serve as an alternative to Pearson correlation when the assumptions of the Pearson correlation are not met by the data. Unfortunately, it is quite difficult to decide if these assumptions are violated so there would be considerable disagreement as to whether to use the Spearman rho correlation coefficient. If the Pearson correlation and Spearman's rho result in much the same conclusion as each other then there is no problem. But if they differ then one might wish to consider the possibility that the statistical assumptions underlying the Pearson correlation are not met by the data.

Versions of the Pearson correlation coefficient can be used when one is not considering the relationship between two sets of scores. For example, if one has a score variable and a binary variable (one with just two alternative categories such as yes and no or male and female) then the point biserial (see section 7.4) correlation coefficient may be calculated. This is the Pearson correlation coefficient applied to the score variable and the binary variable which is coded 1 and 2 for the two binary categories. If one has two binary variables then these can be correlated using the Pearson correlation coefficient though the outcome is conventionally known as the phi coefficient.

7.3 When not to use Pearson and Spearman rho correlation coefficients

Pearson correlation is based on linear (straight-line) relationships hence we draw a straight line through the points on a scattergram or scatterplot when illustrating Pearson correlation. But not all relationships are linear in psychological research. One should always examine the scattergram for the data to assess the extent to which the relationship is non-linear – the best-fitting line on a scatterplot might actually be a curve (i.e. a curvilinear relationship). If this is the case for your data then do not use Pearson correlation since it will be extremely misleading. In these circumstances, there is a correlation coefficient (eta) which may be calculated since it works with curved relationships.

See Howitt, D. and Cramer, D. (2008) *Introduction to Statistics in Psychology* (Harlow: Pearson Education) for a discussion of eta and its calculation.

The Spearman rho also assumes that the relationship is a more-or-less linear one and so this should not be used either where the relationship is a curve not a straight line.

7.4 Data requirements for Pearson and Spearman rho correlation coefficients

The Pearson correlation coefficient requires two score variables as does Spearman's rho. However, the scores should ideally be normally distributed for the Pearson correlation and some would argue, on an equal interval scale. One could consider using Spearman's rho where these requirements are not met though the advantages of doing so may not balance out the costs for anything other than the most simple of research studies because it is a far less flexible statistic.

It is possible to use the Pearson correlation coefficient when one or both variables are in the form of binary variables – that is, there are only two possible response categories. Code these binary variables as 1 for one category and 2 for the other category in SPSS. If you then run the Pearson correlation procedure on these variables the resulting correlations are known as phi (if both variables are binary) and the point biserial (if one variable is binary and the other a score variable).

7.5 Problems in the use of correlation coefficients

Most of the problems involved in using correlation can be identified by carefully looking at the scatterplots of the relationship. The problem of curvilinear relationships has already been discussed and the easiest way of identifying curvilinear relationships is simply by looking at the scatterplot. The alternative is to compare the size of the Pearson correlation on your data with the size of eta calculated on the same data.

Outliers are data points on the scatterplot that are at the extremes of the distribution. They are problematic because they can totally distort the correlation such is their impact; and they can often be identified visually from the scatterplot. However, Spearman's rho is largely unaffected by outliers since they are changed into ranks along with the other scores. So one way of checking for outliers is to compare the Spearman's rho correlation with the Pearson correlation for the same data. If Spearman's rho is much smaller than the Pearson correlation, then suspect the influence of outliers which are making the Pearson correlation appear to be large.

 You can find out more about the correlation coefficient in Chapter 7 of Howitt, D. and Cramer, D. (2008) *Introduction to Statistics in Psychology*. Harlow: Pearson.

7.6 The data to be analysed

We will illustrate the computation of Pearson's correlation, a scatter diagram and Spearman's rho for the data in Table 7.2 (*ISP*, Table 7.1), which gives scores for the musical ability and mathematical ability of 10 children.

Table 7.2 Scores on musical ability and mathematical ability for 10 children

Music score	Mathematics score
2	8
6	3
4	9
5	7
7	2
7	3
2	9
3	8
5	6
4	7

7.7 Entering the data

Step 1:

In 'Variable View' of the 'Data Editor' name the 1st variable 'Music' and the 2nd variable 'Maths'.

Remove the 2 decimal places by changing the figure already here to zero.

	Name	Type	Width	Decimals
1	Music	Numeric	8	0
2	Maths	Numeric	8	0

Step 2:

In 'Data View' of the 'Data Editor' enter 'Music' in the 1st column and 'Maths' in the 2nd column. Save this data as a file to use for Chapter 8.

	Music	Maths
1	2	8
2	6	3
3	4	9
4	5	7
5	7	2
6	7	3
7	2	9
8	3	8
9	5	6
10	4	7

7.8 Pearson's correlation

Step 1:

Select 'Analyze', 'Correlate' and 'Bivariate ...'.

Step 2:

Select 'Music' and 'Maths' either singly or together and the ▶ button to put them in the 'Variables' box as they appear here.

Select 'OK'.

7.9 Interpreting the output

The correlation between 'Maths' and 'Music' is −.900. The two-tailed significance or probability level is .001 or less so the correlation is statistically significant.

The number of cases on which this correlation is based is 10. This information is also given in this cell.

Correlations

		Music	Maths
Music	Pearson Correlation	1	−.900**
	Sig. (2-tailed)		.000
	N	10	10
Maths	Pearson Correlation	−.900**	1
	Sig. (2-tailed)	.000	
	N	10	10

**. Correlation is significant at the 0.01 level

Reporting the output

■ The correlation between music ability and mathematical ability is −.900. It is usual to round correlations to 2 decimal places, which would make it −0.90. This is more than precise enough for most psychological measurements.

■ The exact significance level to 3 decimal places is .000. This means that the significance level is less than 0.001. We would suggest that you do not use a string of zeros, as these confuse people. Always change the third zero to a 1. This means that the significance level can be reported as being $p < 0.001$.

■ It is customary to present the degrees of freedom (*df*) rather than the number of cases when presenting correlations. The degrees of freedom are the number of cases minus 2, which makes them 8 for this correlation. There is nothing wrong with reporting the number of cases instead.

■ In a report, we would write 'There is a significant negative relationship between musical ability and mathematical ability ($r = −0.90$, $df = 8$, $p < 0.001$). Children with more musical ability have lower mathematical ability.'

The significance of the correlation coefficient is discussed in more detail in Chapter 10 of Howitt, D. and Cramer, D. (2008) *Introduction to Statistics in Psychology*. Harlow: Pearson.

7.10 Spearman's rho

As for Pearson's correlation, select 'Analyze', 'Correlate', 'Bivariate' and the variables you want to correlate. Select 'Spearman'.

If you don't want Pearson, deselect it.

7.11 Interpreting the output

Spearman's rho between 'Maths' and 'Music' is –.894. The two-tailed significance level of this correlation is .001 or less so the correlation is statistically significant. The number of cases is 10. This information is also given in this cell.

Correlations

			Music	Maths
Spearman's rho	Music	Correlation Coefficient	1.000	–.894**
		Sig. (2-tailed)		.000
		N	10	10
	Maths	Correlation Coefficient	–.894**	1.000
		Sig. (2-tailed)	.000	.
		N	10	10

**. Correlation is significant at the 0.01 level (2-tailed).

Reporting the output

- The correlation reported to two decimal places is −0.89.
- The probability of achieving this correlation by chance is less than 0.001 (i.e. $p < 0.001$).
- We would report this in the following way: 'There is a statistically significant negative correlation between musical ability and mathematical ability (rho = −0.89, $df = 8$, $p < 0.001$). Those with the highest musical ability tend to be those with the lowest mathematical ability and vice versa.'

7.12 Scatter diagram

Step 1:

Select 'Graphs', 'Legacy Dialogs' and 'Scatter/Dot ...'.

Step 2:

Select 'Define' as 'Simple' has already been selected. It is called the default.

Step 3:

To have 'Music' as the vertical axis, select it and the ▶ button next to the 'Y Axis:' box.

To have 'Maths' as the horizontal axis, select it and the ▶ button next to the 'X Axis:' box.

Select 'OK'.

Step 4:

To fit a correlation line to the scatterplot, double click anywhere in which it opens the 'Chart Editor'.

Select 'Elements' and 'Fit Line at Total'.

Select 'Close' in the 'Properties' box. A correlation line is the same as the regression line.

7.13 Interpreting the output

In this scattergram the scatter of points is relatively narrow, indicating that the correlation is high.
The slope of the scatter lies in a relatively straight line, indicating it is a linear rather than a curvilinear relationship. The line moves from the upper left to the lower right, which signifies a negative correlation. If the relationship is curvilinear, then Pearson's or Spearman's correlations may be misleading.

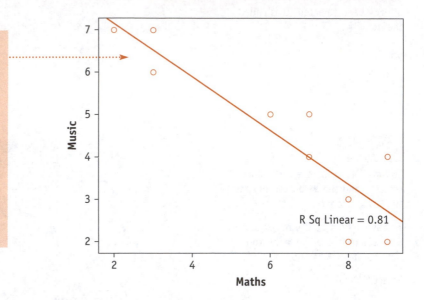

R Sq Linear = 0.81

Reporting the output

■ You should never report a correlation coefficient without examining the scattergram for problems such as curved relationships or outliers (see *ISP*, Chapter 7).

■ In a student project it should always be possible to include graphs of this sort. Unfortunately, journal articles and books tend to be restricted in the numbers they include because of economies of space and cost.

■ We would write of the scattergram: 'A scattergram of the relationship between mathematical ability and musical ability was examined. There was no evidence of a curvilinear relationship or the undue influence of outliers.'

For further resources including data sets and questions, please refer to the CD accompanying this book.

8 Regression
Prediction with precision

Overview

■ Where there is a relationship between two variables, it is possible to estimate or predict a person's score on one of the variables from their score on the other variable. The stronger the correlation, the better the prediction.

■ Regression can be used on much the same data as the correlation coefficient. However, it is far less commonly used, partly because of the problem of comparability between values obtained from different sets of variables. (The beta weight can be used if such comparability is required.)

■ The dependent variable in regression is the variable the value of which is to be predicted. It is also known as the criterion variable, the predicted variable or the *Y*-variable.

■ The independent variable is the variable being used to make the prediction. It is also known as the predictor variable or the *X*-variable.

■ Great care is needed not to get the independent variable and the dependent variable confused. This can easily happen with simple regression. The best way of avoiding problems is to examine the scatterplot or scattergram of the relationship between the two variables. Make sure that the horizontal *x*-axis is the independent variable and that the vertical *y*-axis is the dependent variable. One can then check what the cut point is approximately from the scattergram as well to get an idea of what the slope should be. The cut point is where the slope meets the vertical axis. These estimates may be compared with their calculated values to ensure that an error has not been made. If problems are found, the most likely reason is that the independent and dependent variables have been confused.

■ The simple regression technique described in this chapter expresses relationships in terms of the original units of measurement of the variables involved. Thus, if two different studies use slightly different variables it is difficult to compare the outcomes of the studies using this form of regression.

■ In regression, the relationship between two variables is described mathematically by the slope of the best fitting line through the points of the scattergram together with the point at which this regression line cuts the (vertical) axis of the scattergram. Therefore, the relationship between two variables requires the value of the slope (usually given the symbol *B* or *b*) and the intercept or cut point in the vertical axis (usually given the symbol *a* or described as the constant).

■ Regression becomes a much more important technique when one is using several variables to predict values on another variable. These techniques are known as multiple regression (see Chapters 28 and 29). When the dependent variable is a nominal category variable, then the appropriate statistical analysis will be a form of logistic regression (see Chapters 31 and 32).

8.1   What is simple regression?

One of the most difficult statistical techniques for novices to understand is that of simple regression. It is actually one of the earliest statistical methods and predated historically the correlation coefficient. The first thing to understand is that regression is applied to exactly the same data as the Pearson correlation coefficient. But it does something different. Look at the scatterplot in section 8.11. When we discussed Pearson correlation in Chapter 7, we explained how the correlation coefficient is a measure of how closely the data points fit the straight line through the data points – the bigger the correlation coefficient, the closer the data points tend to be to the straight line. Regression is different in that it describes the characteristics of the straight line itself. In order to describe the best-fitting straight line we need to know two things: (1) where the line cuts the vertical axis of the scatterplot; and (2) what the slope of the line is. The point at which the vertical axis is cut by the straight line is known as the cut point, intercept or constant whereas the slope is the regression weight. The slope is merely the amount that the line goes up (or down) for every unit that one goes along the horizontal axis. The slope can be negative, which indicates that the line goes downwards towards the right of the scatterplot.

The good news is that all of the hard work is done for you on SPSS, The best-fitting straight line is calculated by SPSS so it is not a matter of trial and error.

However, it needs to be understood that regression is affected by which variable you put on the horizontal (or *x*-axis) and which variable you put on the vertical (or *y*-axis). Quite different figures emerge in regression depending on your choice. Why does this matter? One of the functions of regression is to allow the user to make predictions from the value of one variable to the other variable. This is possible if it is established from a sample of data that there is a good correlation between the two variables. For example, if you measured the heights and weights of a sample of participants you would find a correlation between the two. On the basis of this information, you would assume that someone who is tall is likely to be heavier than someone who is small. The only problem is that this is not very precise.

Figure 8.1 gives a scattergram for the relationship between musical and mathematical ability devised from the data in Table 8.1 on page 91, identical to that in Table 7.2 in the previous chapter. The best-fitting straight line (also known as the regression line) has been drawn in. We have added in some extra things: (1) the cut point of the regression line on

Figure 8.1   Scattergram of the relationship between music and maths ability

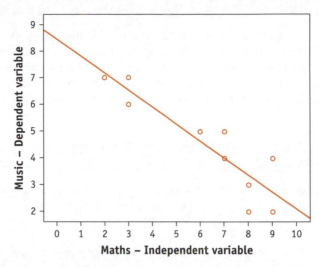

the vertical axis (which, by the way, can be negative – i.e. below the horizontal axis and (2) the words independent and dependent variable that refer to the horizontal and vertical axes respectively. You could predict music ability scores using this scatterplot if you wished simply by drawing a vertical line from the relevant point on the horizontal axis (i.e. a particular individual's maths ability score) to the regression line then horizontally to the vertical axis, The point that the vertical axis is cut is the predicted score on musical ability. It would be more accurate, though, to use the following formula:

Predicted score (Y) = Constant + BX

B is the slope of the regression line and X is a particular score on the x-axis from which the score on the y-axis is to be predicted.

8.2   When to use simple regression

Generally, in psychology, simple regression of this sort would be rarely used. Usually, psychologists would use the correlation coefficient in preference to regression when doing simple regression. Indeed, the regression weight expressed in standardised form is the same as the Pearson correlation coefficient. In terms of learning statistics, it is vital because it introduces the basic ideas of regression. Regression comes into its own when extended into what is termed multiple regression (see Chapters 28 and 29) in which there are several predictor variables involved. It is also closely related conceptually to logistic regression.

However, it can be used on any pair of score variables especially when the data approximate equal-interval measurement, which is the assumption for most score variables in psychology.

8.3 When not to use simple regression

Few psychologists use simple regression in their analyses. It has no advantages over the Pearson correlation coefficient with which it has a lot in common.

In addition, do not use simple regression where one has one or more binary variables (two value or two category variables) since the output may be fairly meaningless – it certainly will not look like a typical scatterplot and so may cause confusion.

8.4 Data requirements for simple regression

Two score variables are needed. It is best if these are normally distributed but some deviation from this ideal will not make much difference.

8.5 Problems in the use of simple regression

Simple regression is beset with the same problems as the Pearson correlation coefficient (see Chapter 7). So non-linear relationships are a problem as are outliers. These can be checked for using a scatterplot of the data.

From a learner's point of view, there is one extremely common mistake – putting the predictor variable in the analysis wrongly so that it is treated as the dependent variable by SPSS. Making a scatterplot should help with this since it is possible to estimate the likely values from this – especially the constant or cut point on the vertical axis. This can be checked against the computed values since this may reveal such a confusion of the independent and dependent variables.

Sometimes the way in which SPSS gives the constant can cause confusion. The constant appears under the column for *B* weights or coefficients which is not what it is. You should have no trouble if you follow the instructions in Section 8.9.

 You can find out more about simple regression in Chapter 8 of Howitt, D. and Cramer, D. (2008) *Introduction to Statistics in Psychology*. Harlow: Pearson.

8.6 The data to be analysed

We will illustrate the computation of simple regression and a regression plot with the data in Table 8.1 (*ISP*, Table 8.2), which gives a score for the musical ability and mathematical ability of 10 children. These data are identical to those used in the previous chapter on correlation. In this way, you may find it easier to appreciate the differences between regression and correlation.

The music scores are the criterion or the dependent variable, while the mathematics scores are the predictor or independent variable. With regression, it is essential to make the criterion or dependent variable the vertical axis (*y*-axis) of a scatterplot and the predictor or independent variable the horizontal axis (*x*-axis).

Table 8.1   Scores on musical ability and mathematical ability for 10 children

Music score	Mathematics score
2	8
6	3
4	9
5	7
7	2
7	3
2	9
3	8
5	6
4	7

8.7   Entering the data

If you have saved the data select the file. Otherwise enter the data again.

Step 1:

In 'Variable View' of the 'Data
Editor' name the 1st variable
'Music' and the 2nd variable 'Maths'.

Remove the 2 decimal places.

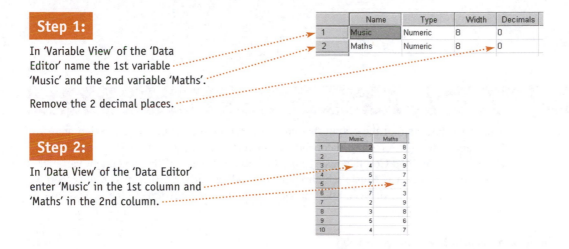

Step 2:

In 'Data View' of the 'Data Editor'
enter 'Music' in the 1st column and
'Maths' in the 2nd column.

8.8   Simple regression

Step 1:

Select 'Analyze',
'Regression' and 'Linear ...'.

Step 2:

Select 'Music' and the ▶ button beside 'Dependent:' to put 'Music' in that box.

Select 'Maths' and the ▶ button beside 'Independent(s):' to put 'Maths' in that box.

Select 'Statistics ...'.

Step 3:

Select 'Confidence intervals'.

Select 'Continue'.

Select 'OK' in the previous box.

8.9 Interpreting the output

This is the last table of the output that has the essential details of the regression analysis. It is very easy to reverse the independent variable and dependent variable accidentally. Check the table titled Coefficients[a]. Under the table the name of the dependent variable is given. In this case it is Music which is our dependent variable. If it read Maths then we would have made a mistake and the analysis would need to be redone as the regression values would be incorrect.

The intercept or constant is 8.425. This is the point at which the regression line cuts the vertical axis.

Coefficients[a]

Model		B	Std. Error	Beta	t	Sig.	Lower Bound	Upper Bound
		Unstandardized Coefficients		Standardized Coefficients			95% Confidence Interval for B	
1	(Constant)	8.425	.725		11.620	.000	6.753	10.097
	Maths	−.633	.109	−.900	−5.832	.000	−.883	−.383

a. Dependent Variable: Music

The unstandardised regression coefficient is −.633. This means that for every increase of 1 on the Maths variable, the score on the Music variable decreases by −.633.

The standardised regression coefficient is −.900. This is more-or-less the Pearson correlation coefficient between maths and music abililty.

The 95% confidence interval ranges from −.883 to −.383. This means that the unstandardised coefficient is very likely to have a population value of between −.883 and −.383.

In simple regression involving two variables, it is conventional to report the regression equation as a slope (*b*) and an intercept (*a*) as explained in *ISP* (Chapter 8). SPSS does not quite follow this terminology. Unfortunately, at this stage the SPSS output is far more complex and detailed than the statistical sophistication of most students:

■ *B* is the slope. The slope of the regression line is called the unstandardised regression coefficient in SPSS. The unstandardised regression coefficient between 'music' and 'maths' is displayed under *B* and is −0.633, which rounded to two decimal places is −0.63. What this means is that for every increase of 1.00 on the horizontal axis, the score on the vertical axis changes by −0.633.

■ The 95% confidence interval for this coefficient ranges from −0.88 (−0.883) to −0.38 (−0.383). Since the regression is based on a sample and not the population there is always a risk that the sample regression coefficient is not the same as that in the population. The 95% confidence interval gives the range of regression slopes within which you can be 95% sure that the population slope will lie.

■ The intercept (*a*) is referred to as the constant in SPSS. The intercept is presented as the (*c*onstant) and is 8.425, which rounded to two decimal places is 8.43. It is the point at which the regression line cuts the vertical (*y*) axis.

■ The 95% confidence interval for the intercept is 6.753 to 10.097. This means that, based on your sample, the intercept of the population is 95% likely to lie in the range of 6.75 to 10.10.

■ The column headed 'Beta' gives a value of −0.900. This is actually the Pearson correlation between the two variables. In other words, if you turn your scores into standard scores (*z*-scores) the slope of the regression and the correlation coefficient are the same thing.

8.10 Regression scatterplot

It is generally advisable to inspect a scattergram of your two variables when doing regression. This involves the steps involved in plotting a scattergram as described in Chapter 7.

Step 1:

Select 'Graphs', 'Legacy Dialogs' and 'Scatter/Dot …'.

Step 2:

Select 'Define' as 'Simple' is the pre-selected default.

Step 3:

Select 'Music' and the ▶ button beside 'Y Axis:' to put it in this box as it is the criterion.

Select 'Maths' and the ▶ button beside 'X Axis:' to put it in this box as it is the predictor.

Select 'OK'.

The output is the same as that for the correlation in section 7.9.

Step 4:

To fit a regression line to the scatterplot, double click anywhere in it which opens the 'Chart Editor'.

Select 'Elements' and 'Fit Line at Total'.

Select 'Close' in 'Properties' box.

8.11   Interpreting the output

The points on the scatterplot are close to the regression line (i.e. the line is a good fit to the data). Furthermore, the points seem to form a straight line (i.e. the relationship is not curvilinear) and there is no sign of outliers (i.e. especially high or low points).

In REGRESSION, the vertical axis is the dependent or criterion variable; in this case Music. It is a common error to mix up the axes in regression. If you have then start again.

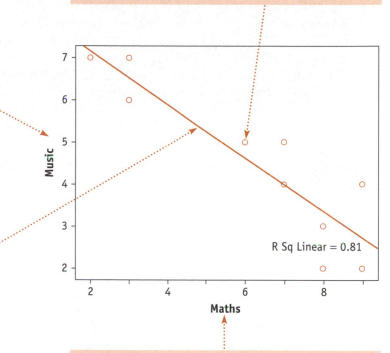

The regression line has a negative slope in this case: i.e. it slopes from top left down to bottom right. The *B* weight therefore has a negative value.

R Sq Linear = 0.81

In REGRESSION, the horizontal axis is the independent or predictor variable; in this case Maths. It is a common error to mix up the axes in regression. If you have then redo the analysis reversing the axes.

■ The regression line sloping from the top left down to bottom right indicates a negative relationship between the two variables. Remember that unless your axes intersect at zero on both the vertical and horizontal axes then your interpretation risks being mistaken.

■ The points seem relatively close to this line, which suggests that beta (correlation) should be a large (negative) numerical value and that the confidence interval for the slope should be relatively small.

Reporting the output

Although all of the output from SPSS is pertinent to a sophisticated user, many users might prefer to have the bare bones at this stage.

■ With this in mind, we would write about the analysis in this chapter: 'The scatterplot of the relationship between mathematical and musical ability suggested a linear negative relationship between the two variables. It is possible to predict accurately a person's musical ability from their mathematical ability. The equation is $Y' = 8.43 + (-0.63X)$ where X is an individual's mathematics score and Y' is the best prediction of their musical ability score.'

■ An alternative is to give the scatterplot and to write underneath $a = 8.43$ and $B = -0.63$.

■ One could add the confidence intervals such as: 'The 95% confidence interval for the slope of the regression line is -0.88 to -0.38. Since this confidence interval does not include 0.00, the slope differs significantly from a horizontal straight line.' However, this would be a relatively sophisticated interpretation for novices in statistics.

For further resources including data sets and questions, please refer to the CD accompanying this book.

Part 3 Significance testing and basic inferential tests

9 Standard error

Overview

- Standard error is an index of the variability of the means of many samples taken from the population. It is nothing other than the standard deviation, but applied to sample means rather than scores. In other words, conceptually, standard error can be regarded as the average amount by which the means of samples differ from the mean of the population from which they came.

- It is mostly used as an intermediate step in other statistical techniques such as the t-test. There is little need to calculate the standard error in its own right since it adds practically nothing more than the standard deviation or variance.

- Nevertheless, it can be used like variance or standard deviation as an index of the amount of variability in the scores on a variable. A knowledgeable researcher will find variance, standard deviation and standard error equally useful as indicators of the variability of scores.

- Standard error is an important concept in the calculation of confidence intervals. Indeed, it will occur in many contexts where the focus is on the characteristics of samples rather than scores.

- There are two versions of standard error: standard error as applied to a set of scores and estimated standard error, which is used when trying to estimate the population standard error from the standard error of a sample. SPSS actually only calculates estimated standard error. Hence, for standard error in SPSS output read estimated standard error.

9.1 What is standard error?

Standard error is a fundamental statistical concept that needs to be understood as part of your development as a statistician. You would rarely need to compute standard error separately as its computation is part of other SPSS procedures you will probably be carrying out.

Standard error is more-or-less the same as the standard deviation (Chapter 5) with one big difference: standard deviation refers to a set of scores whereas the standard error refers to means of samples. In fact, the standard error is essentially the standard deviation of a set of sample means. It is even estimated (calculated) from the standard deviation of the sample of scores that the researcher has information about. This sample is used to make inferences about the characteristics of the population. Basically, but with some slight adjustments, the characteristics of the sample are assumed to be those of the population from which the sample was drawn. Conceptually, you need to imagine that you are drawing samples of a particular size (say 10) from this estimated population of scores (on some measure). Commonsense suggests, and statistical theory insists, that there will be variation in the means of these different samples simply because of the vicissitudes of random selection. The standard deviation calculated on these sample means is the standard error. The standard error is simply a measure of the variation in sample means.

Usually in statistics (and definitely so in SPSS), we do not calculate the standard error but something called the estimated standard error. This is because we usually have just one sample to calculate the standard error from. The steps are that we calculate the standard deviation of the population of scores from the sample (see Figure 9.1). This entails a very small adjustment to the standard deviation formula and yields the estimated standard deviation. Then this estimated standard deviation is used to estimate the standard error of sample means using a very simple formula:

$$(\text{Estimated}) \text{ standard error} = \frac{(\text{Estimated}) \text{ standard deviation of population}}{\sqrt{N}}$$

The value of N is dependent on the sample size for which you wish to obtain the standard error. Which implies, of course, that there is a different standard deviation for each different size of sample.

The standard error gives you an indication of the extent to which sample means can be expected to vary if drawn at random from the same population. It clearly is closely linked to the standard deviation and, often, they are used interchangeably as they are both indicative of the variation in the data. Standard error is important as a key idea in other statistics such as the t-test (Chapters 10 and 11).

Figure 9.1   Estimating the population standard error from a sample of scores

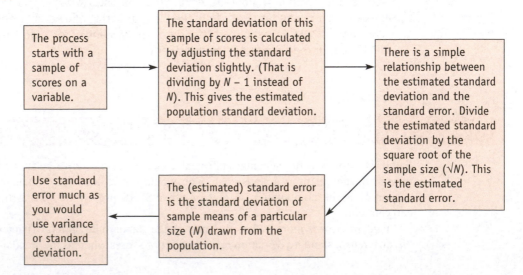

9.2 When to use standard error

Standard error is most likely to be used as an indication of the variability or spread in the data. As such, it vies with standard deviation and variance for that task. There is a close relationship between all of these things and they can be used interchangeably by experienced researchers though, of course, only one of the three should be used for purposes of making comparisons. Ideally the data should be on a scale with equal measurement intervals and normally distributed.

9.3 When not to use standard error

There are few if any circumstances in which it is inappropriate to use standard error if its basic data requirements are met.

9.4 Data requirements for standard error

Standard error can be calculated on any score variable though it is most accurate where the scores are normally distributed and the measurement approaches an equal interval scale.

9.5 Problems in the use of standard error

There are no particular problems associated with standard error.

 You can find out more about standard error in Chapter 11 of Howitt, D. and Cramer, D. (2008) *Introduction to Statistics in Psychology*. Harlow: Pearson.

9.6 The data to be analysed

The computation of the estimated standard error of the mean is illustrated with the set of six scores of self-esteem presented in Table 9.1 (*ISP*, Table 11.3).

Table 9.1   Data for standard error example

Self-esteem scores
5
7
3
6
4
5

9.7 Entering the data

Enter the data in the
'Data Editor'.

Label the variable
'Esteem'.

	Esteem
1	5
2	7
3	3
4	6
5	4
6	5

9.8 Estimated standard error of the mean

Step 1:

Select 'Analyze', 'Descriptive
Statistics' and 'Descriptives ...'.

Step 2:

Select 'Esteem' and the ▶ button
to put 'Esteem' in the 'Variable(s):'
box.

Select 'Options ...'.

Step 3:

Select 'S.E. mean'.

Select 'Continue'.

Select 'OK' in the previous box.

9.9   Interpreting the output

Descriptive Statistics

	N	Minimum	Maximum	Mean		Std.
	Statistic	Statistic	Statistic	Statistic	Std. Error	Statistic
Esteem	6	3	7	5.00	.577	1.414
Valid N (listwise)	6					

> The (estimated) standard error of the mean of this sample of 6 scores is 0.577. It is an indication of the 'average' amount by which sample means differ from the mean of the population from which they came.

The table gives us the value of the standard error of sample means as 0.58, which is rounded to two decimal places. This is the 'average' amount by which means of samples ($N = 6$) differ from the population mean. It is an estimate based on a sample and should really be termed the estimated standard error.

The table includes other information such as the mean (5.00), the estimated population standard deviation based on this sample, and the minimum and maximum values in the data. The final column gives the (estimated) standard deviation of the six scores, which is 1.41.

Reporting the output

Generally, in psychological statistics, one would not report the standard error of sample means on its own. It would be more usual to report it as part of certain tests of significance. However, in many circumstances it is just as informative as the variance or standard deviation of a sample, as it bears a simple relationship to both of these.

For further resources including data sets and questions, please refer to the CD accompanying this book.

10 The *t*-test
Comparing two samples of correlated/related scores

Overview

- The *t*-test is used to assess the statistical significance of the difference between the means of two sets of scores. That is, it helps to address the common research question of whether the average (i.e. mean) score for one set of scores differs significantly from the average score for another set of scores.

- Because in research we invariably deal with samples of people drawn from the potential population, we need to estimate whether any difference we obtain between two sets of scores is statistically significant. That is, is the obtained difference between the two means so very different from a zero difference that it is unlikely that the samples come from the same population?

- Statistical significance is assessed by using the variability in the available data to assess how likely various differences between the two means would be if there was no true difference between the two samples. The null hypothesis suggests that there is no difference between the sample means. Differences between sample means that would be very uncommon by chance if the null hypothesis were true are said to be statistically significant. They lead us to prefer the hypothesis that there is truly a difference between the two means that is unlikely to be a chance effect due to sampling.

- There are two versions of the *t*-test. One is used when the two sets of scores to be compared come from a single set or sample of people or when the correlation coefficient between the two sets of scores is high. This is known as the related or correlated *t*-test. The other version of the *t*-test is used when the two different sets of scores come from different groups of participants. Refer to the next chapter if the two means you wish to compare come from distinct groups of participants.

- If you have used a matching procedure to make pairs of people similar on some other characteristics then you would also use the related *t*-test in this present chapter – especially if the two sets of scores correlate significantly.

- Data entry for related and unrelated variables is very different in SPSS so take care to plan your analysis before entering your data in order to avoid problems and unnecessary work.

- If you have more than two sets of scores to compare then refer to Chapter 18 on the related analysis of variance.

- The *t*-test described in this chapter is known as the related *t*-test. Basically this means that the two sets of scores are obtained from a single sample of participants. There should be a correlation between the scores on the two measures since otherwise the two sets of scores are not related.

- The related *t*-test works at its optimum if the distribution of the differences between the two sets of scores is approximately bell-shaped (that is, if there is a normal distribution). If the distribution is very different from a bell shape, then one might consider using a related non-parametric statistic such as the Wilcoxon matched-pairs test (see Chapter 14).

10.1   What is the related *t*-test?

The related *t*-test gives the statistical significance of the difference between the means of two score variables. Usually, it is based on one group of participants measured twice, which gives the two means. The unrelated *t*-test (Chapter 11) is different and involves two separate groups of participants. Both are based on a statistical distribution known as the *t*-distribution, hence the *t*-test.

The related *t*-test ascertains whether the mean score of one measure is statistically significantly different from the mean on another measure. However, the assumption of the related *t*-test is that the two sets of scores should correlate with each other (hence the name correlated *t*-test). This requirement of correlation is poorly understood but is vital to ensure that the related *t*-test is interpreted properly. The related *t*-test is most likely to be used in psychology in circumstances in which a single group of participants has been measured twice at different points in time on essentially the same variable. The resulting two sets of scores are likely to correlate with each other for the simple reason that some participants will tend to score consistently highly on the variable and others tend to score consistently lowly. This type of design is illustrated in Table 10.1 (see page 108) in which a group of participants are measured at Time A and Time B. To be precise, a group of babies have been assessed at the age of 6 months and then again at the age of 9 months in order to study whether the time that they spend in eye contact with their mothers increases over this three-month period. While we might assume that eye contact increases as the babies get older, we would expect that some babies at Time A tend to be developmentally more advanced than other babies. We might also expect that the developmentally more advanced babies at Time A will tend to be developmentally the more advanced at Time B despite the likelihood that all of the babies develop to some degree over that three-month period. Do the calculations on these data and you will find that the mean eye-contact score at 6 months of age is 5.25 which increases to 6.75 at the age of 9 months. This is in line with the hypothesis guiding the research that eye contact increases with age. Furthermore, if you correlate the two sets of eye-contact scores you find that they correlate at 0.42, which is a moderate sized correlation though (in this case) not statistically significant.

When we measure the same thing twice for a single sample of participants, we actually gain control over more variation in the data. Basically there are two sources of variation in the scores (i.e. the dependent variable) in most research designs:

1. Variation due to the difference between the two means (the independent variable).
2. Variation due to uncontrolled factors (usually called error variance).

However, in the related *t*-test the second source of variance (that due to uncontrolled factors) can be reduced because the measures have been taken twice on a single group of participants. That is, we know that some participants will tend to score highly on both measures whereas other participants tend to get low scores. These 'individual differences' are removed from the error variance in the related *t*-test. The extent of the individual differences is reflected in the size of the correlation between the two sets of scores. The bigger the correlation then the greater reduction there is in the error variance – and the more likely is it that a significant difference will be obtained between the two means as a consequence.

There is a downside, however, since by removing the variance due to individual differences the number of degrees of freedom is reduced too – and the number of degrees of freedom (*df*) affects the statistical significance of the *t*-test. The fewer degrees of freedom, the less likely is it that a significant difference will be obtained. This is fine if the reduction in the error variance due to removing the variation arising from individual differences is sufficient to compensate for the reduction in the degrees of freedom. The bigger the correlation between the two sets of scores then the more likely is this compensation to be achieved. If the correlation is zero then there is just a loss of degrees of freedom with no gains to compensate so there is a consequent reduction in the chance of statistical significance. If there is zero correlation between the two sets of scores, it would actually be totally appropriate to analyse the data with the unrelated *t*-test (Chapter 11) although we have never seen this done by psychologists.

There is another circumstance in which the related *t*-test should be considered the appropriate test of statistical significance. This is where the researcher matches participants in some way between the two groups. Few studies in psychology employ matching so this is rarely an issue. What do we mean by matching? Matching is simply choosing pairs of participants to be similar on a variable(s) believed to correlate with the dependent variable. This is a way of increasing the similarities between the two groups since matching aims to form two groups of participants from pairs of similar individuals. The consequence of effective matching is again that the scores of the two groups should correlate.

10.2 When to use the related *t*-test

- Conventionally, the related *t*-test is used where there is a single group of participants that has been measured twice – once at each of two different points in time. Usually the same measure is used twice or sometimes alternative forms of the same measure are used (with counterbalancing of the order). However, for the related *t*-test to be effective, the scores on the two measures should correlate with each other.

- If participants have been matched in a number of pairs and one member of each pair assigned to Group 1 and the other member of the pair assigned to Group 2 (usually at random), then the related *t*-test can be used to analyse these data though one should make sure that the two sets of scores correlate when arranged in the pairs. If they do not correlate then the matching procedure was not effective, probably because the variable the pairs were matched on did not correlate with the dependent variable.

- Whatever design is used, you should make sure that the measures being compared in terms of their means can be meaningfully compared. If they are the same measure then this condition is met.

- Ideally, the data should be normally distributed in terms of the distribution of the differences between the pairs of scores on the dependent variable.

- The related *t*-test is a version of the one-sample *t*-test in which a single sample of scores is compared with the population of scores. In the related *t*-test this single sample is essentially created by taking the differences between each pair of scores to give a single sample of difference scores.

10.3 When not to use the related *t*-test

One common mistake is to use the related *t*-test to compare two sets of scores that cannot be meaningfully compared despite the fact that they are measured on a single group of participants. For example, it is meaningless to compare scores on a measure of intelligence with scores on a measure of extraversion even though these two measures came from the same group of participants. SPSS will do the calculation but why is it helpful to know that the mean score on intelligence differs significantly from the mean score on extraversion? Intelligence and extraversion are different measures which might be expected to have different means. So make sure that you are comparing comparable measures. (Of course, it is meaningful to correlate intelligence with extraversion since correlation coefficients do not test for differences in mean scores but the strength of the association between two variables.)

You should not use the related *t*-test if the two measures do not correlate as this is to reduce the likelihood of obtaining significant differences. Where there is a zero correlation then it is perfectly correct to use the unrelated *t*-test instead (though your data would have to be re-entered in the correct format to do this). However, what if there is a modest correlation between the two measures rather than a large correlation? Our advice is given in section 10.5.

10.4 Data requirements for the related *t*-test

Two sets of scores on the same dependent variable are usually measured at two different points in time. However, the scores could be from two groups of matched pairs of participants. The scores should be normally distributed though ideally the crucial thing is that the differences between the pairs of scores should form a normal (bell-shaped) distribution.

10.5   Problems in the use of the related *t*-test

Careful thought should prevent most of the problems with the related *t*-test, especially the problem of making meaningless comparisons between two variables that are very different from each other. The solution is to make sure that you are using the same variable measured twice, which generally is straightforward.

The other problem is where the two measures correlate poorly, which has the consequence of reducing the significance level. If you have any such worries, probably the simplest thing would be for you to analyse your data with both the related and the unrelated *t*-test, although you need to remember that these use very different data entry methods. If both *t*-tests are significant then there is no major problem. If the related *t*-test is more significant than the unrelated *t*-test then all is well and good. If the unrelated *t*-test is significant but the related *t*-test not significant (or less significant) then the related *t*-test is problematic since the basic assumptions of the test are not being met.

It is always important to remember that the related *t*-test compares two different means. You need to know the means for each of the groups in order to assess whether the mean is increasing, decreasing or staying the same.

 You can find out more about the correlated or paired *t*-test in Chapter 12 of Howitt, D. and Cramer, D. (2008) *Introduction to Statistics in Psychology*. Harlow: Pearson.

10.6   The data to be analysed

The computation of a related *t*-test is illustrated with the data in Table 10.1, which shows the number of eye contacts made by the same babies with their mothers at 6 and 9 months (*ISP*, Table 12.6). The purpose of the analysis is to see whether the amount of eye contact changes between these ages.

Table 10.1   Number of one-minute segments with eye contact at different ages

Baby	Six months	Nine months
Clara	3	7
Martin	5	6
Sally	5	3
Angie	4	8
Trevor	3	5
Sam	7	9
Bobby	8	7
Sid	7	9

10.7 Entering the data

Step 1:

In 'Variable View' of the 'Data Editor' label the 1st variable 'Six_mths' and the 2nd variable 'Nine_mths'.

Remove the 2 decimal places by changing the figure for the decimals to 0.

	Name	Type	Width	Decimals
1	Six_mths	Numeric	8	0
2	Nine_mths	Numeric	8	0

Step 2:

In 'Data View' of the 'Data Editor' enter the data in the first 2 columns. (Save this data file to use in Chapter 14.)

	Six_mths	Nine_mths
1	3	7
2	5	6
3	5	3
4	4	8
5	3	5
6	7	9
7	8	7
8	7	9

10.8 The related *t*-test

Step 1:

Select 'Analyze', 'Compare Means' and 'Paired-Samples T Test ...'.

Step 2:

Select 'Six_mths' and the ▶ button to put it in the 'Paired Variables' box. Do the same for 'Nine_mths'.

Select 'OK'.

10.9 Interpreting the output

Paired Samples Statistics

		Mean	N	Std. Deviation	Std. Error Mean
Pair 1	Six_mths	5.25	8	1.909	.675
	Nine_mths	6.75	8	2.053	.726

The 1st table shows the mean, the number of cases and the standard deviation of the two groups. The mean for 'Six_mths' is 5.25 and its standard deviation is 1.909. The two standard deviations are very similar which is an advantage.

Paired Samples Correlations

		N	Correlation	Sig.
Pair 1	Six_mths & Nine_mths	8	.419	.301

The 2nd table shows the degree to which the two sets of scores are correlated. The correlation between them is .419. This is a moderate correlation although it is not significant as the significance is greater than .05. Correlated tests such as the related *t*-test should have a substantial correlation between the two sets of scores. Be careful, this table is *not* the test of significance. It is a common mistake, among novices, to confuse this correlation between two variables with the significance of the difference between the two variables.

The first three columns containing figures are the basic components of the calculation of the related *t*-test. The mean of −1.500 is actually the difference between the six-month and nine-month means. So it is really the mean difference. The value of *t* is based on this mean difference (−1.500 divided by the standard error of the mean (.756)). This calculation gives us the value of *t* (−1.984).

Paired Samples Test

		Paired Differences							
					95% Confidence Interval of the Difference				Sig. (2-tailed)
		Mean	Std. Deviation	Std. Error Mean	Lower	Upper	t	df	
Pair 1	Six_mths – Nine_mths	−1.500	2.138	.756	−3.287	.287	−1.984	7	.088

The 3rd and last table shows the *t* value (−1.984), the degrees of freedom (7) and the two-tailed significance level (.088). As the significance level is greater than .05 this difference is not significant. The one-tailed level is obtained by dividing it by 2 which is .044 and significant. (However, unless the difference has been predicted in advance of data collection on the basis of strong theoretical and/or empirical reasons, only the two-tail test is appropriate.)

- In the first table of the output, the mean number of eye contacts at 6 months ('Six_mths') and at 9 months ('Nine_mths') is displayed under Mean. Thus the mean amount of eye contact is 5.25 at 6 months and 6.75 at 9 months.

- In the second table of the output is the (Pearson) correlation coefficient between the two variables (eye contact at 6 months and eye contact at 9 months). *Ideally*, the value of this should be sizeable (in fact it is 0.419) and statistically significant (which it is not, with a two-tailed significance level of 0.301). The related *t*-test assumes that the two variables are correlated, and you might consider an unrelated *t*-test (Chapter 11) to be more suitable in this case.

- In the third table of the output the difference between these two mean scores is presented under the 'Mean' of 'Paired Differences' and the standard error of this mean under 'Std. Error Mean'. The difference between the two means is −1.50 and the estimated standard error of means for this sample size is 0.76.

- The *t*-value of the difference between the sample means, its degrees of freedom and its two-tailed significance level are also shown in this third table. The *t*-value is −1.984, which has an exact two-tailed significance level of 0.088 with 7 degrees of freedom.

Reporting the output

■ We could report these results as follows: 'The mean number of eye contacts at 6 months (M = 5.25, SD = 1.91) and at 9 months (M = 6.75, SD = 2.05) did not differ significantly ($t = -1.98$, *df* = 7, two-tailed $p = 0.088$).'

■ In this book, to be consistent, we will report the exact probability level for non-significant results as above. However, it is equally acceptable to report them as '$p > 0.05$' or 'ns' (which is short for non-significant).

■ Notice that the findings would have been statistically significant with a one-tailed test. However, this would have to have been predicted with sound reasons prior to being aware of the data. In this case one would have written to the effect: 'The two means differed significantly in the predicted direction ($t = -1.98$, *df* = 7, one-tailed $p = 0.044$).'

■ A one-tailed test should only be used if prior to data collection the direction of the difference between means had been predicted on the basis of strong theoretical reasons or a strong consistent trend in the previous research. These requirements are rarely met in student research so, generally, two-tailed significance testing should be the norm.

■ Once again, to be consistent throughout this book, we will report the exact probability level for significant findings where possible. Note that when SPSS displays the significance level as '.000', we need to present this as '$p < 0.001$' since the exact level is not given. It is equally acceptable to report significant probabilities as '$p < 0.05$', '$p < 0.01$' and '$p < 0.001$' as appropriate.

■ If you prefer to use confidence intervals (Chapter 12), you could report your findings as: 'The mean number of eye contacts at 6 months was 5.25 (SD = 1.91) and at 9 months was 6.75 (SD = 2.05). The difference was 1.50. The 95% confidence interval for this difference is −3.29 to 0.29. Since the confidence interval passes through 0.00, the difference is not statistically significant at the two-tailed 5% level.'

■ Some statisticians advocate the reporting of confidence intervals rather than significance levels. However, it remains relatively uncommon to give confidence intervals.

For further resources including data sets and questions, please refer to the CD accompanying this book.

11 The *t*-test
Comparing two groups of unrelated/ uncorrelated scores

Overview

■ The uncorrelated or unrelated *t*-test is used to calculate whether the means of two sets of scores are significantly different from each other. It is the most commonly used version of the *t*-test. Statistical significance indicates that the two samples differ to an extent which is unlikely to be due to chance factors as a consequence of sampling. The variability inherent in the available data is used to estimate how likely it is that the difference between the two means would be if, in reality, there is no difference between the two samples.

■ The unrelated *t*-test is used when the two sets of scores come from two different samples of people. (Refer to the previous chapter on the related *t*-test if your scores come from just one set of people or if you have employed a matching procedure.)

■ Data entry for related and unrelated variables are very different in SPSS. So take care to plan your analysis before entering your data in order to avoid problems and unnecessary work. SPSS, however, is very flexible and errors of this sort are usually straightforward to correct using cut-and-paste and similar features.

■ SPSS procedures for the unrelated *t*-test are very useful and go beyond usual textbook treatments of the topic. That is, they include an option for calculating the *t*-test when the variances of the two samples of scores are significantly different from each other. Most textbooks erroneously suggest that the *t*-test is too inaccurate to use when the variances of the two groups are unequal. This additional version of the unrelated *t*-test is rarely mentioned in statistics textbooks but is extremely valuable.

■ If you have more than two sets of scores to compare, then refer to Chapter 17 on the unrelated analysis of variance.

11.1   What is the unrelated *t*-test?

The unrelated *t*-test simply tests the statistical significance of the difference between two different group (i.e. sample) means (see Box 1.1 on page 17 for a discussion of statistical significance). That is, it addresses the question of whether the average score for one group (e.g. males) is significantly different from the average score for the other group (females). It is much more commonly used than the related *t*-test discussed in Chapter 10. It is called the *t*-test because the computation is based on a mathematical distribution known as the *t*-distribution.

The unrelated *t*-test basically involves the difference between the two sample means. Of course, scores vary and this variation may be responsible for the apparent difference between the sample means. So a formula based on combining the variances of the two separate samples is calculated. This is known as the standard error of the differences between two sample means. The smaller this is compared to the size of the difference between the two sample means then the more likely it is for the two means to be statistically significantly different from each other. This is illustrated in Figure 11.1.

Table 11.1 gives data from a study for which the unrelated *t*-test is an appropriate test of significance. The data consist of scores on a single variable coming from two groups of participants – the important criterion for using the unrelated *t*-test. If you have just one group of participants then it is possible that the related *t*-test (Chapter 10) is the appropriate technique. Group 1 consists of children brought up in two-parent families and Group 2 consists of those brought up in lone-parent families. The researcher wishes to know whether these two groups differ on a measure of emotionality. It is easy to see that the two groups differ from the mean scores for each group shown in Table 11.1. Quite clearly, children from two-parent families have higher emotionality scores (mean = 13.42) than those from the lone-parent families (mean = 9.50). The question is whether this difference is statistically significant that is hard to explain on the basis of chance.

There is a slight problem in the calculation of the standard error of the difference between the two group means. If the two variances are very different, then combining them is problematic in terms of statistical theory. It is possible to test whether two variances are statistically significantly different using the *F*-ratio (see Chapter 16). SPSS uses

Figure 11.1   The unrelated *t*-test

Table 11.1 Emotionality scores in two-parent and lone-parent families

Two-parent family X_1	Lone-parent family X_2
12	6
18	9
14	4
10	13
19	14
8	9
15	8
11	12
10	11
13	9
15	
16	
Mean = 13.42	Mean = 9.50

Levene's test of homogeneity to do this. If the two variances differ significantly then SPSS also provides a version of the unrelated *t*-test 'equal variances not assumed'. This should be used instead in these circumstances.

11.2 When to use the unrelated *t*-test

The unrelated *t*-test can be used where there are two separate groups of participants for which you have scores on any score variable. It is best if the scores are normally distributed and correspond to an equal interval level of measurement, though any score data can be used with a loss of accuracy. SPSS provides two versions of the unrelated *t*-test: one where the variances of the two sets of scores are equal and the other where the two variances are significantly different.

11.3 When not to use the unrelated *t*-test

Do not use the unrelated *t*-test where you have three or more groups of participants – the mean of each group you wish to compare with the mean of each other group. ANOVA is a more suitable statistic in these circumstances since multiple comparisons using an unrelated *t*-test increase the likelihood of having one or more comparisons significant by chance.

Some researchers would prefer to use a non-parametric or distribution-free test of significance (Chapter 14) if the scores are not measured on an equal interval scale of measurement. Mostly, however, considerable violations of the assumptions of the unrelated *t*-test are tolerated.

If your two sets of scores come from one group of participants, then you might need the related *t*-test in preference (see Chapter 10).

11.4 Data requirements for the unrelated *t*-test

One single score variable and two distinct groups of participants are required.

11.5 Problems in the use of the unrelated *t*-test

SPSS causes users some problems. The common problem is confusing the significance of the *F*-ratio comparing the variances of the two groups of scores with the significance of the *t*-test. They are quite distinct but very close together in SPSS output.

There are two versions of the unrelated *t*-test. One is used if the two sets of scores have similar variances. This is described as 'Equal variances assumed' in SPSS. Where the *F*-ratio shows a statistically significant difference in the variances then the output for 'Equal variances not assumed' should be used.

As is often the case in statistical analysis, it is useful to be clear what the difference in the two group means indicates prior to the test of significance. The test of significance then merely confirms whether this is a big enough difference to be regarded as statistically reliable. It is very easy to get confused by SPSS output giving mean differences otherwise.

 You can find out more about the unrelated *t*-test in Chapter 13 of Howitt, D. and Cramer, D. (2008) *Introduction to Statistics in Psychology*. Harlow: Pearson.

11.6 The data to be analysed

The computation of an unrelated *t*-test is illustrated with the data in Table 11.1 on page 115, which shows the emotionality scores of 12 children from two-parent families and 10 children from single-parent families (*ISP*, Table 13.8). In SPSS this sort of *t*-test is called an independent samples *t*-test. The purpose of the analysis is to assess whether emotionality scores are different in two-parent and lone-parent families.

11.7 Entering the data

Step 1:

In 'Variable View' of the 'Data Editor', label the 1st variable 'Family'. This defines the two types of family.

Label the 2nd variable 'Emotion'. These are the emotionality scores. Remove the 2 decimal places by changing the value here to 0 if necessary.

	Name	Type	Width	Decimals
1	Family	Numeric	8	0
2	Emotion	Numeric	8	0

Step 2:

In 'Data View' of the 'Data Editor' enter the values of the 2 variables in the 1st two columns. Save the data as a file to use in Chapter 14.

	Family	Emotion
1	2	12
2	2	18
3	2	14
4	2	10
5	2	19
6	2	8
7	2	15
8	2	11
9	2	10
10	2	13
11	2	15
12	2	16
13	1	6
14	1	9
15	1	4
16	1	13
17	1	14
18	1	9
19	1	8
20	1	12
21	1	11
22	1	9

■ Take a good look at step 2. Notice that there are two columns of data. The second column ('emotion') consists of the 22 emotionality scores from *both* groups of children. The data are not kept separate for the two groups. In order to identify to which group the child belongs, the first column ('family') contains lots of 1 s and 2 s. These indicate, in our example, children from a lone-parent family (they are the rows with 1 s in 'family') and children from two-parent families (they are the rows with 2 s in 'family'). Thus a single column is used for the dependent variable (in this case, emotionality, 'emotion') and another column for the independent variable (in this case, type of family, 'family'). So each row is a particular child, and their independent variable and dependent variable scores are entered in two separate columns in the Data Editor.

11.8 Carrying out the unrelated *t*-test

Step 1:

Select 'Analyze', 'Compare Means' and 'Independent-Samples T Test ...'.

Step 2:

Select 'Emotion' and the ▶ button for the 'Test Variable(s):' box to put it there.

Select 'Family' and the ▶ button for the 'Grouping Variable:' box to put it there.

Select 'Define Groups …' to define the two groups.

Step 3:

Enter '1' (code for one-parent) besides 'Group 1:' and '2' (code for two-parent) besides 'Group 2:'. Which group goes in which box is arbitrary.

Select 'Continue'.

Select 'OK' in the previous box.

11.9 Interpreting the output

Group Statistics

	Family	N	Mean	Std. Deviation	Std. Error Mean
Emotion	1	10	9.50	3.100	.980
	2	12	13.42	3.370	.973

This 1st table shows for each group the number of cases, the mean and the standard deviation. The mean for the lone parents is 9.50. There is obviously a difference, therefore, between the two types of family. The question next is whether the two means differ significantly.

The value of t is simply the mean difference (−3.917) divided by the standard error of the difference (1.392) which yields the value of −2.813.

Independent Samples Test

| | | Levene's Test for Equality of Variances | | t-test for Equality of Means | | | | | | |
| | | F | Sig. | t | df | Sig. (2-tailed) | Mean Difference | Std. Error Difference | 95% Confidence Interval of the Difference | |
									Lower	Upper
Emotion	Equal variances assumed	.212	.650	−2.813	20	.011	−3.917	1.392	−6.821	−1.013
	Equal variances not assumed			−2.836	19.768	.010	−3.917	1.381	−6.800	−1.034

If the significance of Levene's test is greater than .05, which it is here at .650, use the information on this 1st row. If the significance of the Levene's test is .05 or less, use the information on the 2nd row. The 2nd row gives the figures for when the variances are significantly different.

For equal variance, t is −2.813, which with 20 degrees of freedom is significant at .011 for the two-tailed level. To obtain the one-tailed level, divide this level by 2 which gives .006 rounded to 3 decimal places.

The output for the uncorrelated/unrelated t-test on SPSS is particularly confusing even to people with a good knowledge of statistics. The reason is that there are two versions of the uncorrelated/unrelated t-test. Which one to use depends on whether or not there is a significant difference between the (estimated) variances for the two groups of scores.

■ Examine the first table of the output. This contains the means and standard deviations of the scores on the dependent variable (emotionality) of the two groups. Notice that an additional figure has been added by the computer to the name of the column containing the dependent variable. This additional figure indicates which of the two groups the row refers to. If you had labelled your values, these value labels would be given in the table.

■ For children from two-parent families ('family 2') the mean emotionality score is 13.42 (see the first table above) and the standard deviation of the emotionality scores is 3.37. For the children of lone-parent families ('family 1') the mean emotionality score is 9.50 and the standard deviation of emotionality is 3.10.

■ In the second table, look at the columns under 'Levene's Test for Equality of Variances'. If the probability value is statistically significant then your variances are *unequal*. Otherwise they are regarded as equal.

■ Levene's test for equality of variances in this case tells us that the variances are equal because the p value of .650 is not statistically significant.

- Consequently, you need the row for 'Equal variances assumed'. The *t* value, its degrees of freedom and its probability are displayed. The *t* value for equal variances is −2.813, which with 20 degrees of freedom has an exact two-tailed significance level of .011.

- Had Levene's test for equality of variances been statistically significant (i.e. .05 or less), then you should have used the second row of the output which gives the *t*-test values for unequal variances.

Reporting the output

- We could report the results of this analysis as follows: 'The mean emotionality scores of children from two-parent families (M = 13.42, SD = 3.37) is significantly higher ($t = -2.81$, *df* = 20, two-tailed $p = 0.011$) than that of children in lone-parent families (M = 9.50, SD = 3.10).'

- It is unusual to see the *t*-test for unequal variances in psychological reports. Many psychologists are unaware of its existence. So what happens if you have to use one? In order to clarify things, we would write: 'Because the variances for the two groups were significantly unequal ($F = 8.43$, $p < 0.05$), a *t*-test for unequal variances was used . . .'

- If you prefer to use the confidence intervals (Chapter 12), you might write: 'The difference between the emotionality scores for the children from two-parent families (M = 13.42, SD = 3.37) and lone-parent families (M = 9.50, SD = 3.10) is −3.92. The 95% confidence interval for this difference is −6.82 to −1.01. Since this interval does not include 0.00, the difference is statistically significant at the two-tailed 5% level.'

For further resources including data sets and questions, please refer to the CD accompanying this book.

12 Confidence intervals

Overview

- Confidence intervals are advocated as an alternative and, perhaps, better way of conceptualising inferential statistics since they better reflect the fact that statistical analyses are subject to a certain amount of uncertainty.

- A confidence interval is basically a range of a statistic within which the population value is likely to lie. Conventionally, single-point statistics such as the mean are given, which fail to reflect the likely variability of the estimate. The confidence interval would suggest that the population mean is likely to lie between two points or limits (e.g. 2.3 and 6.8).

- The most common confidence interval is the 95% value. This gives the interval between the largest and smallest values that cut off the extreme 2.5% of values in either direction. That is, the 95% confidence interval includes the 95% of possible population values in the middle of the distribution.

12.1 What are confidence intervals?

The idea of confidence intervals is an important one but too little used in psychological reports. Professional statistical practice demands that they are used though, as yet, they are far from universally employed. They can be regarded as an alternative to the point estimate approach which is very familiar since it is the conventional approach. Point estimates can be made of any statistic including the mean, the slope of a regression line, and so on. This book is full of examples of such point statistics. But point estimates fail to emphasise appropriately the extent to which statistical estimates are imprecise. To estimate the mean of a population from a sample as 8.5 suggests a degree of precision which is a little misleading. So the confidence interval approach does something different – that is, it gives the most likely range of the population values of the statistics.

Although expert statisticians recommend the greater use of confidence intervals in psychology they still tend to be supplementary rather than central to most analyses if, indeed, they appear at all. Nevertheless, the underlying concept is relatively easy to understand and, thanks to SPSS, involves little or no labour. In inferential statistics, we use all sorts of statistics from a sample or samples to estimate the characteristics of the population from which the sample was drawn. Few of us will have any difficulty understanding that if the mean age of a sample of participants is 23.5 years then our best estimate of the mean age of the population is exactly the same at 23.5 years. This estimate is known as a point estimate simply because it consists of a single figure (or point). Most of us will also understand that this single figure is simply the best estimate and that it is likely that the population mean will be, to a degree, different. We know this because we know that when we randomly sample from a population the sample mean is likely to be similar to the population mean but generally will be a little different. So it follows that if we use a sample to estimate a population characteristic then our estimate will be subject to the variation due to sampling.

Confidence intervals simply are the most likely spread of values of a population characteristic (parameter) when it is estimated from a sample characteristic (statistic). So instead of an estimate of the mean population age of 23.5 one would get a confidence interval of, say, 20.0 years to 27.0 years. Actually the confidence interval gives the spread of the middle 95% of means in the case of the 95% confidence interval or the middle 99% of means in the case of the 99% confidence interval.

The value of the confidence interval is essentially dependent on the spread of scores in the original sample of data – the bigger the spread of scores then the wider will be the confidence interval. So the variability in the scores is used to estimate the standard deviation of the population. This standard deviation can then be used to estimate the standard error of the population. Then it is simply a matter of working out the number of standard errors that cover the middle 95% of the distribution of sample means which could be drawn from that population. The number of standard errors can be obtained from something known as the *t*-distribution for any sample size but, as we are using SPSS, we can leave the computer to do the calculation.

SPSS calculates confidence intervals automatically as part of certain statistical procedures. Although we have dwelt on the confidence interval for the mean in this chapter, there are other statistics for which confidence intervals are provided, as listed at the end of this chapter.

Sometimes the concept *confidence limits* is used. Confidence limits are merely the extreme values of the *confidence interval*. In the above example, the 95% confidence limits are 4.64 and 15.36.

12.2 The relationship between significance and confidence intervals

At first sight, statistical significance and confidence intervals appear dissimilar concepts. This is incorrect since they are both based on much the same inferential process. Remember that in significance testing we usually test the null hypothesis of no relationship between two variables. This usually boils down to a zero (or near-zero) correlation or to a difference of zero (or near-zero) between sample means. If the confidence interval does not contain this zero value then the obtained sample mean is statistically significant at 100% minus the confidence level. So if the 95% confidence interval is 2.30 to 8.16 but the null hypothesis would predict the population value of the statistic to be 0.00, then the null hypothesis is rejected at the 5% level of significance. In other words, confidence intervals contain enough information to judge statistical significance. However, statistical significance alone does not contain enough information to calculate confidence intervals.

You can find out more about confidence intervals in Chapter 37 of Howitt, D. and Cramer, D. (2008) *Introduction to Statistics in Psychology*. Harlow: Pearson.

12.3 Confidence intervals and limits in SPSS

Confidence intervals have been presented in the output for the following tests described in this book:

- Regression *B*: see the table on page 92.
- Related *t*-test: see the table on page 111.
- Unrelated *t*-test: see the table on page 119.
- One-way unrelated ANOVA: see the table on page 169.
- Multiple-comparison tests: see the table on page 193.
- One-way ANCOVA: see the table on page 209.

Confidence intervals can also be readily obtained for the following statistics when using SPSS:

- One-sample *t*-test.
- One-way related ANOVA.
- Two-way unrelated ANOVA.
- Two-way mixed ANOVA.
- Regression – predicted score.

For further resources including data sets and questions, please refer to the CD accompanying this book.

13 Chi-square
Differences between samples of frequency data

Overview

■ Chi-square is generally used to assess whether two or more samples each consisting of frequency data (nominal data) differ significantly from each other. In other words, it is the usual statistical test to analyse cross-tabulation or contingency tables based on two nominal category variables.

■ It can also be used to test whether a single sample differs significantly from a known population. The latter application is the least common because population characteristics are rarely known in research.

■ It is essential to remember that chi-square analyses frequencies. These should *never* be converted to *percentages* for entry into SPSS as they will give misleading outcomes when calculating the value and significance of chi-square. This should be clearly distinguished from the use of percentages when one is trying to interpret what is happening in a contingency table.

■ Also remember that a chi-square analysis needs to include the data from every individual only once. That is, the total frequencies should be the same as the number of people used in the analysis.

■ The analysis and interpretation of 2 × 2 contingency tables is straightforward. However, interpretation of larger contingency tables is not quite so easy and may require the table to be broken down into a number of smaller tables. Partitioning chi-square, as this is known, usually requires adjustment to the significance levels to take into account the number of sub-analyses carried out.

■ This chapter also includes the Fisher exact test, which can be useful in some circumstances when the assumptions of the chi-square are not met by your data (especially when the expected frequencies are too low).

■ The McNemar test for significance of changes, which is closely related to chi-square, is also discussed. This looks at changes from one nominal category to another over two different points in time.

■ Versions of chi-square are used as measures of goodness-of-fit in some of the more advanced statistical techniques discussed later in this book such as logistic regression. A test of goodness-of-fit simply assesses the relationship between the available data and the predicted data based on a set of predictor variables. Consequently, it is essential to understand chi-square adequately, not simply because of its simple application but because of its role in more advanced statistical techniques.

13.1 What is chi-square?

Chi-square is a test of statistical significance that is used when the data consist of only nominal (category) variables (see Figure 13.1). It can be used with a single nominal variable (one-sample chi-square) but it is much more usual to use it with two nominal variables. If you have three or more nominal variables then it is likely that log-linear analysis (Chapter 30) is the solution though it is a much more complex statistic. It has to be said that many psychologists never collect data in the form of nominal category data rather than score data. As a consequence, despite its familiarity among psychologists, chi-square is not as commonly used as this might imply.

The basic principle underlying chi-square is the comparison of the frequencies of cases of members of samples with what might be expected to be the frequencies in the population from which the samples are drawn:

- In the one-sample chi-square, the population distribution is usually based on some known population (e.g. the national statistics on the number of males and females) or some theoretical distribution (e.g. the population distribution of heads and tails for tosses of a coin can be said to be 50% heads and 50% tails). (If you only have one sample then your best estimate of the population characteristics is therefore exactly the same as that sample, which is not very helpful.) There are very few circumstances in which a researcher would need to carry out a one-sample chi-square.

- In the two-sample chi-square, the population distribution is estimated from the available data since you will have two or more separate samples. This is simply done by combining the characteristics of two or more samples of data.

This is illustrated by the data in Table 13.1, which is sometimes known as a cross-tabulation table or contingency table. This table shows the data from a study in which a sample of males and a sample of females (i.e. the nominal variable gender) have been asked about their favourite television programme (i.e. the nominal variable favourite type of programme). Some mention soap operas, some crime dramas and others mention neither of these. The researcher wants to know if males and females differ in terms of their

Figure 13.1   Basics of chi-square

Table 13.1 Relationship between favourite TV programme and sex

Respondents	Soap opera	Crime drama	Neither
Males	27	14	19
Females	17	33	9

favourite types of programme – which is exactly the same thing as asking whether there is a relationship between a respondent's gender and their favourite type of TV programme. In chi-square, the assumption is that there is no relationship between the two nominal variables. In terms of our example this means that there is no difference between one group of respondents (males) in terms of their favourite TV programmes and the other (females). That is, the male and females come from the same population so far as favourite type of TV programme is concerned. The chi-square for the data can be referred to as a 2×3 chi-square as there are two rows and three columns of data.

What this amounts to is that it is possible to estimate the population characteristics simply by combining the findings for the males with the findings for females. Thus the 'population' distribution is 44 (i.e. $27 + 17$) for Soap opera, 47 for Crime drama, and 28 for Neither. The total size of the 'population' is 119.

But what if there is a relationship between gender and favourite type of TV programme – that is, what if there is a difference between males and females in terms of their favourite type of TV programme? If this were the case then the 'population' distribution will be very different from the distribution of favourite types of TV programmes for males and females separately. If males and females are no different in terms of their favourite type of TV programme then they should show the same distribution as the estimated 'population' distribution (which, after all, was simply the separate samples combined). In the terminology of chi-square, the cell frequencies are called the observed frequencies and the population frequencies are called the expected frequencies (since they are what we would expect on the basis that there is no difference between the samples).

The only complication is that the population frequencies have to be scaled down to the sample sizes in question, which do not have to be equal. So the expected frequency of males in the Soap opera condition in Table 13.1 is calculated on the basis that in the population there are 44/119 who prefer Soap operas and that there is a total of 60 (i.e. $27 + 14 + 19$) males. So the expected frequency of males who like Soap operas is 44/119 of 60 which equals 22.185. Notice that this expected value is different from the obtained value of 27 which can be seen in Table 13.1. The more that the obtained and expected values differ for all of the entries in the table, then the more that the male participants and the female participants differ. Chi-square is based on the sum of the squared differences between the obtained frequencies and the expected frequencies.

Chi-square is subject to a range of restrictions which mean that the data may need to be modified to make them suitable for analysis or a different analysis performed. The Fisher exact probability can be used, for example, instead of a 2×2 chi-square in some circumstances – that is where there are two rows and two columns of data. It is also available for the 2×3 case.

There is a variant of chi-square known as the McNemar test of significance of changes. This is a test of the change over time of the categories of a nominal variable in which a sample is placed. The nominal variable can only have two different categories. It is the chi-square equivalent of a related test. An example is given later in this chapter.

13.2 When to use chi-square

There are few alternatives to the use of chi-square when dealing solely with nominal (category) variables. Chi-square can only be used with nominal (category) data. It can be used where there is just one nominal variable but also where there are two different nominal variables. There may be any *practical* number of categories (values) of each of the nominal variables though you will probably wish to restrict yourself to just a few categories as otherwise the analysis may be very difficult to interpret. Chi-square is not used for three or more nominal variables where log-linear analysis may be the appropriate statistic.

13.3 When not to use chi-square

There are a number of limitations on the use of chi-square. The main problem is when there are too many expected frequencies which are less than five. Any more than 20–25% of the expected frequencies below five indicates that chi-square would be problematic. Sometimes a Fisher exact test can be used instead because low expected frequencies do not invalidate this test in the same way. An alternative is to combine categories of data together if this is appropriate, thus increasing the expected frequencies to five or above (hopefully). However, it is not always meaningful to combine categories with each other. Sometimes the alternative is simply to delete the small categories. This is all based on judgement and it is difficult to give general advice other than to be as thoughtful as possible (see section 13.5).

13.4 Data requirements for chi-square

Each participant in the research contributes just one to the frequencies of each value of the nominal variable. It is difficult to violate this requirement using SPSS but even then it is wise to check that the number of participants you have in your analysis is the same as the total number of frequencies in the chi-square if you are inputting your own contingency or cross-tabulation table into SPSS.

13.5 Problems in the use of chi-square

Chi-square is not an easy statistical test to use well. Fortunately, psychologists tend to prefer score data so the problems with chi-square are not routinely experienced by researchers. The main difficulties with chi-square are as follows:

■ Usually it is necessary to have a fairly substantial numbers of participants to use chi-square appropriately. This is because having small expected frequencies invalidates the test. Usually if you have more than about 20% or 25% expected frequencies of less than five then you should not use chi-square. You may be able to use the Fisher exact test instead in the 2×2 case. Otherwise it is a case of trying to rejig the contingency table in some way. But the main implication is to avoid categories of the nominal variable that attract few cases. These could be deleted or put with other categories into a combined 'other category'.

■ A major problem in using chi-square is what happens when the analysis is of something larger than a 2×2 contingency table. The problem is that an overall significant chi-square tells you that the samples differ, it does not entirely tell you in what way the samples differ. So, for example, do women tend to prefer soap operas and men tend to prefer crime drama? It is possible to analyse the data as a 2×2 chi-square by dropping the category 'neither', for example. Indeed it is possible to form as many 2×2 analyses out of a bigger cross-tabulation table as you wish though it would be usual to adjust the significance level for the number of separate chi-squares carried out.

■ One thing that gets students confused is that it is possible to enter a cross-tabulation table directly in SPSS using a weighting procedure. This would be useful in circumstances where you have carried out a study and already have your data in the form of a simple table. However, if your data are part of a bigger SPSS spreadsheet then this weighting procedure would not be used. It all depends on what form your data are in.

You can find out more about chi-square in Chapter 14 of Howitt, D. and Cramer, D. (2008) *Introduction to Statistics in Psychology*. Harlow: Pearson.

13.6 The data to be analysed

The computation of chi-square with two or more samples is illustrated with the data in Table 13.1 on page 126 (*ISP*, Table 14.8). This table shows which one of three types of television programme is favoured by a sample of 119 teenage boys and girls. To analyse a table of data like this one with SPSS, first we have to input the data into the Data Editor and weight the cells by the frequencies of cases in them.

■ As we are working with a ready-made table, it is necessary to go through the 'Weighting Cases' procedure first (see section 13.7). Otherwise, you would enter Table 13.1 case by case, indicating which category of the row and which category of the column each case belongs to (see section 13.8). We need to identify each of the six cells in Table 13.1. The rows of the table represent the sex of the participants, while the columns represent the three types of television programme. We will then weight each of the six cells of the table by the number of cases in them.

■ The first column, called 'Sex' in Step 1 of section 13.7, contains the code for males (1) and females (2). (These values have also been labelled.)

■ The second column, called 'Program', holds the code for the three types of television programme: soap opera (1), crime drama (2) and neither (3). (These values have also been labelled.)

13.7 Entering the data of Table 13.1 using the 'Weighting Cases' procedure

Step 1:

In 'Variable view' of the 'Data Editor' label the 1st 3 variables 'Sex', 'Program' and 'Freq' respectively.

Remove the 2 decimal places.

Label the values of 'Sex' and 'Program'.

Step 2:

In 'Data view' of the 'Data Editor' enter the appropriate values. Each row represents one of the 6 cells in Table 13.1.

Step 3:

To weight these cells, select 'Data' and 'Weight Cases ...'.

Step 4:

Select 'Freq', 'Weight cases by' and the ▶ button.

Select 'OK'.

13.8   Entering the data of Table 13.1 case by case

Enter the values for the two ·······
variables for each of the 119 cases. ·····

13.9   Conducting a chi-square on Table 13.1

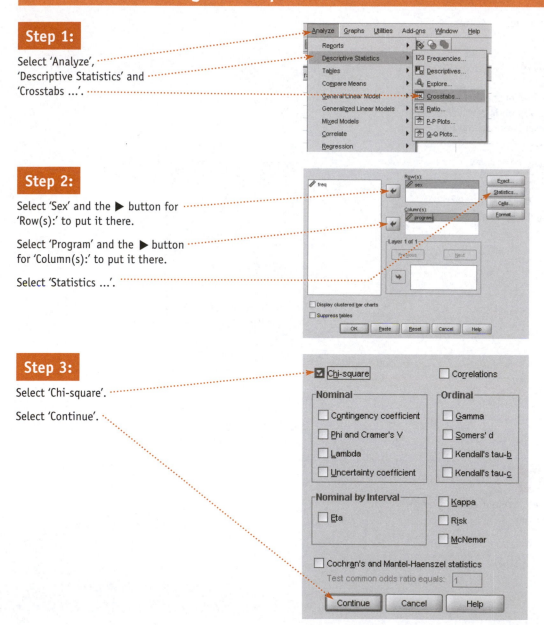

Step 1:

Select 'Analyze', ·······
'Descriptive Statistics' and ·······
'Crosstabs ...'. ·······

Step 2:

Select 'Sex' and the ▶ button for ·······
'Row(s):' to put it there.

Select 'Program' and the ▶ button ·······
for 'Column(s):' to put it there.

Select 'Statistics ...'. ·······

Step 3:

Select 'Chi-square'. ·······

Select 'Continue'. ·······

Step 4:

Select 'Cells'.

Step 5:

Select 'Expected' under 'Counts'.
Select 'Unstandardized' under 'Residuals'. Residuals means differences.

Select 'Continue'.

Select 'OK' in the previous box.

13.10 Interpreting the output for the chi-square

This second table of the output gives the frequency (count), the expected frequency (expected count) and the difference (residual) between the two for each of the six cells of the table.

Sex * Program Crosstabulation

			Program Soap	Program Crime	Program Neither	Total
Sex	Males	Count	27	14	19	60
		Expected Count	22.2	23.7	14.1	60.0
		Residual	4.8	−9.7	4.9	
	Females	Count	17	33	9	59
		Expected Count	21.8	23.3	13.9	59.0
		Residual	−4.8	9.7	−4.9	
Total		Count	44	47	28	119
		Expected Count	44.0	47.0	28.0	119.0

For example, the count or number of females saying they prefer 'soaps' is 17, the number expected by chance is 21.8 and the difference between these is −4.8.

You must understand what the figures for count for the gender by program cross-tabulation mean. This is equivalent to the original data table (Table 13.1). You could turn the figures into percentages. (See the screenshot in step 5 that gives three different options – Row, Column and Total percentages.) Choosing column percentages would probably help you see that males tend to prefer Soap operas and Neither more than females. Females tend to prefer Crime programmes more than do males.

The 3rd and last table gives the value of (Pearson's) chi-square (13.518), the degrees of freedom (2) and the two-tailed significance (.001). As this value is less than .05, this chi-square is significant.

Chi-Square Tests

	Value	df	Asymp. Sig. (2-sided)
Pearson Chi-Square	13.518[a]	2	.001
Likelihood Ratio	13.841	2	.001
Linear-by-Linear Association	.000	1	.987
N of Valid Cases	119		

a. 0 cells (.0%) have expected count less than 5. The minimum expected count is 13.88.

- The second (middle) table shows the observed and expected frequencies of cases and the difference (residual) between them for each cell. The observed frequency (called Count) is presented first and the expected frequency (called Expected Count) second. The observed frequencies are always whole numbers, so they should be easy to spot. The expected frequencies are always expressed to one decimal place, so they are easily identified. Thus the first cell of the table (males liking Soap opera) has an observed frequency of 27 and an expected frequency of 22.2.

- The final column in this table (labelled 'Total') lists the number of cases in that row followed by the expected number of cases in the table. So the first row has 60 cases, which will always be the same as the expected number of cases (i.e. 60.0).

- Similarly, the final row in this table (labelled 'Total') first presents the number of cases in that column followed by the expected number of cases in the table for that column. Thus the first column has 44 cases, which will always be equal to the expected number of cases (i.e. 44.0).

- The chi-square value, its degrees of freedom and its significance level are displayed in the third table on the line starting with the word 'Pearson', the man who developed this test. The chi-square value is 13.518 which, rounded to two decimal places, is 13.52. Its degrees of freedom are 2 and its exact two-tailed probability is .001.

- Also shown underneath this table is the 'minimum expected count' of any cell in the table, which is 13.88 for the last cell (females liking neither). If the minimum expected frequency is less than 5.0 then we should be wary of using chi-square. If you have a 2×2 chi-square and small expected frequencies occur, it would be better to use the Fisher exact test which SPSS prints in the output in these circumstances.

Reporting the output

There are two ways of describing these results. To the inexperienced eye they may seem very different but they amount to the same thing:

1. We could describe the results in the following way: 'There was a significant difference between the observed and expected frequency of teenage boys and girls in their preference for the three types of television programme ($\chi^2 = 13.51$, $df = 2$, $p = 0.001$).'

2. Alternatively, and just as accurate: 'There was a significant association between sex and preference for different types of television programme ($\chi^2 = 13.51$, $df = 2$, $p = 0.001$).'

In addition, we need to report the direction of the results. One way of doing this is to state that: 'Girls were more likely than boys to prefer crime programmes and less likely to prefer soap operas or both programmes.'

13.11   Fisher exact test

The chi-square procedure computes the Fisher exact test for 2×2 tables when one or more of the four cells has an expected frequency of less than 5. The Fisher exact test would be computed for the data in Table 13.2 (*ISP*, Table 14.14).

Table 13.2   Photographic memory and sex

	Photographic memory	No photographic memory
Males	2	7
Females	4	1

13.12 Interpreting the output for the Fisher exact test

Sex * Memory Crosstabulation

			Memory		
			Photographic	Non-photographic	Total
Sex	Males	Count	2	7	9
		Expected Count	3.9	5.1	9.0
		Residual	−1.9	1.9	
	Females	Count	4	1	5
		Expected Count	2.1	2.9	5.0
		Residual	1.9	−1.9	
Total		Count	6	8	14
		Expected Count	6.0	8.0	14.0

This is the 2nd of 3 tables in the output showing the observed (Count) and expected (Expected Count) frequencies of the 4 cells.

Chi-Square Tests

	Value	df	Asymp. Sig. (2-sided)	Exact Sig. (2-sided)	Exact Sig. (1-sided)
Pearson Chi-Square	4.381[b]	1	.036		
Continuity Correction[a]	2.340	1	.126		
Likelihood Ratio	4.583	1	.032		
Fisher's Exact Test				.091	.063
Linear-by-Linear Association	4.069	1	.044		
N of Valid Cases	14				

a. Computed only for a 2×2 table.
b. 3 cells (75.0%) have expected count less than 5. The minimum expected count is 2.14.

The 3rd and last table in the SPSS output. It shows the values of the statistics, their degrees of freedom and their significance levels. The significance of the Fisher exact test for this table is .091 at the two-tailed level and .063 at the one-tailed level.

Reporting the output

We would write: 'There was no significant relationship between sex and the possession of a photographic memory (two-tailed Fisher exact $p = 0.091$)' or 'Males and females do not differ in the frequency of possession of a photographic memory (two-tailed Fisher exact $p = 0.091$)'. However, with such a small sample size, the finding might best be regarded as marginally significant and a strong recommendation made that further studies should be carried out in order to establish with more certainty whether girls actually do possess photographic memories more frequently.

13.13 One-sample chi-square

We will illustrate the computation of a one-sample chi-square with the data in Table 13.3 (*ISP*, Table 14.16), which shows the observed and expected frequency of smiling in 80 babies. The expected frequencies were obtained from an earlier large-scale study.

Table 13.3 Data for a one-sample Chi-square

	Clear smilers	Clear non-smilers	Impossible to classify
Observed frequency	35	40	5
Expected frequency	40	32	8

Step 1:

Enter the data in 'Data View' of the 'Data Editor' having named the variables and removed the 2 decimal places. Label the 3 categories.

Weight the cells or cases with 'Freq'.

Step 2:

Select 'Analyze', 'Nonparametric Tests' and 'Chi-Square ...'.

Step 3:

Select 'Category' and the ▶ button to put it in the 'Test Variable List:' box.

Type in the expected frequencies one at a time in the 'Values:' box following each one with 'Add'.

Select 'OK'.

13.14 Interpreting the output for a one sample chi-square

Category

	Observed N	Expected N	Residual
Smilers	35	40.0	−5.0
Non-smilers	40	32.0	8.0
Unclassifiable	5	8.0	−3.0
Total	80		

The 1st of the two tables in the output shows the observed and the expected frequencies for the three categories together with the difference or residual between them. The 1st column shows the three categories, the 2nd column the Observed *N* or frequencies, the 3rd column the Expected *N* or frequencies and the 4th column the Residual or difference between the observed and the expected frequencies. The observed frequency of smilers is 35 and the expected frequency 40.0.

Test Statistics

	Category
Chi-Square[a]	3.750
df	2
Asymp. Sig.	.153

The 2nd table shows the value of chi-square (3.750), the degrees of freedom (2) and the significance level (.153). As the significance level is greater than .05, the observed frequencies do not differ significantly from those expected by chance.

a. 0 cells (.0%) have expected frequencies less than 5. The minimum expected cell frequency is 8.0.

Reporting the output

We could describe the results of this analysis as follows: 'There was no statistical difference between the observed and expected frequency for the three categories of smiling in infants ($\chi^2 = 3.75$, *df* = 2, *p* = 0.153).'

13.15 McNemar test

We will illustrate the computation of McNemar's test with the data in Table 13.4, which shows the number of teenage students who changed or did not change their minds about going to university after listening to a careers talk favouring university education (*ISP*, Table 14.17). The table gives the numbers who wanted to go to university before the talk and after it (30), those who wanted to go before the talk but not after it (10), those who wanted to go to university after the talk but not before it (50), and the numbers not wanting to go to university both before and after the talk (32).

Table 13.4   Students wanting to go to university before and after a careers talk

	1 Before talk 'yes'	2 Before talk 'no'
1 After talk 'yes'	30	50
2 After talk 'no'	10	32

Step 1:

Enter the data in 'Data View' of the 'Data Editor' having named the variables and removed the 2 decimal places.

Label value 1 as 'Yes' and value 2 as 'No'.

Weight the cells or cases with 'Freq'.

	After	Before	Freq
1	1	1	30
2	1	2	50
3	2	1	10
4	2	2	32

Step 2:

Select 'Analyze', 'Nonparametric Tests' and '2 Related Samples ...'.

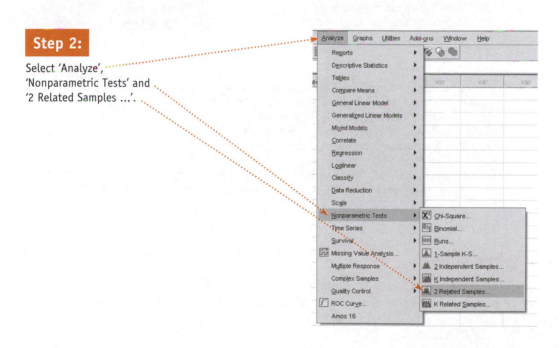

Step 3:

Select 'After', 'Before' and the ▶ button to put these 2 variables in the 'Test Pair(s) List:' box.

Select 'Wilcoxon' to deselect it.

Select 'McNemar'.

Select 'OK'.

13.16 Interpreting the output for a McNemar test

The first of the two tables shows the frequencies of cases in the four cells as in Table 13.4. The two values, 1 and 2, have not been labelled.

After & Before

After	Before 1	Before 2
1	30	50
2	10	32

The number who changed from wanting to go to university before hearing the talk to *not* wanting to go after hearing the talk (i.e. 10).

The number who changed from not wanting to go to university before hearing the talk to wanting to go after hearing the talk (i.e. 50).

The 2nd table in the output shows the total number (N) of cases (122), the value of chi-square (25.350) and the significance level (.000). Technically the significance level can never be 0: it is less than .001. As it is less than .05 it is significant. This means that there has been a significant change in the number of teenagers changing their minds about going to university after listening to a careers talk favouring university education.

Test Statistics[b]

	After & Before
N	122
Chi-Square[a]	25.350
Asymp. Sig.	.000

a. Continuity Corrected
b. McNemar Test

Reporting the output

We can report the results of this analysis as follows: 'There was a significant increase in the number of teenagers who wanted to go to university after hearing the talk ($\chi^2 = 25.35$, $df = 1$, $p < 0.001$).'

13.17 Chi-square without ready-made tables

In this chapter we have concentrated on how one can analyse data from pre-existing contingency tables. This is why we need the weighting procedure. However, you will not always be using ready-made tables. Any variables which consist of just a small number of nominal categories can be used for chi-square. For example, if one wished to examine the relationship between sex (coded 1 for male, 2 for female) and age (coded 1 for under 20 years, 2 for 20–39 years and 3 for 40 years and over), the procedure is as follows:

- Enter the age codes for your, say, 60 cases in the first column of the Data Editor.
- Enter the age categories for each of these cases in the equivalent row of the next column.

You can then carry out your chi-square as follows.

- You do not go through the weighting procedure first.
- The frequencies in the cells are calculated for you by SPSS.

For further resources including data sets and questions, please refer to the CD accompanying this book.

14 Ranking tests for two groups
Non-parametric statistics

Overview

■ Sometimes you may wish to know whether the means of two different sets of scores are significantly different from each other but feel that the requirement that the scores on each variable are roughly normally distributed (bell-shaped) is not fulfilled. Non-parametric tests can be used in these circumstances.

■ Non-parametric tests are ones that make fewer assumptions about the characteristics of the population from which the data came. This is unlike parametric tests (such as the *t*-test) which makes more assumptions about the nature of the population from which the data came. The assumption of normality (bell-shaped frequency curves) is an example of the sort of assumptions incorporated into parametric statistics.

■ Strictly speaking, non-parametric statistics do not test for differences in means. They cannot, since, for example, they use scores turned into ranks. Usually they test whether the ranks in one group are typically larger or smaller than the ranks in the other groups.

■ We have included the sign test and Wilcoxon's test for related data. In other words, they are the non-parametric equivalents to the related *t*-test. The Wilcoxon test should be used in preference to the sign test when comparing score data.

■ The Mann–Whitney *U*-test is used for unrelated data. That is, it is the non-parametric equivalent to the unrelated *t*-test.

14.1 What are non-parametric tests?

There is a whole variety of statistical techniques which were developed to use in circumstances in which data do not meet the standards required of other more commonly used statistical techniques. These are known as non-parametric or distribution free methods. By this is meant that they do not depend mathematically on standard distributions such as the normal distribution, the *t*-distribution and so on, unlike the *t*-test and similar techniques. Many statistical techniques were developed on the assumption that the data are normally distributed. To the extent that this is not the case, the results of the analysis using these tests may be to a degree misleading. Non-parametric tests are often referred to as ranking tests since many of them are based on turning the scores into ranks (where 1, 2, 3, etc. refer to the smallest score, second smallest score and third smallest score, etc.). However, not all non-parametric tests use ranking.

The other issue that results in the use of non-parametric tests is the scale of measurement involved. The interval scale of measurement assumes that the distances between each point on the scale are equal. If you think of a rule then the marks on the scale (e.g. millimetres) are of equal size no matter where you look on the rule. That is basically what an interval (or equal interval) scale is. It is possible to do things like work out the average length of things using such a scale. Imagine that the rule is made of plastic and it is heated such that it can be pulled and stretched. Now following this, the millimetres will not all be the same size anymore. Strictly speaking, the rule is now inaccurate and some would say useless. It is no longer possible to work out the average length of things because the rule has stretched more in some places than others. If the stretching had been constant then the rule would still be able to measure lengths though no longer in millimeters but some other unit. Since the stretching is not even, the question is whether the rule can serve any purpose at all. It could still be used to say which things are longer than which other things, for example.

What has this to do with psychological measurements? Psychologists have in the past argued that it has a lot to do with such measures as intelligence, extraversion and other measures. So unless they felt that their measures were on an interval scale then they would use non-parametric tests that do not assume equal intervals but only that a higher score on the scale would indicate greater intelligence, for example. The trouble with this is how do we know that psychological measures have equal intervals? The answer is that we don't.

So does that mean that we should never use statistics that assume equal intervals? Well some would argue that case. On the other hand, psychologists regularly seem to ignore the equal interval requirement. One reason is that they might feel that psychological measures are more-or-less roughly equal intervals so it does not matter that much. This is not much more than an article of faith and it has no factual basis. Others argue that the underlying psychological scale of measurement does not matter since mathematically it is the numbers (scores) which we do the statistical analysis on. So we do not need to bother about equal intervals and psychological measurement. This is the view that we take.

The parametric tests that are built on the equal interval assumption are among the most powerful statistical techniques available for psychologists to use. It would be extremely restricting not to use them.

If you wish to use a non-parametric test then there is no particular problem with this in simple analyses. Unfortunately for complex data it may result in a weaker analysis being employed and the statistical question may not be so well addressed. Some may regard this as statistical heresy but overwhelmingly it is clear that psychologists largely proceed on the assumption that their measures are on an interval scale – more-or-less.

SPSS has a range of non-parametric statistical tests for one sample cases, two sample cases and multiple sample cases. These are generally analogous to a parametric equivalent such as the *t*-tests or ANOVA:

■ The Mann-Whitney *U*-test is equivalent to the unrelated *t*-test and can be applied to exactly the same data.

■ The Wilcoxon matched pairs test is equivalent to the related *t*-test and can be applied to exactly the same data.

■ The sign test is a weaker test than the Wilcoxon matched pairs test and cannot generally be recommended as a substitute for the related *t*-test.

SPSS has these under 'Analyze ... Non-parametric tests'. That is also where the one-sample chi-square is to be found though this is not strictly a non-parametric test.

14.2 When to use non-parametric tests

Generally speaking, use non-parametric tests only when you have a very clear and strong reason for doing so. Quite what would be sufficient reason is not obvious. Before computers non-parametric tests would often be recommended as they are easier to compute by hand than parametric tests in general. But these circumstances are unlikely to occur nowadays. You might find it a useful exercise to compare the results of equivalent parametric and non-parametric analyses on the same data. It is unlikely that your interpretation will be very different and, where it is, these will be marginal circumstances close to the dividing line between statistical significance and non-significance.

However, you might find non-parametric tests useful in circumstances where you suspect that outliers might be affecting your results. These are uncommonly high or low scores that may disproportionately affect your findings. Because of the way they work, non-parametric tests are less prone to the influence of outliers. So, if you suspect the influence of outliers, then it would be useful to compare the results of a parametric and the equivalent non-parametric test on the same data. The non-parametric test will be likely to be much less statistically significant if outliers are confusing the parametric test.

14.3 When not to use non-parametric tests

Generally speaking, non-parametric tests are less powerful than their parametric equivalents. Basically this means that when applied to the same data, the non-parametric test is somewhat less likely to give statistically significant results. Unfortunately, it is not possible to give a rule of thumb which indicates the extent of this. If significance is being strictly interpreted as the 5% or 0.05 level then this may make a difference. However, it is our observation that psychologists are increasingly prepared to consider marginally significant findings (e.g. the 6% and 0.06 levels). This implies that the loss of power from using non-parametric tests may not be quite so important as it once was.

14.4 Data requirements for non-parametric tests

The data requirements for non-parametric tests are similar to their parametric equivalents. However, assumptions that the scores are normally distributed or that the measurement is equal interval need not be met.

14.5 Problems in the use of non-parametric tests

There are few problems in using non-parametric tests other than their reduced power compared to their parametric equivalents. In the past, before SPSS, they were considered student-friendly techniques because they were so easy to calculate. SPSS has put an end to that advantage and replaced them in the affections of teachers of statistics.

 You can find out more about non-parametric tests for two groups in Chapter 18 of Howitt, D. and Cramer, D. (2008) *Introduction to Statistics in Psychology*. Harlow: Pearson.

14.6 The data to be analysed

The computation of two non-parametric tests for related scores is illustrated with the data in Table 14.1, which was also used in Chapter 10, and which shows the number of eye contacts made by the same babies with their mothers at 6 and 9 months. Notice that the sign test (section 14.7) and the Wilcoxon matched-pairs test (section 14.9) produce different significance levels. The sign test seems rather less powerful at detecting differences than the Wilcoxon matched-pairs test.

Table 14.1 Number of one-minute segments with eye contact at different ages

Baby	Six months	Nine months
Clara	3	7
Martin	5	6
Sally	5	3
Angie	4	8
Trevor	3	5
Sam	7	9
Bobby	8	7
Sid	7	9

14.7 Related scores: sign test

Step 1:

Select the file of this data if you saved it. Otherwise enter the data.

	Six_mths	Nine_mths
1	3	7
2	5	6
3	5	3
4	4	8
5	3	5
6	7	9
7	8	7
8	7	9

Step 2:

Select 'Analyze', 'Nonparametric Tests' and '2 Related Samples ...'.

Step 3:

Select 'Six_mths', 'Nine_mths' and the ▶ button to put these 2 variables into the 'Test Pair(s) List:' box.

Select 'Wilcoxon' to deselect it.

Select 'Sign'.

Select 'OK'.

14.8 Interpreting the output for the sign test

Frequencies

		N
Nine_mths – Six_mths	Negative Differences[a]	2
	Positive Differences[b]	6
	Ties[c]	0
	Total	8

a. Nine_mths < Six_mths
b. Nine_mths > Six_mths
c. Nine_mths = Six_mths

The first of the two tables of output can be ignored. It shows the number of negative (2), positive (8) and no (0) differences in smiling between the two ages.

Test Statistics^b

	Nine_mths – Six_mths
Exact Sig. (2-tailed)	.289^a

a. Binomial distribution used.
b. Sign Test.

The 2nd table shows the significance level of this test. The two-tailed probability is .289 or 29%, which is clearly not significant at the 5% level. The binomial distribution refers to the statistical technique by which probabilities can be found for samples consisting of just two different possible values, as is the case with the sign test (given that we ignore ties).

Reporting the output

We could report these results as follows: 'There was no significant change in the amount of eye contact between 6 and 9 months (sign test, $N = 8$, $p = 0.289$).'

14.9 Related scores: Wilcoxon test

The 'Wilcoxon' test is the default option on the '2 Related Samples' tests dialog box. If you have previously deselected it, reselect it. Then OK the analysis to obtain the Wilcoxon test output.

14.10 Interpreting the output for the Wilcoxon test

The 1st of the two tables of output can be ignored. It shows the number of negative (2), positive (6) and no (0) differences in the ranked data for the two ages as well as the mean and the sum of the negative and positive ranked data. The values of 'Nine_mths' are bigger than those for 'Six_mths'.

Ranks

		N	Mean Rank	Sum of Ranks
Nine_mths – Six_mths	Negative Ranks	2^a	3.00	6.00
	Positive Ranks	6^b	5.00	30.00
	Ties	0^c		
	Total	8		

a. Nine_mths < Six_mths
b. Nine_mths > Six_mths
c. Nine_mths = Six_mths

Test Statistics[b]

	Nine_mths – Six_mths
Z	−1.706[a]
Asymp. Sig. (2-tailed)	.088

a. Based on negative ranks.
b. Wilcoxon Signed Ranks Test.

The 2nd table shows the significance level of this test. Instead of using tables of critical values, the computer uses a formula that relates to the z-distribution. The z-value is −1.706, which has a two-tailed probability of .088. This means that the difference between the two variables is not statistically significant at the 5% level.

Reporting the output

We could report these results as follows: 'There was no significant difference in the amount of eye contact by babies between 6 and 9 months (Wilcoxon, $N = 8$, $z = -1.71$, two-tailed $p = 0.088$).'

14.11 Unrelated scores: Mann–Whitney U-test

We will illustrate the computation of a non-parametric test for unrelated scores with the data in Table 14.2, which shows the emotionality scores of 12 children from two-parent families and 10 children from single-parent families.

Table 14.2   Emotionality scores in two-parent and lone-parent families

Two-parent family X_1	Lone-parent family X_2
12	6
18	9
14	4
10	13
19	14
8	9
15	8
11	12
10	11
13	9
15	
16	

Step 1:

Select the file of these data if you saved it. Otherwise enter the data.

	Family	Emotion
1	2	12
2	2	18
3	2	14
4	2	10
5	2	19
6	2	8

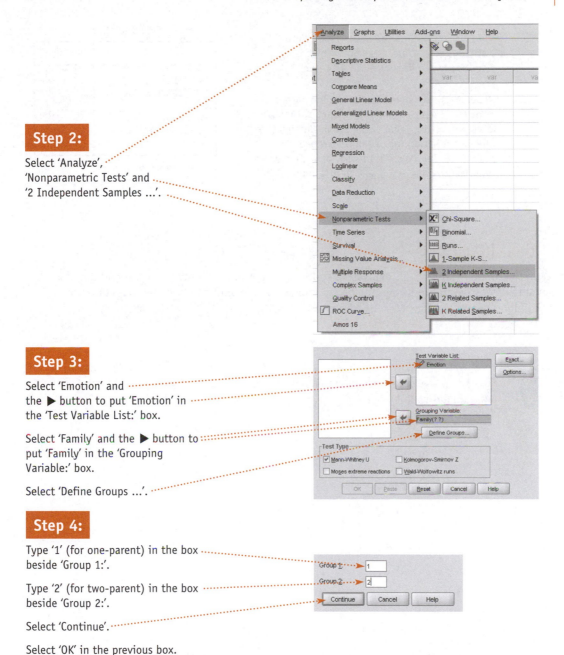

Step 2:

Select 'Analyze',
'Nonparametric Tests' and
'2 Independent Samples ...'.

Step 3:

Select 'Emotion' and
the ▶ button to put 'Emotion' in
the 'Test Variable List:' box.

Select 'Family' and the ▶ button to
put 'Family' in the 'Grouping
Variable:' box.

Select 'Define Groups ...'.

Step 4:

Type '1' (for one-parent) in the box
beside 'Group 1:'.

Type '2' (for two-parent) in the box
beside 'Group 2:'.

Select 'Continue'.

Select 'OK' in the previous box.

14.12 Interpreting the output for the Mann–Whitney *U*-test

The 1st of the two tables of the output can be
ignored. It shows that the average rank given to
'Emotion' for the first group (i.e. value = 1) is 7.85,
and the average rank given to the second group (i.e.
value = 2) is 14.54. This means that the scores for
Group 2 tend to be larger than those for Group 1.

Ranks

	Family	N	Mean Rank	Sum of Ranks
Emotion	1	10	7.85	78.50
	2	12	14.54	174.50
	Total	22		

The 2nd table shows the basic Mann–Whitney statistic, the U value, is 23.500, which is statistically significant at the .014 level.

In addition, the computer has printed out a Z value of −2.414, which is significant at the .016 level. This is the value of the Mann–Whitney test when a correction for tied ranks has been applied. As can be seen, this has only altered the significance level marginally to .016 from .014.

Test Statistics[b]

	Emotion
Mann-Whitney U	23.500
Wilcoxon W	78.500
Z	−2.414
Asymp. Sig. (2-tailed)	.016
Exact Sig. [2*(1-tailed Sig.)]	.014[a]

a. Not corrected for ties.
b. Grouping Variable: Family.

Reporting the output

We could report the results of this analysis as follows: 'The Mann–Whitney U-test found that the emotionality scores of children from two-parent families were significantly higher than those of children in lone-parent families ($U = 23.5$, $N_1 = 10$, $N_2 = 12$, two-tailed $p = 0.016$).'

For further resources including data sets and questions, please refer to the CD accompanying this book.

15 Ranking tests for three or more groups

Non-parametric statistics

Overview

- Sometimes you may wish to know whether the means of three or more different sets of scores are significantly different from each other but feel that the requirement that the scores on each variable are roughly normally distributed (bell-shaped) is not fulfilled. Non-parametric tests can be used in these circumstances.

- Non-parametric tests are ones which make fewer assumptions about the characteristics of the population from which the data came. This is unlike parametric tests (such as the *t*-test) that make fairly stringent assumptions about the distribution of the population from which the data came. The assumption of normality (bell-shaped frequency curves) is an example of the sort of assumptions incorporated into parametric statistics.

- Very few sets of data would meet the requirements of parametric testing exactly. However, some variation makes little difference. The problem is knowing just how much the assumptions of parametric tests can be violated without it having a major impact on the outcome of the study.

- Strictly speaking, non-parametric statistics do not test for differences in means. They cannot, since, for example, they use scores turned into ranks. Usually they test whether the ranks in one group are typically larger or smaller than the ranks in the other groups.

- We have included the Friedman test for related data. In other words, it is the non-parametric equivalent to the related ANOVA.

- The Kruskal–Wallis test is used for unrelated data. That is, it is the non-parametric equivalent to the unrelated ANOVA.

15.1 What are ranking tests?

Several non-parametric tests were described in Chapter 14. However, these dealt with circumstances in which only two sets of scores were compared. If you have three or more sets of scores there are other tests of significance that can be used. These are nowhere near as flexible and powerful as the analyses of variance described in Chapters 17–21 although they could be applied to the same data as some of the ANOVAs discussed in subsequent chapters. Nevertheless, in circumstances in which you have three or more sets of data to compare, then these ranking tests might be appropriate. There are unrelated and related versions of these ranking methods so they can be applied to the data in Chapter 17 on unrelated ANOVA and Chapter 18 on related ANOVA.

The decision to use non-parametric tests, then, does have an impact in that the analysis is less likely to be statistically significant than where the parametric equivalent is used – all other things being equal. Generally speaking, in simple research designs the non-parametric test will be adequate. The problem is that there is no non-parametric equivalent to many of the variants of ANOVA discussed later in this book – so SPSS does not have non-parametric equivalents of MANOVA, ANCOVA, mixed-design ANOVA, and so forth. So the researcher may have no choice but to use the parametric test. If it were possible to clearly specify the circumstances in which parametric tests are too risky to apply then it would be less of a problem but, unfortunately, such information is generally not available. The best advice is to try to ensure that the data collected are of as good a quality as possible. Problems such as highly skewed data distributions may reflect that the researcher's measures have been poorly designed, for example.

It needs to be understood that the non-parametric techniques generally use ranks rather than the original scores. This results in a situation in which it is not strictly speaking true to discuss the differences in group means though, of course, the ranks do reflect differences in the means.

The statistical tests discussed in this chapter are equivalent to the parametric ANOVAs described later in this book. So the Kruskal–Wallis test is used as an alternative to the unrelated one-way ANOVA (Chapter 17) and the Friedman test is the alternative to the related one-way ANOVA (Chapter 18).

15.2 When to use ranking tests

The tests described in this chapter can be used in simple one-way unrelated and related ANOVA designs. They can be employed when the data do not meet the requirements of the parametric equivalents. However, this is a very subjective matter to assess and no hard-and-fast rules can be given. There is a loss of power when choosing the non-parametric version and often a loss of the flexibility offered by the parametric versions. For example, you will have to carry out multiple comparisons tests using non-parametric versions of the *t*-test (see Chapter 14) with adjustments for the number of comparisons made. It is also important to remember that there are no non-parametric versions of some variants of ANOVA.

15.3 When not to use ranking tests

We would avoid using the ranking (non-parametric) version of the test wherever possible. As a way of learning about the practical limitations of these, we would suggest that you compare the outcomes of the parametric and non-parametric analyses on your data. You may be surprised how little difference it makes.

15.4   Data requirements for ranking tests

Given the loss of power when ranking tests are used, then researchers should satisfy them-selves that the data do not correspond to a normal distribution and that the data cannot be regarded as being on an equal interval scale. Other than that, the data requirements are the same as for the parametric equivalent.

15.5   Problems in the use of ranking tests

One major problem is that student research is often carried out on relatively small samples. This means that there is insufficient data to decide whether the data are normally dis-tributed, skewed and so on.

The limited variety of ranking tests on SPSS are a further limitation to their use.

You can find out more about non-parametric tests for three or more groups in Appendix B2 of Howitt, D. and Cramer, D. (2008) *Introduction to Statistics in Psychology*. Harlow: Pearson.

15.6   The data to be analysed

The computation of the non-parametric test for related scores is illustrated with the data in Table 15.1 overleaf, which shows the recall of the number of pairs of nonsense syllables for the same participants under the three conditions of high, medium and low distraction. The computation of the non-parametric test for related scores is illustrated with the data in Table 15.2 on page 154, which shows the reading ability of three separate groups of chil-dren under the three conditions of high, medium and low motivation.

15.7   The Friedman three or more related samples test

This test is used in circumstances in which you have three or more *related* samples of scores. The scores for each participant in the research are ranked from smallest to largest separately. In other words the scores for Joe Bloggs are ranked from 1 to 3 (or however many conditions there are), the scores for Jenny Bloggs are also ranged from 1 to 3, and so on for the rest. The test essentially examines whether the average ranks in the several conditions of the experiment are more or less equal, as they should be if the null hypo-thesis is true.

Table 15.1 gives the scores in an experiment to test the recall of pairs of nonsense syllables under three conditions – high, medium and low distraction. The same participants were used in all conditions of the experiment.

Table 15.1 Scores on memory ability under three different levels of distraction

	Low distraction	Medium distraction	High distraction
John	9	6	7
Mary	15	7	2
Shaun	12	9	5
Edmund	16	8	2
Sanjit	22	15	6
Ann	8	3	4

Step 1:

Enter the data. ⋯⋯⋯⋯⋯⋯⋯⋯⋯⋯⋯⋯⋯⋯⋯⋯

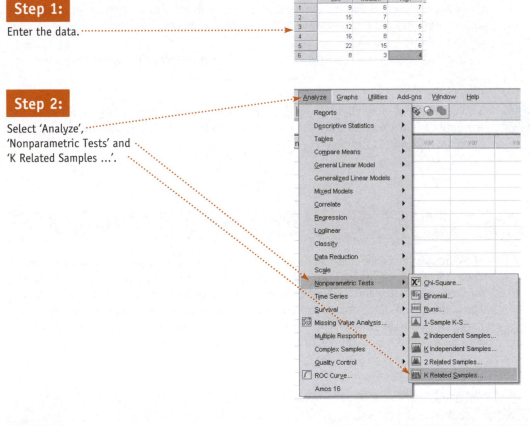

Step 2:

Select 'Analyze',
'Nonparametric Tests' and
'K Related Samples …'.

Step 3:

Select 'Low', 'Medium', 'High' and
the ▶ button to put these 3
variables into the 'Test Variables
List:' box.

Make sure that 'Friedman' is selected.

Select 'OK'.

15.8 Interpreting the output for the Friedman test

The first of the two tables of output can be ignored. It shows the mean rank for the three conditions.

Ranks

	Mean Rank
Low	3.00
Medium	1.67
High	1.33

Test Statistics[a]

N	6
Chi-Square	9.333
df	2
Asymp. Sig.	.009

a. Friedman Test

The 2nd table shows the significance level of this test. The two-tailed probability is .009 or 0.9%, which is significant at the 5% level. We would then need to determine which of these 3 groups differed significantly. We could use a Wilcoxon matched-pairs signs test (Chapter 14) to do this.

Reporting the output

We could report these results as follows: 'There was a significant difference in recall in the three conditions (Friedman $\chi^2 = 9.33$, $N = 6$, $p < .009$).'

15.9 The Kruskal–Wallis three or more unrelated conditions test

The Kruskal–Wallis test is used in circumstances where there are *more than two* groups of independent or unrelated scores. All of the scores are *ranked* from lowest to highest irrespective of which group they belong to. The average rank in each group is examined. If the null hypothesis is true, then all groups should have more or less the same average rank.

Imagine that the reading abilities of children are compared under three conditions: (1) high motivation, (2) medium motivation and (3) low motivation. The data might be as in Table 15.2. Different children are used in each condition so the data are unrelated. The scores on the dependent variable are on a standard reading test.

Table 15.2 Reading scores under three different levels of motivation

High motivation	Medium motivation	Low motivation
17	10	3
14	11	9
19	8	2
16	12	5
18	9	1
20	11	7
23	8	6
21	12	
18	9	
	10	

Step 1:

Enter the data.

Step 2:

Select 'Analyze', 'Nonparametric Tests' and 'K Independent Samples …'.

Step 3:

Select 'Reading' and the ▶ button to put 'Reading' in the 'Test Variable List:' box.

Select 'Conditions' and the ▶ button to put 'Conditions' in the 'Grouping Variable:' box.

Select 'Define Range …'.

Step 4:

Type '1' (for High) in the box beside 'Minimum:'.

Type '3' (for Low) in the box beside 'Maximum:'.

Select 'Continue'.

Select 'OK' in the previous box.

15.10 Interpreting the output for the Kruskal–Wallis test

The 1st of the two tables of the output can be ignored. It shows that the mean rank given to 'Reading' for the first group (i.e. High) is 22.00, the 2nd group (i.e. Medium) is 12.20 and the 3rd group (i.e. Low) is 4.43. This means that the scores for High tend to be larger than those for Medium which in turn tend to be higher than those for Low.

Ranks

	Conditions	N	Mean Rank
Reading	High	9	22.00
	Medium	10	12.20
	Low	7	4.43
	Total	26	

The 2nd table shows that the Kruskal–Wallis chi-square is 21.317, which is statistically significant at the .000 level. We would then need to determine which of these three groups differed significantly. We could use a Mann–Whitney U-test (Chapter 14) to do this.

Test Statistics[a,b]

	Reading
Chi-Square	21.317
df	2
Asymp. Sig.	.000

a. Kruskal Wallis Test
b. Grouping Variable: Conditions

Reporting the output

We could report the results of this analysis as follows: 'The Kruskal-Wallis test found that the reading scores in the three motivation conditions differed significantly ($\chi^2 = 21.31$, $df = 2$, two-tailed $p = 0.001$).'

For further resources including data sets and questions, please refer to the CD accompanying this book.

Part 4 Analysis of variance

16 The variance ratio test
Using the *F*-ratio to compare two variances

Overview

■ The variance ratio test (*F*-test) indicates whether two unrelated sets of scores differ in the variability of the scores around the mean: i.e. are the variances significantly different?

■ This is clearly not the same question as asking whether two means are different, and one should remember that variances can be significantly different even though the means for the two sets of scores are the same. Consequently, examining the variances of the variables can be as important as comparing the means.

■ Because few research questions are articulated in terms of differences in variance, researchers tend to overlook effects on variances and concentrate on differences between sample means. This should be avoided as far as possible.

■ The *F*-test is probably more commonly found associated with the *t*-test and the analysis of variance.

16.1 What is the variance ratio test?

One of the conceptual clichés which is hard to break is the idea that the main function of statistical analysis in psychology is to compare groups in terms of the mean scores on a particular variable. Is it not possible to imagine circumstances in which two groups differ not in terms of their means but in terms of the spread of their scores? For example, what about eating behaviour when under emotional stress? We have probably all heard people say that they eat more when they are stressed (e.g. comfort eating) but others say that they can't eat when they are stressed. So if we compared the eating behaviour of a group of participants suffering from stress with that of a group not suffering stress then we would not necessarily expect the mean amounts of food eaten to be different between the two groups. What we might expect is that some stressed individuals eat a lot more and other stressed individuals eat a lot less. In contrast, those who are not stressed should show no such tendency. In other words, eating behaviour may be more extreme in both directions for the stressed group than for the non-stressed group. The mean amount of food eaten in both groups may average out the same. So it would be quite wrong to suggest that stress has no effect on eating behaviour simply because the mean amounts eaten are the same.

How can one detect this difference between the groups? The variance ratio (or *F*-ratio) is one way of identifying that the variability of scores in one group is greater than for the other group. The variance ratio is simply the ratio of the larger variance divided by the smaller variance. If the variances are significantly different, then this means that the variability of scores is different for the two samples. It is called the *F*-ratio because this statistic is distributed like the *F*-distribution, which is a statistical distribution like the *t*- and *z*-distributions.

The variance ratio is part of other statistical techniques. For example, it is a crucial statistic in analysis of variance (although SPSS actually calculates Levene's test which is slightly different). Levene's test is also calculated as part of the unrelated *t*-test procedure. The *t*-test assumes that the variances of the two samples are statistically similar. If they are not, then a different version of the *t*-test must be used from the SPSS output.

16.2 When to use the variance ratio test

It is legitimate to compare the variances of scores for different groups of participants. Routinely a researcher would obtain the variance (or standard deviation or standard error) for each sample of scores as part of the basic descriptive statistics reported in any study. Any large differences in variance could be tested using the variance ratio test.

It is good practice to check that the variances on a particular variable are similar for the different groups in the study. Normally variance (or the related measures of standard deviation or standard error) are routinely calculated for each variable or sample as part of the basic descriptive statistics for the data. It would be appropriate to test for differences in variances if they seemed very different, say, for two different samples of participants. Most tests of differences between means routinely include variance ratios (*F*-ratios) in the SPSS output.

16.3 When not to use the variance ratio test

So long as the data are score data, use of the variance ratio test will be helpful in general.

16.4 Data requirements for the variance ratio test

The variance ratio needs to be computed on score data.

16.5 Problems in the use of the variance ratio test

There are no particular problems except that it is easily forgotten that variance is variation around the mean score of a sample. The value of the variance does not say anything about the mean score as such.

You can find out more about the variance ratio test in Chapter 19 of Howitt, D. and Cramer, D. (2008) *Introduction to Statistics in Psychology*. Harlow: Pearson.

16.6 The data to be analysed

To compute the variance ratio – or *F*-ratio – we divide the larger variance estimate by the smaller variance estimate. The variance estimate is produced by the descriptives procedure first introduced in Chapter 5. The computation of the variance ratio is illustrated with the data in Table 16.1 (*ISP*, Table 19.2), which reports the emotional stability scores of patients who have had an electric current passed through either the left or the right hemisphere of their brains. In this chapter, the method involves a little manual calculation. However, it provides extra experience with SPSS.

An alternative way of achieving the same end is to follow the *t*-test procedures in Chapter 11. You may recall that the Levene *F*-ratio test is part of the output for that *t*-test. Although Levene's test is slightly different, it is a useful alternative to the conventional *F*-ratio test.

Table 16.1 Emotional stability scores from a study of ECT to different hemispheres of the brain

Left hemisphere	Right hemisphere
20	36
14	28
18	4
22	18
13	2
15	22
9	1
Mean = 15.9	Mean = 15.9

16.7 Variance estimate

Step 1:

Enter the data. Code left hemisphere as '1' and right hemisphere as '2'. Label these two values. Call this variable 'Spheres' for short.

	Spheres	Emotion
1	1	20
2	1	14
3	1	18
4	1	22
5	1	13
6	1	15
7	1	9
8	2	36
9	2	28
10	2	4
11	2	18
12	2	2
13	2	22
14	2	1

Step 2:

Select 'Analyze',
'Compare Means' and
'Means …'.

Step 3:

Select 'Emotion' and the ▶ button
beside the 'Dependent List:' box to
put it there.

Select 'Spheres' and the ▶ button
beside the 'Independent List:' box
to put it there.

Select 'Options …'.

Step 4:

Select 'Variance' and
the ▶ button to put it in
the 'Cell Statistics:' box.

Select 'Continue'.

Select 'OK' in the
previous box.

Report

Emotion

Spheres	Mean	N	Std. Deviation	Variance
Left	15.86	7	4.451	19.810
Right	15.86	7	13.837	191.476
Total	15.86	14	9.875	97.516

The variances for the two
groups is in the last column
of this table. It is 19.810 for
the left hemisphere group.

16.8 Calculating the variance ratio from the output

■ Divide the larger variance estimate in the output by the smaller variance estimate. The
larger variance estimate is 191.476 (for 'Right'), which divided by the smaller one of
19.810 (for 'Left') gives a variance or F-ratio of 9.6656. This ratio is 9.66 when
rounded *down* to two decimal places.

- We need to look up the statistical significance of this ratio in a table of critical values of F-ratios where the degrees of freedom for the numerator (191.48) and the denominator (19.81) of the ratio are both 6.

- The 0.05 critical value of the F-ratio with 6 degrees of freedom in the numerator and denominator is 4.28.

- The F-ratio we obtained is 9.66, which is larger than the 0.05 critical value of 4.28 (see *ISP* Significance Table 19.1 where the nearest critical value is 4.4 with 5 degrees of freedom in the numerator).

Reporting the output

We would report these findings as: 'The variance of emotionality scores of patients in the right hemisphere condition (191.48) was significantly larger than those of patients in the left hemisphere condition (19.81) ($F_{6,6} = 9.66$, $p < 0.05$).'

For further resources including data sets and questions, please refer to the CD accompanying this book.

17 Analysis of variance (ANOVA)

Introduction to the one-way unrelated or uncorrelated ANOVA

Overview

- The unrelated/uncorrelated analysis of variance indicates whether several (two or more) groups of scores have very different means. It assumes that each of the sets of scores comes from different individuals. It is not essential to have equal numbers of scores for each set of scores.

- The different groups correspond to the independent variable. The scores correspond to the dependent variable.

- Basically the analysis of variance calculates the variation between scores and the variation between the sample means. Both of these can be used to estimate the variation in the population. If between samples variation is much bigger, it means that the variation due to the independent variable is greater than could be expected on the basis of the variation between scores. If this disparity is big enough, the difference in variability is statistically significant. This means that the independent variable is having an effect on the scores.

- The interpretation of the analysis of variance can be difficult when more than two groups are used. The overall analysis of variance may be statistically significant, but it is difficult to know which of the three or more groups is significantly different from the other groups.

- The solution is to break the analysis into several separate comparisons to assess which sets of scores are significantly different from other sets of scores. That is, which of the groups are significantly different from other groups.

- Ideally an adjustment should be made for the number of comparisons being made (see Chapter 20 on multiple comparisons for information on more sophisticated methods for doing this than those described in this chapter). This adjustment is necessary because the more statistical comparisons that are made, the more likely it is that some of the comparisons will be statistically significant.

17.1　What is one-way ANOVA?

One-way ANOVA is essentially an extension of the unrelated *t*-test to cover the situation in which the researcher has three or more groups of participants. Indeed, one could use one-way ANOVA instead of the unrelated *t*-test where one has just two groups of participants but convention is against this. The sort of data which could be analysed using one-way ANOVA are illustrated in Table 17.1. This shows the data for a study that investigated the effect of different hormone treatments on depression scores. Do the mean scores for the groups differ significantly? It would appear from looking at Table 17.1 that the mean score for Group 1 is higher than those of the other two groups since if we calculate the means we find that they are: Group 1 mean = 9.67, Group 2 mean = 3.67 and Group 3 mean = 4.00.

It is known as the one-way ANOVA since there is just one independent variable – that is, a single nominal variable forms the basis of the groups. In this case, that single variable is the drug treatment (Hormone 1, Hormone 2 and Placebo control). It is possible to extend this design to have a second (or third, etc.) independent variable as discussed in Chapter 19 on the two-way ANOVA.

Essentially ANOVA works by comparing the variation in the group means with the variation within the groups using the variance or *F*-ratio. The more variation there is between the group means compared to the variation within the groups then the more likely it is that the analysis will be statistically significant. The variation between the group means is the *between groups variance*; the variation within the groups is the *within groups variance* though it can be referred to as the *error variance* since it is the variation in scores which is unaccounted for. The bigger the error variance then the greater the possibility that we get variation between the cell means by chance. The calculation is a little more complex than this description implies but this will serve you well enough conceptually. Figure 17.1 shows the basic steps in one-way ANOVA.

Confusingly, ANOVA does not use the terms 'between groups variance' and 'error variance'. Instead terms such as *mean square between groups* and *mean square error* are used. This is merely a convention as they are, in fact, the *variance estimate between groups* and the *variance estimate error*. They are variance estimates because one is trying to calculate the variance in the population of scores using information from a sample of scores.

The language used in ANOVA can be somewhat arcane – terms such as levels of treatment, split-plot designs, blocks and so on reflect the origins of ANOVA in agricultural research. Gradually the terminology is changing but this takes a lot of time in psychological statistics.

Table 17.1　Data for a study of the effects of hormones

Group 1 Hormone 1	Group 2 Hormone 2	Group 3 Placebo control
9	4	3
12	2	6
8	5	3

Figure 17.1   The steps in one-way ANOVA

ANOVA, like other statistical techniques, makes use of the concept of degrees of freedom. This is closely related to the number of participants in the study though it is not always apparent. This is because the total number of degrees of freedom (which is always one less than the number of scores) gets divided up in various ways. Fortunately, SPSS does all of this for you.

Finally, you need to understand that a significant ANOVA simply means that the variation in the group means is bigger than can be accounted for simply on the basis of the variation due to using samples. In other words, the independent variable (the groups) makes a difference to the dependent variable (the scores). It does not mean that all of the groups have means that are significantly different from each other. In our example, the means are 9.67, 3.67 and 4.00. It is obvious that the last two means are not very different from each other whereas both are very different from the first mean. As part of ANOVA, it is usual to do some sort of test of which means are significantly different from each other. These are discussed in Chapter 20 on multiple comparisons. However, we do suggest simple procedures in this chapter that may be more readily understood by novices.

17.2 When to use one-way ANOVA

One-way ANOVA can be used when the means of three or more groups are to be compared. These must be independent groups in the sense that a participant can only be in one group and contribute one score to the data being analysed.

Conventionally, one-way ANOVA is not used when there are just two groups to be compared. A *t*-test is usually employed in these circumstances. However, it is perfectly proper to use one-way ANOVA in these circumstances. It will give exactly the same significance level as the *t*-test on the same data when the variances do not differ. When the variances differ it may be more appropriate to use an unrelated *t*-test where the variances are pooled together more appropriately.

17.3 When not to use one-way ANOVA

The main indication that there may be problems is when the test of the homogeneity of variances is statistically significant. This is discussed later in this chapter. This means that the variances of the different groups are very different which makes it difficult to combine them. The extent to which this is a problem is not well documented but it is probably not so important where the group sizes are equal. If the variances do differ significantly, then some researchers might prefer to use the Krusal–Wallis three or more unrelated conditions test which is available under 'Nonparametric' tests on SPSS (see Chapter 15).

17.4 Data requirements for one-way ANOVA

One-way ANOVA requires three or more independent groups of participants each of which contributes a single score to the analysis. Since one-way ANOVA essentially tests for differences between the means of the groups of participants, ideally the scores correspond to the theoretically ideal equal interval scale of measurement. The variances of the various groups need to be approximately equal.

17.5 Problems in the use of one-way ANOVA

Confusion arises because of the traditional advice that if the one-way ANOVA is not significant, then no further analysis should be carried out comparing the different group means with each other. This may have been sound advice once but it is somewhat outmoded. It is perfectly appropriate to use the Newman–Keuls test and the Duncan's new multiple range test as multiple-comparisons tests (see Chapter 20) even if the ANOVA is not significant. This begs the question whether ANOVA adds anything in these circumstances – the answer is probably no. If ANOVA is significant, then any multiple-range test is appropriate.

 You can find out more about one-way ANOVA in Chapter 20 of Howitt, D. and Cramer, D. (2008) *Introduction to Statistics in Psychology*. Harlow: Pearson.

17.6 The data to be analysed

The computation of a one-way unrelated analysis of variance is illustrated with the data in Table 17.1 on page 165 (*ISP*, Table 20.2), which shows the scores of different participants in three conditions. It is a study of the effect of different hormone and placebo treatments on depression. So drug is the independent variable and depression the dependent variable.

17.7 One-way unrelated ANOVA

Step 1:

Enter the data. Code the 3
conditions '1', '2' and '3'
respectively. Label them
'Hormone 1', 'Hormone 2' and
'Placebo control'.
Save this file to use in
Chapters 20 and 22.

Step 2:

Select 'Analyze',
'Compare Means' and
'One-Way ANOVA ...'.

Step 3:

Select 'Depression' and the ▶ button
beside the 'Dependent List:' box to
put it there.

Select 'Condition' and the ▶ button
beside the 'Factor:' box to put it
there.

Select 'Options ...'.

Step 4:

Select 'Descriptive' and
'Homogeneity of variance test'.

Select 'Continue'.

Select 'OK' from previous box.

17.8 Interpreting the output

The 1st table provides various descriptive statistics such as the number (*N*) of cases, the mean and the standard deviation for the three conditions and the total sample.

Descriptives

Depression

	N	Mean	Std. Deviation	Std. Error	95% Confidence Interval for Mean		Minimum	Maximum
					Lower Bound	Upper Bound		
Hormone 1	3	9.67	2.082	1.202	4.50	14.84	8	12
Hormone 2	3	3.67	1.528	.882	−.13	7.46	2	5
Placebo control	3	4.00	1.732	1.000	−.30	8.30	3	6
Total	9	5.78	3.308	1.103	3.23	8.32	2	12

Test of Homogeneity of Variances

Depression

Levene Statistic	df1	df2	Sig.
.293	2	6	.756

The 2nd table gives Levene's test of how similar the variances are. As this test is not significant (with a significance of .756), the variances are similar or homogeneous. If the variances were not similar, we should try to transform the scores to make them so. Otherwise there may be problems in interpreting the analysis of variance.

The 3rd table shows the results of the analysis of variance. The *F*-ratio is significant at .011 as it is less than .05.

ANOVA

Depression

	Sum of Squares	df	Mean Square	F	Sig.
Between Groups	68.222	2	34.111	10.586	.011
Within Groups	19.333	6	3.222		
Total	87.556	8			

- The *F*-ratio is the between groups mean square divided by the within group mean square, which gives an *F*-ratio of 10.586 (34.111/3.222 = 10.5869).

- This indicates that there is a significant difference between the three groups. However it does not necessarily imply that all the means are significantly different from each other. In this case, one suspects that the means 3.67 and 4.00 are not significantly different.

- Which of the means differs from the others can be further determined by the use of multiple comparison tests such as the unrelated *t*-test. To do this, follow the procedure for the unrelated *t*-test described in Chapter 10. You do not have to re-enter your data. However, do an unrelated *t*-test defining the groups as 1 and 2, then redefine the groups as 1 and 3, and finally you would redefine the groups as 2 and 3. For our example, group 1 is significantly different from groups 2 and 3, which do not differ significantly from each other. (See *ISP* Chapter 11 for more details.)

- Because we are doing three comparisons, the exact significance level of each *t*-test should be multiplied by 3 to obtain the Bonferroni significance level.

- It is useful to know how much variance the independent variable accounts for or explains. This is given by a statistic called eta squared. This statistic is not available with the one-way ANOVA SPSS procedure. It is available with the general linear model SPSS procedure described in Chapters 18–22. If you use the univariate option of the general linear model you will see that eta squared for this analysis is about 0.78. This means that the three conditions account for about 80% of the variance in the depression scores. Psychologists are encouraged to report this statistic as it gives an indication of the size of an effect.

Reporting the output

We could report the results of the output as follows: 'The effect of the drug treatment was significant overall ($F_{2,6} = 10.58$, $p = 0.011$, $\eta^2 = 0.78$). When a Bonferroni adjustment was made for the number of comparisons, the only significant difference was between the means of hormone treatment 1 and hormone treatment 2 ($t = 4.02$, $df = 4$, two-tailed $p < 0.05$). The mean of hormone treatment 1 (M = 9.67, SD = 2.08) was significantly greater than that for hormone treatment 2 (M = 3.67, SD = 1.53). There was no significant difference between the mean of the placebo control and the mean of either hormone treatment 1 or hormone treatment 2.'

For further resources including data sets and questions, please refer to the CD accompanying this book.

18 Analysis of variance for correlated scores or repeated measures

Overview

- The correlated/related analysis of variance indicates whether several (two or more) sets of scores have very different means. However, it assumes that a single sample of individuals has contributed scores to each of the different sets of scores and that the correlation coefficients between sets of scores are large. It is also used in designs where matching has taken place.

- If your data do not meet these requirements then turn back to Chapter 17 on the unrelated analysis of variance.

- Changes in scores on a variable over time is a typical example of the sort of study which is appropriate for the correlated/related analysis of variance.

- If properly used, correlated/related designs can be extremely effective in that fewer participants are required to run the study. The reason is that once participants are measured more than once, it becomes possible to estimate the individual differences component of the variation in the data. In a study of memory, for example, some participants will tend to do well whatever the condition and others will tend to do poorly. These individual differences can be identified and adjusted for in the analysis. What would be classified as error variation in an unrelated analysis of variance is separated into two components – the individual differences component (within subjects error) and residual error. Effectively this means that the error term is reduced because the individual difference component has been removed. Since the error term is smaller, it is possible to get significant results with smaller numbers of participants than would be possible with an unrelated design.

18.1 What is repeated-measures ANOVA?

Just as the one-way ANOVA was an extension of the unrelated *t*-test, the repeated-measures ANOVA is an extension of the related *t*-test to cover three or more measures taken (usually) at different points in time. It is mainly used to investigate how scores change on a measure for a sample of cases over a period of investigation but can be used where participants in three groups are matched. It could be used as an alternative to the related *t*-test since exactly the same level of significance would be obtained. However, conventionally this is not done.

The whole point of repeated-measures, related-scores and correlated-scores tests is that they can be very effective designs since they capitalise on the fact that participants are serving 'as their own controls'. That is to say, because individuals are measured at several different points in time, it is possible to estimate the tendency for individuals to give, say, particularly high scores or particularly low scores irrespective of the time that they are measured. In other words, it is possible to adjust the calculation for the consistencies in the responses of individuals measured at different points in time. This can be seen in the data in Table 18.1. As you can see, there are five participants who are given one of two drug treatments or an inert placebo. The scores are the amount of relief from pain felt in these three conditions. The greatest relief from pain is experienced in the Product-X condition where the average score is 8.00 compared to 6.00 in the Aspirin condition and 4.00 in the control Placebo condition. Thus the treatment condition does seem to have an effect.

But it is equally important to notice that Bob Robertson tends to get the highest relief from pain scores irrespective of the drug treatment condition. Bert Entwistle gets the lowest scores on average. The repeated-measures ANOVA simply takes this information and adjusts the scores to take account of these individual differences. In doing so, essentially it deals with some of the variance which would have been attributed to error in the unrelated measures one-way ANOVA. In other words, the error variance is essentially reduced. What this means is that the research findings have an increased chance of being significant simply because the error variance is smaller – that is, all things being equal.

Unfortunately, and this is largely overlooked by psychologists, all things are *not* equal. What happens is that the degrees of freedom associated with the error variance are reduced because of these individual difference adjustments. Depending on the size of the correlations between the scores in the different conditions, the analysis may be statistically significant (if the correlations are strong) but it may be statistically non-significant if the correlations are poor. But the researcher has to check on this.

The repeated-measures ANOVA introduces yet more new terminology. This is because the error variance (error mean square) no longer contains the variance due to individual differences compared to the ANOVA in the previous chapter. This adjusted error variance is known as the residual variance though it is usually used as the measure of error. The individual difference variance is known as the *between subjects* or *between people variance*.

The basic steps in the correlated samples ANOVA are shown in Figure 18.1.

Table 18.1   Pain relief scores from a drugs experiment

	Aspirin	**'Product X'**	**Placebo**
Bob Robertson	7	8	6
Mavis Fletcher	5	10	3
Bob Polansky	6	6	4
Ann Harrison	9	9	2
Bert Entwistle	3	7	5

Figure 18.1   Steps in the correlated samples ANOVA

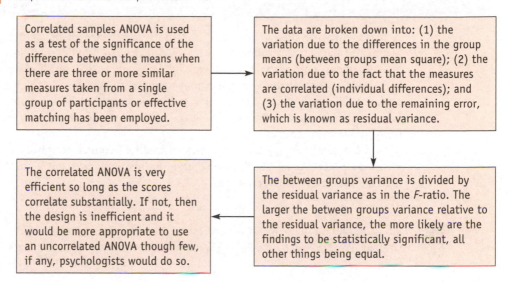

18.2   When to use repeated-measures ANOVA

Correlated-scores designs are relatively uncommon in psychology but do have some advantages in terms of their power in appropriate circumstances. They are, of course, essential if a group of participants is being studied over time on several occasions. Matching is harder to use though is perfectly appropriate as a way of achieving the requirement of correlated scores. It is essential that the dependent variable (the scores) is comparable at different points in time. Usually this is achieved by using the same measure on each occasion (or possibly alternative forms of the same measure).

18.3   When not to use repeated-measures ANOVA

We would argue that the repeated-measures ANOVA should only be used where the data show substantial correlations between the scores measured, for example, at different points in time. Otherwise, it is a form of analysis that has lower power compared to the unrelated samples ANOVA. That is to say, the findings may be non-significant for the correlated scores ANOVA but significant if the same data are put through an unrelated ANOVA analysis. Unfortunately, except for carrying out the two analyses and comparing the outcomes, it is not possible to say just how much the scores need to correlate.

18.4   Data requirements for repeated-measures ANOVA

The repeated-measures ANOVA requires a complete set of scores from each participant. It cannot be done using partial data. The scores in each condition should ideally have similar variances. Overall, the scores should correlate between conditions.

18.5 Problems in the use of repeated-measures ANOVA

A major difficulty lies in the view that the research design rather than the statistical features of the data determine that a repeated-measures ANOVA should be used. Unfortunately, there is no guarantee that matching, for example, will result in strong correlations between the scores in different conditions – unless it is known that the matching variable correlates highly with the dependent variable. Furthermore, it is just an assumption that individuals will serve as their own controls – it can only be the case for measures that are fairly stable over time.

A more common problem is the lack of multiple comparison measures for repeated-measures ANOVAs on SPSS. One solution to this is to carry out a number of related *t*-tests on selected pairs of conditions.

 You can find out more about the correlated ANOVA in Chapter 21 of Howitt, D. and Cramer, D. (2008) *Introduction to Statistics in Psychology*. Harlow: Pearson.

18.6 The data to be analysed

The computation of a one-way correlated analysis of variance is illustrated with the data in Table 18.1 on page 172, which shows the scores of the same participants in three different conditions (*ISP*, Table 21.10).

18.7 One-way correlated ANOVA

Step 1:

Enter the data. As the data are related the values for the 3 conditions are in 3 columns.

Step 2:

Select 'Analyze', 'General Linear Model' and 'Repeated Measures ...'.

Step 3:

Type '3' in the 'Number of Levels:' box.

Select 'Add'.

Select 'Define'.

Step 4:

Select each variable individually or all 3 together and the ▶ button beside the 'Within-Subjects Variables:' box to put them there.

Select 'Options …'.

Step 5:

Select 'Descriptive statistics'.

Select 'Estimates of effect size'.

Select 'Continue'.

Select 'OK' in the previous box.

18.8 Interpreting the output

The output gives seven tables. Only the more important ones are shown below.

Descriptive Statistics

	Mean	Std. Deviation	N
Aspirin	6.00	2.236	5
ProductX	8.00	1.581	5
Placebo	4.00	1.581	5

The 2nd table gives the mean and standard deviation for the groups.

Mauchly's Test of Sphericity[b]

Measure: MEASURE_1

Within Subjects Effect	Mauchly's W	Approx. Chi-Square	df	Sig.	Epsilon[a] Greenhous e-Geisser	Huynh-Feldt	Lower-bound
factor1	.862	.444	2	.801	.879	1.000	.500

Tests the null hypothesis that the error covariance matrix of the orthonormalized transformed dependent variables is proportional to an identity matrix.

a. May be used to adjust the degrees of freedom for the averaged tests of significance. Corrected tests are displayed in the Tests of Within-Subjects Effects table.

b. Design: Intercept
   Within Subjects Design: factor1

The 4th table gives the results for Mauchly's test of sphericity. As this test is not significant, sphericity is assumed and we do not have to adjust the significance levels for the analysis. If it is significant, then one of the alternative tests in the next output box should be used.

The 5th table gives the significance of the *F*-ratio. It is .037 when sphericity is assumed.

Partial eta squared is .561.

Tests of Within-Subjects Effects

Measure: MEASURE_1

Source		Type III Sum of Squares	df	Mean Square	F	Sig.	Partial Eta Squared
factor1	Sphericity Assumed	40.000	2	20.000	5.106	.037	.561
	Greenhouse-Geisser	40.000	1.758	22.752	5.106	.045	.561
	Huynh-Feldt	40.000	2.000	20.000	5.106	.037	.561
	Lower-bound	40.000	1.000	40.000	5.106	.087	.561
Error(factor1)	Sphericity Assumed	31.333	8	3.917			
	Greenhouse-Geisser	31.333	7.032	4.456			
	Huynh-Feldt	31.333	8.000	3.917			
	Lower-bound	31.333	4.000	7.833			

Very little of the output is needed. Mostly it consists of similar analyses using slightly different tests. These are used when Mauchly's test is significant in the previous output table.

■ The F-ratio is the mean square (MS) for 'factor1' (20.000) divided by Error(factor1) Mean Square (3.917). It is 5.106 (20.000/3.917 = 5.1059).

■ The exact significance level of this F-ratio is 0.037. Since this value is smaller than 0.05, we would conclude that there is a significant difference in the mean scores of the three conditions overall.

■ In order to interpret the meaning of the ANOVA as it applies to your data, you need to consider the means of each of the three groups of scores which are displayed in the second table. They are 6.00, 8.00 and 4.00. Which of these means are significantly different from the other means?

■ You also need to remember that if you have three or more groups, you need to check where the significant differences lie between the pairs of groups. The related t-test procedure in Chapter 10 explains this. For the present example, only the difference between the means for 'Product X' and the 'Placebo' was significant. Because you are doing several t-tests, each exact probability for the t-tests should be multiplied by the number of t-tests being carried out. In our example, there are three comparisons, so each exact probability should be multiplied by 3. This is known as the Bonferroni adjustment or correction (see Chapter 20).

Reporting the output

We could describe the results of this analysis in the following way: 'A one-way correlated analysis of variance showed a significant treatment effect for the three conditions ($F_{2,8} = 5.10$, $p = 0.037$, partial $\eta^2 = 0.56$). The Aspirin mean was 6.00, the Product X mean 8.00, and the Placebo mean was 4.00. None of the three treatments differed from one another with related t-tests when a Bonferroni adjustment was made for the number of comparisons.'

This could be supplemented by an analysis of variance summary table such as Table 18.2. Drugs is factor1 in the output, and Residual error is Error(factor1) from the fifth table in the output.

Table 18.2 Analysis of variance summary table

Source of variation	Sum of squares	Degrees of freedom	Mean square	F-ratio
Drugs	40.00	2	20.00	5.11*
Residual error	31.33	8	3.92	

* Significant at 5% level.

For further resources including data sets and questions, please refer to the CD accompanying this book.

19 Two-way analysis of variance for unrelated/uncorrelated scores

Overview

- Two-way analysis of variance allows you to compare the means of a dependent variable when there are *two* independent variables.

- If you have more than one *dependent* variable then you simply repeat the analysis for each dependent variable separately. On the other hand, if the several dependent variables are measuring much the same thing then they could be combined into a single overall measure using the summing procedures described in Chapter 36 or use MANOVA (Chapter 23).

- With SPSS, you do *not* need equal numbers of scores in each condition of the independent variable. If it is possible to have equal numbers in each condition, however, then the analysis is optimal statistically.

- Although the two-way ANOVA can be regarded as an efficient design insofar as it allows two different independent variables to be incorporated into the study, its ability to identify interactions may be more important. An interaction is simply a situation in which the combined effect of two variables is greater than the sum of the effects of each of the two variables acting separately.

- The two-way ANOVA can be tricky to interpret. It is important to concentrate on the means in each condition and not simply on the complexities of the statistical output. It is important to note that ANOVAs proceed according to certain rules. The main effects are identified prior to the interactions. Sometimes, unless care is taken, the interaction is mistaken for the main effects – simply because variation is claimed for the main effects before it is claimed for the interaction. As with most statistical analyses, it is important to concentrate as much on the patterns of means in the data as the statistical probabilities.

19.1 What is two-way ANOVA?

ANOVA can be extended to include two or more independent variables. This is illustrated by the data in Table 19.1 which relates to a study of the effects of sleep deprivation on the number of mistakes that participants make on a task (the dependent variable).

Table 19.1 Data for sleep deprivation experiment: number of mistakes on video test

| | Sleep deprivation | | |
	4 hours	12 hours	24 hours
Alcohol	16	18	22
	12	16	24
	17	25	32
No alcohol	11	13	12
	9	8	14
	12	11	12

There are three groups of participants on the basis of the independent variable Sleep deprivation. One group is deprived of sleep for four hours, one is deprived of sleep for 12 hours, and the third is deprived of sleep of 24 hours. However, there is a second independent variable – alcohol. Some of the participants are given alcohol as part of the study and another group are not given alcohol. As can be seen, every combination of the alcohol variable and the sleep deprivation variable is used in the study. This is known as a two-way ANOVA because there are two independent variables. In each combination, in this case, data has been collected from three different participants – a total of 18 different participants. (If it were decided to consider male and female participants separately in addition, then this would be a three-way ANOVA because there are three independent variables – sleep deprivation, alcohol and gender.)

It is possible to regard the data in Table 19.1 as two separate studies:

1. The effects of sleep deprivation on the number of mistakes made. In order to do this, one essentially ignores the alcohol condition so that there are six participants in the four-hour sleep deprivation condition, six participants in the 12-hour sleep deprivation condition, and six participants in the 24-hour sleep deprivation condition. One would compare the average number of mistakes made in these three conditions.

2. The effects of alcohol on the number of mistakes made. In this case, the sleep deprivation condition is ignored so that there are nine participants in the alcohol condition and another nine participants in the no-alcohol condition. One would compare the average number of mistakes made in the alcohol condition with the average number of mistakes made in the no-alcohol condition.

Thus really there are two separate studies contained within the one overall study. If it were two entirely separate studies, then one could compare the average errors in the sleep deprivation study using the one-way ANOVA discussed in Chapter 17 and the average errors for the alcohol study either using the unrelated *t*-test (Chapter 11) or the one-way ANOVA which is essentially the same thing for just two groups. This is more or less what happens in two-way ANOVA. Each of the separate studies, though, is called a *main effect*. So we would speak of the main effect of sleep deprivation and the main effect of alcohol. In the two-way ANOVA, the main effects are computed almost as if they were separate studies with one slight difference. That is, the degrees of freedom are slightly reduced for the error variance. The consequence of this is that the main effects are slightly less statistically significant than they would have been if the data had been analysed separately. In other words, there is a slight negative consequence involved in doing two studies essentially for the price of one.

Figure 19.1   A chart illustrating the interaction of sleep deprivation with alcohol consumption

However, there is nothing wrong in regarding each main effect as if it were a separate study.

There is an advantage in the use of two-way ANOVA. This is something known as the *interaction*. There is just one interaction for the two-way ANOVA but there would be four interactions for the three-way ANOVA. The number of interactions escalates with increasing numbers of independent variables in the design. Interaction is a difficult concept to understand. Looking at Table 19.1, it might be noticed that the number of errors made in the 24-hour sleep deprivation with alcohol condition seems to be disproportionately large. This is an indication that there may be an interaction since the scores in that condition are bigger than generally one would expect on the basis of the influence of alcohol acting alone and the effect of 24 hours of sleep deprivation acting alone. This becomes clearer if we put the means calculated from Table 19.1 on a chart (Figure 19.1). Notice that there are two lines on the chart – one for the alcohol condition and the other for the no-alcohol condition. The vertical axis on the chart is the average number of mistakes.

If we look at the four-hour sleep conditions first, it can be seen that on average a few more mistakes are made in the alcohol condition than the no alcohol condition. The 12-hour sleep deprivation conditions also indicate that even more mistakes are made on average in the alcohol condition than the no-alcohol condition. Finally, the 24-hour sleep deprivation conditions also show that more mistakes are made when alcohol is consumed but the difference is bigger than for any of the other sleep deprivation conditions. That is to say, the effect of being given alcohol is *not* consistently the same for each sleep deprivation condition. It is greater for some conditions than others. This is indicative of an interaction between the amount of sleep deprivation and whether or not alcohol had been consumed. The reason for this is that in statistics it is assumed that the effects of a variable are additive. In other words, there is an effect of being given alcohol which adds a certain amount to the effects of the different amounts of sleep deprivation. The crucial thing is that this effect of alcohol should be constant (the same amount) irrespective of the effect of the different amounts of sleep deprivation. This clearly is not the case in Figure 19.1 since more mistakes can be attributed to the influence of alcohol when participants have been sleep deprived for 24 hours than for those who had been sleep deprived, say, for four hours. This inconsistency of effect is the interaction. That is, alcohol has greater influence at some levels of sleep deprivation than others or, in other words, amount of sleep deprivation and

Figure 19.2   A chart illustrating a situation in which there is no interaction

alcohol interact to produce greater effects (greater numbers of mistakes) than the effects of alcohol alone plus the effects of the amount of sleep deprivation alone can account for.

Figure 19.2 illustrates one case where there is no interaction. Notice that the lines are parallel to each other. This means that alcohol has exactly the same effect on mistakes made irrespective of the amount of sleep deprivation.

In ANOVA, the main effects are calculated before the interaction is calculated. This means that priority is given to the main effects. Thus variation is attributed to the main effects as a priority and only the variation which is left over can potentially be attributed to the interaction. This is important when interpreting two-way ANOVA designs and others that involve potential interactions.

19.2   When to use two-way ANOVA

Two-way ANOVA, like other forms of ANOVA, are ideally suited to randomised experimental studies. ANOVA was initially developed to analyse the data from agricultural experiments. Of course, ANOVA can be used in other contexts but care has to be taken to avoid making the analysis too cumbersome. Survey data are usually too complex to use ANOVA on, though not in every case.

It should be noted that ANOVA is very closely related to multiple regression which may be preferred for survey-type data.

19.3   When not to use two-way ANOVA

While two-way ANOVA does have fairly restricted data requirements, it is actually difficult to avoid using it when interactions may be an important aspect of the analysis. This is because SPSS has no non-parametric alternatives to two-way ANOVA.

19.4   Data requirements for two-way ANOVA

The independent (grouping) variables should consist of relatively small numbers of categories otherwise the data analysis will be exceedingly cumbersome. This is not usually a problem for researchers designing randomised experiments as the practicalities of the research will place limits on what can be done.

It is best if the scores in each condition have more-or-less similar variances which SPSS can test is the case. As usual, many psychologists believe that it is better if the scores approximate an equal interval scale of measurement.

There does not have to be the same number of participants in each condition of the study though it is generally better if there are when the requirements of ANOVA are violated, such as when the variances of scores in each condition are different.

19.5   Problems in the use of two-way ANOVA

The major problem is the interpretation of the two-way ANOVA. It has to be appreciated that the calculation gives priority to finding main effects to such an extent that it can attribute to a main effect influences that really are due to the interaction. Take Figure 19.3. If you look at the No alcohol line you will see that there are no differences in terms of mistakes between any of the three sleep deprivation conditions. This would seem to indicate that there is no main effect for the variable sleep deprivation simply because all of the means are the same. If we look at the line for the Alcohol condition, there is no difference between the four-hour and the 12-hour period of sleep deprivation which again would indicate no main effect for sleep deprivation. The number of mistakes is the same for both conditions. This would suggest that there is no main effect of sleep deprivation. It is only when we consider the 24-hour sleep deprivation group given alcohol that we find that the number of mistakes changes. We would say much the same of the alcohol variable. If we consider the four-hour and the 12-hour periods of sleep deprivation, there is virtually no difference between the alcohol groups and the no-alcohol groups. This would be

Figure 19.3   A case where an interaction may be confused with a main effect indicative of no main effect for alcohol. Only when we consider the 24-hour sleep deprivation groups do we get a big difference due to alcohol.

If the ANOVA tells us that there is a significant main effect for either or both alcohol and sleep deprivation, we need to be very cautious since this is at odds with what the pattern of the data in Figure 19.3 tells us. We suspect an interaction. However, it is possible that the interaction is not significant according to the SPSS output.

The message is that the ANOVA may be confusing things and we need to be very cautious when interpreting the output. This is a case where simple descriptive statistics are vital to the interpretation of our data.

Anyone contemplating more complex ANOVAs than this should be wary that three-way, four-way, and so on ANOVAs generate massive numbers of interactions that are extremely difficult to interpret. We would suggest that very complex ANOVAs should be avoided unless you have a very good reason for using them and until your level of statistical skill is well developed.

You can find out more about two-way ANOVA in Chapter 22 of Howitt, D. and Cramer, D. (2008) *Introduction to Statistics in Psychology*. Harlow: Pearson.

19.6 The data to be analysed

The computation of a two-way unrelated analysis of variance is illustrated with the data in Table 19.1 on page 179. The table shows the scores of different participants in six conditions, reflecting the two factors of sleep deprivation and alcohol (*ISP*, Table 22.11). The purpose of the analysis is to evaluate whether the different combinations of alcohol and sleep deprivation differentially affect the mean number of mistakes made.

19.7 Two-way unrelated ANOVA

Step 1:

Enter the data. The 2 codes for 'Alcohol' (1 = Alcohol and 2 = No alcohol) are in the 1st column. The 3 codes for 'SleepDep' are in the 2nd column (1 = 4 hrs, 2 = 12 hrs and 3 = 24 hrs). The errors are in the 3rd column. Label these codes in this way. Remove the decimal places in 'Variable View'.

	Alcohol	SleepDep	Errors
1	1	1	16
2	1	1	12
3	1	1	17
4	1	2	18
5	1	2	16
6	1	2	25
7	1	3	22
8	1	3	24
9	1	3	32
10	2	1	11
11	2	1	9
12	2	1	12
13	2	2	13
14	2	2	8
15	2	2	11
16	2	3	12
17	2	3	14
18	2	3	12

Step 2:

Select 'Analyze',
'General Linear Model' and
'Univariate ...'.

Step 3:

Select 'Errors' and the ▶ button
beside the 'Dependent Variable:' box
to put it there.

Select 'Alcohol' and 'SleepDep' either
singly or together and the ▶ button
beside 'Fixed Factor(s):' to put them
there.

Select 'Options ...'.

Step 4:

Select 'Descriptive statistics',
'Estimates of effect size' and
'Homogeneity tests'.

Select 'Continue'.

Select 'Plots ...' from
the previous screen,
which reappears.

Step 5:

Select 'Alcohol' and the ▶ button beside
the 'Horizontal Axis:' box to put it there.

Select 'SleepDep' and the ▶ button beside
the 'Separate Lines:' box to put it there.

Select 'Add'.

Select 'Continue'.

Select 'OK' in the previous box which
reappears.

19.8 Interpreting the output

Descriptive Statistics

Dependent Variable: Errors

Alcohol	SleepDep	Mean	Std. Deviation	N
Alcohol	4 hrs	15.00	2.646	3
	12 hrs	19.67	4.726	3
	24 hrs	26.00	5.292	3
	Total	20.22	6.099	9
No alcohol	4 hrs	10.67	1.528	3
	12 hrs	10.67	2.517	3
	24 hrs	12.67	1.155	3
	Total	11.33	1.871	9
Total	4 hrs	12.83	3.061	6
	12 hrs	15.17	5.981	6
	24 hrs	19.33	8.066	6
	Total	15.78	6.330	18

The 2nd table provides the means, standard deviations and number (N) of cases for the two variables of 'Alcohol' and 'Sleep deprivation' separately and together. So the mean for the 'Alcohol' condition is given against the 'Total' (i.e. 20.22). The mean for the '4 hrs' 'Sleep deprivation' is given against the 'Total' (i.e. 12.83).

Levene's Test of Equality of Error Variances[a]

Dependent Variable: Errors

F	df1	df2	Sig.
2.786	5	12	.068

Tests the null hypothesis that the error variance of the dependent variable is equal across groups.

    a. Design: Intercept+Alcohol+SleepDep+Alcohol
      * SleepDep.

The 3rd table gives Levene's test to see if the variances are similar. As the significance of this test is .068 (which is above .05), the variances are similar. If this test was significant, the scores should be transformed say by using a logarithmic scale to make the variances similar. This is a matter of trial and error – try different transformations until the variances become the same.

Tests of Between-Subjects Effects

Dependent Variable: Errors

Source	Type III Sum of Squares	df	Mean Square	F	Sig.	Partial Eta Squared
Corrected Model	546.444[a]	5	109.289	9.739	.001	.802
Intercept	4480.889	1	4480.889	399.287	.000	.971
Alcohol	355.556	1	355.556	31.683	.000	.725
SleepDep	130.111	2	65.056	5.797	.017	.491
Alcohol * SleepDep	60.778	2	30.389	2.708	.107	.311
Error	134.667	12	11.222			
Total	5162.000	18				
Corrected Total	681.111	17				

a. R Squared = .802 (Adjusted R Squared = .720)

The 4th table gives the significance levels for the two variables of 'Alcohol' and 'SleepDep' and their interaction as well as their partial etas squared. Partial eta squared is the sum of squares for an effect (e.g. 355.556 for alcohol) divided by the sum of squares for that effect added to the sum of squares for the error (355.556 + 134.667). In other word, it does not take account of the variance explained by the other effects.

- In the analysis of variance table the *F*-ratio for the two main effects ('Alcohol' and 'SleepDep') is presented first.

- For the first variable of alcohol the *F*-ratio is 31.683, which is significant at less than the 0.0005 level. Since there are only two conditions for this effect we can conclude that the mean score for one condition is significantly higher than that for the other condition.

- For the second variable of sleep deprivation it is 5.797, which has an exact significance level of 0.017. In other words, this *F*-ratio is statistically significant at the 0.05 level, which means that the means of the three sleep conditions are dissimilar.

- Which of the means differ from the others can be further determined by the use of multiple-comparison tests such as the unrelated *t*-test.

- The *F*-ratio for the two-way interaction between the two variables (Alcohol * SleepDep) is 2.708. As the exact significance level of this ratio is 0.107 we would conclude that there was no significant interaction.

This plot is shown for the means of the six conditions. It has been edited with the 'Chart Editor'. The style of the different coloured lines has been changed so that they can be more readily distinguished.

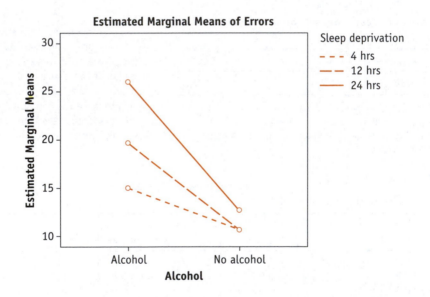

19.9 Editing the graph

Step 1:

To change the style of line, double click on the plot to select the 'Chart Editor'.

Select the line in the legend to be changed.

Step 2:

Select the ▼ button next to 'Style' and select the style of line desired.
Change the size of the line if desired.
Change the colour if desired.

Select 'Apply' and then 'Close'

Select the next line to be edited and repeat these steps.

Reporting the output

■ We could report the results of the output as follows: 'A two-way unrelated ANOVA showed that significant effects were obtained for alcohol ($F_{2,12} = 31.68$, $p < 0.001$, partial $\eta^2 = 0.73$) and sleep deprivation ($F_{2,12} = 5.80$, $p = 0.017$, partial $\eta^2 = 0.49$) but not for their interaction ($F_{2,12} = 2.70$, $p = 0.107$, partial $\eta^2 = 0.31$).'

■ It is usual to give an analysis of variance summary table. A simple one, like that shown in Table 19.2, would leave out some of the information in the third table in the output, which is unnecessary.

■ Because the 'SleepDep' factor has more than two conditions, we need to use an appropriate multiple-comparison test to determine the means of which groups differ significantly (see Chapter 20).

■ We also need to report the means and standard deviations of the groups which differ significantly. These descriptive statistics are given in the second table of the output.

Table 19.2 Analysis of variance summary table

Source of variation	Sums of squares	Degrees of freedom	Mean square	F-ratio	Probability
Alcohol	355.56	1	355.56	31.68	< .001
Sleep deprivation	130.11	2	65.06	5.80	< .05
Alcohol with sleep deprivation	60.78	2	30.39	2.71	Not significant
Error	134.67	12	11.22		

For further resources including data sets and questions, please refer to the CD accompanying this book.

20 Multiple comparisons in ANOVA

Overview

- This chapter extends the coverage of multiple *t*-tests from Chapters 17 and 18. It explains how to decide which particular pairs of means are significantly different from each other in the analysis of variance.

- The technique is used when you have more than two means. It adds no further information if there are only two means.

- ANOVAs with three or more means to compare are almost certain to benefit from employing multiple comparison methods.

- It is not possible to give definitive advice as to which multiple comparison test to use in different situations as there is no clear consensus in the literature.

20.1 What is multiple comparisons testing?

ANOVA brings problems of interpretation when the independent variable (the grouping variable) has three or more categories. The problem arises because if the ANOVA is significant, this does not indicate that all of the means are significantly different from each other – it merely implies that the pattern of means is unlikely to have occurred by chance as a consequence of random sampling from a population in which the groups do not differ. If the independent variable has just two categories, then a significant ANOVA indicates that the two means involved do differ significantly from each other.

Take the data in Table 20.1 which we have previously discussed in Chapter 17. We have added the group means on the dependent variable Depression in each case. What is obvious is that the mean depression score is higher in the Hormone 1 condition than in the other two conditions. Indeed, there seems to be little difference between the Hormone 2 group and the Placebo control group. If any comparison is statistically significant, it is likely to be the comparison between the Hormone 1 group and the Hormone 2 group. The comparison between the Hormone 1 group and the Placebo control group is the next most likely significant difference. It is very unlikely that the comparison between the Hormone 2 group and the Placebo control group will be statistically significant.

Table 20.1   Data for a study of the effects of hormones

Group 1 Hormone 1	Group 2 Hormone 2	Group 3 Placebo control
9	4	3
12	2	6
8	5	3
Mean = 9.667	Mean = 3.667	Mean = 4.000

It would seem to be obvious to compare the pairs of means using the t-test in these circumstances. There is just one problem with what is otherwise a good idea – that is, the more statistical analyses one carries out on any data the more likely that one is to get at least one statistically significant finding by chance. So if that method is to be used, then some adjustment should be made to deal with this problem. One way of doing this is the Bonferroni procedure which basically involves adjusting the significance level for the number of t-tests used. However, there is little point in doing this as SPSS has far better multiple comparisons tests available.

The problem is generally to decide which one(s) to use. It has to be said that there is little clarity in the literature on this matter. One way of dealing with this would be to use all of the available multiple comparisons tests on SPSS on the grounds that if they all lead to the same conclusion there is no problem – a problem only arises if they give different conclusions. However, we would recommend instead that you consider using the Newman–Keuls test (S-N-K in SPSS) or Duncan's new multiple range test, which are both available on SPSS. There are two reasons as follows:

1. These are among the more powerful multiple range tests and are not prone to problems.

2. They can be used when the ANOVA is not statistically significant overall. This is important because in the past it used to be claimed that ANOVA had to be significant before any paired comparisons could be tested for. This produced obvious anomalous situations in which certain means were clearly very different but had to be disregarded because of this unfortunate 'rule'. It should be added that some of the multiple comparisons tests were developed as alternatives to ANOVA anyway so it is legitimate to use them on their own.

These two tests assume that each condition has the same number of cases in them. A test that does not assume this is the Scheffé test. However, it is a more conservative test which means that differences are less likely to be significant.

Of course, the issue of multiple-comparisons disappears when the independent variables in the ANOVA only have two different values. With a one-way ANOVA then it is easy to obtain multiple comparisons. However, with the two-way ANOVA and more complex versions one has to resort to breaking the analysis up into individual one-way ANOVAs in order to employ multiple comparisons. It is probably sound advice, wherever possible, then to plan the two-way ANOVA in a way in which each independent variable has only two values, which circumvents the problem. However, this is not always desirable, of course. SPSS will calculate the multiple comparisons tests for two-way (and more complex) ANOVAs simply by doing two (or more) separate one-way ANOVAs.

20.2 When to use multiple comparisons testing

It is appropriate to carry out Newman–Keuls test (S-N-K in SPSS) or Duncan's new multiple range test whenever one is doing an unrelated samples one-way ANOVA irrespective of the outcome of the ANOVA. Generally, it is helpful to calculate multiple comparisons tests for one-way unrelated ANOVAs of the sort described in Chapter 17. If the variances of your groups depart markedly from being equal, it is possible to select a multiple comparisons test which does not assume equal variances. The Games–Howell would be a good choice in these circumstances. SPSS will calculate a homogeneity of variance test as one of the procedure's options.

Multiple comparisons testing is available for two-way and more complex ANOVAs. However, be aware that SPSS will not attempt to calculate these where there are only two conditions of the independent (grouping) variable.

20.3 When not to use multiple comparisons testing

Unfortunately, there is no point trying to do multiple comparisons tests on SPSS when dealing with correlated data as in the correlated ANOVA (Chapter 18). It simply does not have any available. In these circumstances you could resort to multiple related *t*-tests between pairs of means.

20.4 Data requirements for multiple comparisons testing

There is a flexible choice of multiple comparisons tests in SPSS. Some of these do not require equality of variances. It is a simple matter to go into Options in SPSS for ANOVA analyses and select 'Homogeneity test'. If this is statistically significant then one should choose a multiple comparisons test that does not assume that the variances are equal.

20.5 Problems in the use of multiple comparisons testing

The output from SPSS for multiple comparisons tests is not entirely consistent for each of the tests. Choosing more then one test can make the output seem much more complicated so you may find it easier to check for homogeneity before running the multiple comparison test of your choice. This does mean running the analysis twice but this is a minor chore for SPSS.

 You can find out more about multiple comparison tests in Chapter 23 of Howitt, D. and Cramer, D. (2008) *Introduction to Statistics in Psychology*. Harlow: Pearson.

20.6 The data to be analysed

Knowing precisely where significant differences lie between different conditions of your study is important. The overall trend in the ANOVA may only tell you part of the story. SPSS has a number of post hoc procedures which are, of course, applied after the data are collected and not planned initially. They all do slightly different things. There is a thorough discussion of them in Howell, D. (2007) *Statistical Methods for Psychology* (6th edition), Belmont, CA: Wadsworth. We will illustrate the use of these multiple comparison procedures (using the data in Table 20.1 on page 190, which were previously discussed in Chapter 17).

20.7 Multiple comparison tests

Step 1:

Select the data file if you saved it. Otherwise enter the data.

Step 2:

Select 'Analyze', 'Compare Means' and 'One-Way ANOVA ...'.

Step 3:

Select 'Depression' and the ▶ button beside the 'Dependent List:' box to put it there.

Select 'Condition' and the ▶ button beside the 'Factor:' box to put it there.

Select 'Post Hoc ...'.

Step 4:

Select 'S-N-K', 'Duncan' and 'Scheffe'.

Select 'Continue'.

Select 'OK' in the previous box.

20.8 Interpreting the output

ANOVA

Depression

	Sum of Squares	df	Mean Square	F	Sig.
Between Groups	68.222	2	34.111	10.586	.011
Within Groups	19.333	6	3.222		
Total	87.556	8			

The 1st table shows the results for the analysis of variance. The *F*-ratio for the Between Groups effect (i.e. the effects of hormones) is 10.586, which has an exact significance level of .011. In other words, the Between Groups effect is significant. Overall the means for the three groups differ.

The second and last table gives the results for the three multiple comparison tests.

Multiple Comparisons

Dependent Variable: Depression

	(I) Condition	(J) Condition	Mean Difference (I-J)	Std. Error	Sig.	95% Confidence Interval	
						Lower Bound	Upper Bound
Scheffe	Hormone 1	Hormone 2	6.000*	1.466	.018	1.30	10.70
		Placebo control	5.667*	1.466	.023	.97	10.37
	Hormone 2	Hormone 1	−6.000*	1.466	.018	−10.70	−1.30
		Placebo control	−.333	1.466	.975	−5.03	4.37
	Placebo control	Hormone 1	−5.667*	1.466	.023	−10.37	−.97
		Hormone 2	.333	1.466	.975	−4.37	5.03

*. The mean difference is significant at the .05 level.

For example, using the Scheffé test, the Hormone 1 mean is significantly different from the Hormone 2 mean (sig. = .018) and the Placebo control mean (sig. = .023).

Homogeneous Subsets

Depression

	Condition	N	Subset for alpha = .05	
			1	2
Student-Newman-Keuls[a]	Hormone 2	3	3.67	
	Placebo control	3	4.00	
	Hormone 1	3		9.67
	Sig.		.828	1.000
Duncan[a]	Hormone 2	3	3.67	
	Placebo control	3	4.00	
	Hormone 1	3		9.67
	Sig.		.828	1.000
Scheffe[a]	Hormone 2	3	3.67	
	Placebo control	3	4.00	
	Hormone 1	3		9.67
	Sig.		.975	1.000

Means for groups in homogeneous subsets are displayed.
a. Uses Harmonic Mean Sample Size = 3.000.

Hormone 2 and Placebo control are in the same subset – i.e. not significantly different.

Hormone 1 is the only group in this 2nd subset. Consequently it is significantly different from the other two group means.

■ The last table, entitled 'Homogeneous Subsets', lists the sets of means which do not *differ* significantly from each other. So taking the section for the Student–Newman–Keuls test, there are two subsets of means. Subset 1 indicates that the Hormone 2 and Placebo control means of 3.67 and 4.00 do not differ significantly. Subset 2 contains just the Hormone 1 mean of 9.67. Thus the mean of Hormone 1 differs significantly from the means of both Hormone 2 and the Placebo control. However, the means of Hormone 2 and the Placebo control do not differ significantly. The pattern is identical for the Duncan and Scheffé tests in this case – but it is not always so.

■ Therefore the three multiple comparison tests all suggest the same thing: that there are significant differences between Hormone 1 and Hormone 2, and between Hormone 1 and the Placebo control. There are no other differences. So, for example, it is not possible to say that Hormone 1 and Hormone 2 are significantly different.

■ The choice between the three tests is not a simple matter. Howell, D. (2007) *Statistical Methods for Psychology* (6th edition), Belmont, CA: Wadsworth makes some recommendations.

Reporting the output

We could report the results of the output as follows: 'A one-way unrelated analysis of variance showed an overall significant effect for the type of drug treatment ($F_{2,6} = 10.59$, $p = 0.011$). Scheffé's range test found that the Hormone 1 group differed from the Hormone 2 group ($p = 0.018$) and the Placebo control ($p = 0.023$) but no other significant differences were found.'

For further resources including data sets and questions, please refer to the CD accompanying this book.

21 Two-way mixed analysis of variance (ANOVA)

Overview

- A mixed analysis of variance design is merely a two-way (or three-way, etc.) research design which contains *both* unrelated and related independent variables.

- Mixed designs generate rather more complex measures of error estimates compared to other forms of the ANOVA. This means that special care needs to be taken when producing appropriate summary tables.

- Apart from that, concepts from related and unrelated ANOVAs apply.

21.1 What is two-way mixed analysis of variance?

So long as you understand the two-way ANOVA (Chapter 19) and the concept of related data (Chapter 18), there is little new to learn for the mixed analysis of variance. It is simply a two-way ANOVA in which one of the two independent variables is based on repeated measures of the same variable such as when a group of participants is measured at several different points in time, for example. An example of a mixed design is shown in Table 21.1.

The study consists of two separate groups of children – the experimental and the control conditions or the experimental and control groups. These are unrelated groups since

Table 21.1   Pre- and post-test self-esteem scores in two conditions

Conditions	Children	Pre-test	Post-test
Control	1	6	5
	2	4	6
	3	5	7
Experimental	4	7	10
	5	5	11
	6	5	12

any child can be in either the experimental or control condition but not in both. That is, we have an unrelated independent variable. The other independent variable is a pre-test/post-test measure. Now, in this particular study, children are measured in both the pre-test and the post-test situations. In other words, pre-test/post-test is a related independent variable. What is happening in the study is that the self-esteem of children is being measured on two occasions – one before the experimental manipulation and the other after the experimental manipulation. The children in the experimental condition were praised whenever they exhibited good behaviour whereas there was no feedback for the children in the control condition. It should be fairly obvious that the self-esteem of the children in the experimental condition increases between the pre-test and the post-test.

Of course, all other things being equal, the fact that there is a related independent variable means that the error term can be adjusted for individual differences since participants have been measured more than once. If there is a strong individual difference component to the data then adjusting for this will make the ANOVA more powerful – that is, more able to detect significant differences if they exist.

There is little more that needs to be known since mixed ANOVA would be looking for the main effect of the pre-test/post-test variable and main effect of the control/experimental variable together with any interaction between the two. Actually the interaction is crucial in this study since it is this which actually tests the hypothesis that praise raises self-esteem. The main effects are of relatively little interest in this example though this will not always be the case.

21.2 When to use two-way mixed analysis of variance

A two-way mixed design ANOVA will be particularly appropriate for studies that investigate change over a period of time. So it will be used when a single group of participants are studied at different time points. It can also be used where a group of participants serves in a number of different conditions of an experiment (though counterbalancing of the order of serving in the different conditions would be a design improvement).

Such a design is readily turned into a mixed design simply by, for example, breaking the sample down into two separate samples – males and females. Of course, there may be other unrelated independent variables that could be used.

21.3 When not to use two-way mixed analysis of variance

The usual strictures about related measures apply to the mixed analysis of variance. That is, where the data are supposed to be related scores, then the scores should correlate. In our example, the pre-test scores should correlate with the post-test scores. If they don't, then it is not advantageous to use the mixed analysis of variance and it can be counterproductive.

You may find it useful to try both the two-way ANOVA and the mixed ANOVA on your data since this can be informative. If you get more significant results with the two-way ANOVA than the mixed ANOVA then it may be that your related measure is not in fact a related measure. In these circumstances, it would be acceptable to use the results of the two-way ANOVA though we know of no cases where researchers have done that.

21.4 Data requirements for two-way mixed analysis of variance

A two-way mixed ANOVA requires a related and an unrelated independent variable. The variances should be similar for all conditions though the test used (the Box test of equality of covariance matrices) actually checks that the covariances in the data are similar.

As discussed above, the scores on the repeated measures should correlate with each other for this form of analysis to be maximally effective.

21.5 Problems in the use of two-way mixed analysis of variance

The mixed design ANOVA on SPSS produces a particularly bewildering array of output. It is helpful to dispense with as much of this as possible and just concentrate on the essentials if you are new to the procedure. Our step-by-step instructions should help you with this.

What is particularly confusing is that different error terms are used in different parts of the analysis.

You can find out more about mixed ANOVA in Chapter 24 of Howitt, D. and Cramer, D. (2008) *Introduction to Statistics in Psychology*. Harlow: Pearson.

21.6 The data to be analysed

A two-way mixed analysis of variance has one unrelated factor and one related factor. Factors are independent variables. This analysis is illustrated with the data in Table 21.1 on page 196 (*ISP*, Table 24.1), which consists of the self-esteem scores of children measured before and after an experimental manipulation in which half the children (chosen at random) were praised for good behaviour (experimental condition) while the other half were given no feedback (control condition).

21.7 Two-way mixed ANOVA

Step 1:

Enter the data. The codes for the two conditions (1 = Control and 2 = Experimental) are in the 1st column. Label these values as such. The pre-test and post-test scores are in the 2nd and 3rd columns.

	Condition	Pretest	Posttest
1	1	6	5
2	1	4	6
3	1	5	7
4	2	7	10
5	2	5	11
6	2	5	12

Step 2:

Select 'Analyze',
'General Linear Model' and
'Repeated Measures ...'.

Step 3:

Type '2' in the 'Number of Levels:' box.

Select 'Add'.

Select 'Define'.

Step 4:

Select 'Pretest' and 'Posttest' either
alone or together and the ▶ button
beside the 'Within-Subjects
Variables:' box to put them there.

Select 'Condition' and the ▶ button
beside the 'Between-Subjects
Factor(s):' box to put it there.

Select 'Options ...'.

Step 5:

Select 'Descriptive statistics',
'Estimates of effect size' and
'Homogeneity tests'.

Select 'Continue'.

Select 'Plots ...' from
the previous screen,
which reappears.

Step 6:

Select 'factor1' ('Pretest' 'Posttest') and the ▶ button beside the 'Horizontal Axis:' box to put it there.

Select 'Condition' and the ▶ button beside the 'Separate Lines:' box to put it there.

Select 'Add'.

Select 'Continue'.

Select 'OK' in the previous box.

21.8 Interpreting the output

The output gives ten tables and a plot. Only the more important tables are shown here. The second table gives the mean and standard deviation for the two groups.

Descriptive Statistics

	Condition	Mean	Std. Deviation	N
Pretest	Control	5.00	1.000	3
	Experimental	5.67	1.155	3
	Total	5.33	1.033	6
Posttest	Control	6.00	1.000	3
	Experimental	11.00	1.000	3
	Total	8.50	2.881	6

The third table shows whether the covariances matrices of the post-test are equal across the two conditions. This analysis of variance assumes that they are. As the significance level of 0.951 is greater than 0.05, the matrices are similar and this assumption is met.

Box's Test of Equality of Covariance Matrices[a]

Box's M	.757
F	.115
df1	3
df2	2880.000
Sig.	.951

Check that this value is *not* less than .05. It is not significant and therefore the covariances of the post-test groups are equal.

Tests the null hypothesis that the observed covariance matrices of the dependent variables are equal across groups.

   a. Design: Intercept+Condition
      Within Subjects Design: factor1

The ninth table shows whether the error variance of the two variables is similar across the two conditions. A significance level of more than 0.05 indicates that these variances are similar.

Levene's Test of Equality of Error Variances[a]

	F	df1	df2	Sig.
Pretest	.308	1	4	.609
Posttest	.000	1	4	1.000

Tests the null hypothesis that the error variance
of the dependent variable is equal across groups.
a. Design: Intercept+Condition
   Within Subjects Design: factor1

Check these for significance.
Significance means that the
error variances are significantly
different for the two or more
conditions – either for the pre-
test or the post-test.

The eighth table contains information for the F-test. The F-test that is of particular interest to us is that for the interaction between the within-subjects and between-subjects factor (factor1 * Condition). This F-ratio is 7.682 and has a probability value of 0.05. In other words, this interaction is just significant. If we look at the means for the four groups we can see that while the mean for the control condition increases little from pre-test (5.00) to post-test (6.00), the mean for the experimental condition shows a larger increase from pre-test (5.67) to post-test (11.00).

Tests of Within-Subjects Contrasts

Measure: MEASURE_1

Source	factor1	Type III Sum of Squares	df	Mean Square	F	Sig.	Partial Eta Squared
factor1	Linear	30.083	1	30.083	16.409	.015	.804
factor1 * Condition	Linear	14.083	1	14.083	7.682	.050	.658
Error(factor1)	Linear	7.333	4	1.833			

This indicates a just significant interaction between pre-test/post-test and experimental condition. In other words, there are differences between the cells that cannot be explained by the pre-existing differences between the groups of participants or simply by changes in all conditions between the pre-test and the post-test. Take a look at Table 21.3 which will help clarify the trends in the means.

These are the partial etas squared.

To determine whether these increases were statistically significant we could run a related t-test between the pre- and post-test scores for the two conditions separately (with Bonferroni adjustment for the number of comparisons carried out). We could also see whether the two conditions differed at pre-test and at post-test with an unrelated t-test for the two test periods separately.

The plot or graph on the following page shows the means of the four cells which may help you to grasp more quickly the relationships between them.

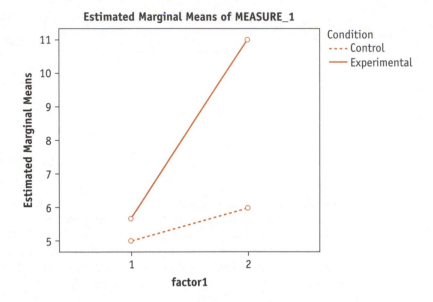

Estimated Marginal Means of MEASURE_1

Reporting the output

■ We could report the results of the output as follows: 'The interaction between the two conditions and the change over time was statistically significant ($F_{1,4} = 7.68$, $p = 0.05$, partial $\eta^2 = 0.66$). While the pre-test means did not differ significantly ($t = 0.76$, $df = 4$, two-tailed $p = 0.492$), the post-test mean for the experimental condition (M = 11.00, SD = 1.00) was significantly higher ($t = 6.12$, $df = 4$, two-tailed $p = 0.004$) than that for the control condition (M = 6.00, SD = 1.00). The increase from pre-test (M = 5.67, SD = 1.15) to post-test (M = 11.00, SD = 1.00) was significant for the experimental condition ($t = 4.44$, $df = 2$, two-tailed $p = 0.047$) but not for the control condition ($t = 1.00$, $df = 2$, two-tailed $p = 0.423$).'

■ An analysis of variance table for this analysis is presented in Table 21.2.

■ It is also useful to include a table of means (M) and standard deviations (SD) as shown in Table 21.3.

Table 21.2 ANOVA summary table for a two-way mixed design

Source of variance	Sums of squares	Degrees of freedom	Mean square	*F*-ratio
Between-subjects factor	24.08	1	24.08	72.25*
Between-subjects error	1.33	1	1.33	
Within-subjects factor	30.08	1	30.08	16.41*
Within-subjects error	7.33	4	1.83	
Interaction	14.08	1	14.08	7.68*

* Significant at 0.05 level.

Table 21.3   Means and standard deviations of the pre- and post-tests for the control and experimental conditions

Conditions	Pre-test		Post-test	
	M	SD	M	SD
Control	5.00	1.00	6.00	1.00
Experimental	5.67	1.15	11.00	1.00

For further resources including data sets and questions, please refer to the CD accompanying this book.

22 Analysis of covariance (ANCOVA)

Overview

- The analysis of covariance is a variant of ANOVA. Analysis of covariance allows the researcher to control or adjust for variables that correlate with the dependent variable before comparing the means on the dependent variable. These variables are known as covariates of the dependent variable.

- To the extent that the levels of the covariates are different for the different research conditions, unless you adjust your dependent variable for the covariates you will confuse the effects of your independent variables with the influence of the pre-existing differences between the conditions caused by different levels of the covariates.

- By controlling for the covariates, essentially you are taking their effect away from your scores on the dependent variable. Thus having adjusted for the covariates, the remaining variation between conditions cannot be due to the covariates.

- One common use of ANCOVA is in pre-test/post-test designs. Assume that the pre-test suggests that the different conditions of the experiment have different means prior to testing (e.g. the experimental and control groups are different), ANCOVA may be used to adjust for these pre-test differences.

22.1 What is analysis of covariance (ANCOVA)?

Analysis of covariance (ANCOVA) basically allows the researcher to control (adjust for) variables that are not part of the main ANOVA design but may be correlated with both the independent and the dependent variables and so produce a spurious relationship in the ANOVA analysis. In randomised experiments, it is assumed that random assignment of participants to various conditions of the study equates the conditions in terms of all influences other than the independent variables. Of course, randomisation only works in the long run – it may not fully equate the participants in each of the conditions prior to the experimental treatment.

Furthermore, ANOVA can also be used to analyse non-experimental studies. In this case, it is perfectly possible that participants in the different conditions of the experiment

Table 22.1 Data for a study of the effects of hormones (analysis of covariance)

Group 1 Hormone 1		Group 2 Hormone 2		Group 3 Placebo control	
Pre	Post	Pre	Post	Pre	Post
5	9	3	4	2	3
4	12	2	2	3	6
6	8	1	5	2	3

are different in some respect related to the dependent variable. ANCOVA allows you to explore possible influential variables that are not part of the basic ANOVA design.

Table 22.1 contains data that can be used to illustrate the use of ANCOVA. The study is the one we used in Chapter 17 though it has been extended. We have three groups of participants who have been given one of three hormone treatments (Hormone 1, Hormone 2 or Placebo control). The dependent variable is a measure of depression. The study has been changed such that it now includes a pre-test measure of depression as well as a post-treatment measure. Ideally, the pre-test measures should have the same mean irrespective of the condition. But you will notice that the mean pre-test score for the Hormone 1 group is higher than for the other two groups. It is possible that the higher post-test scores of the Hormone 1 group is simply a consequence of them starting with higher levels of depression and not an effect of the hormone treatment.

It is possible to compute an ANOVA for these data but treat the pre-test measure of depression as a covariate. Two important things can be achieved:

1. ANCOVA on SPSS will give you the means on the dependent variable adjusted for the covariate. In other words, it will equate all the participants on the covariate and make adjustments to the scores of the dependent variable to reflect this equality.

2. ANCOVA adjusts the error variance to take into account the tendency for individual differences to affect the dependent variable. This gives a new significance level which can be more statistically significant though, of course, this does not have to be so.

22.2 When to use ANCOVA

The analysis of covariance needs to be used with restraint. It is undesirable to have more than a few covariates, for example. These covariates should be selected because it is known that they correlate with the dependent variable – if not then there is no point in using it. Covariates should correlate poorly with each other to be effective in ANCOVA.

22.3 When not to use ANCOVA

There is a requirement that the relationship between the covariate and the dependent variable should be the same throughout the data. It should not be the case that the regression slope is different in the different conditions of the study because ANCOVA works with the average slope, which may not be appropriate within a particular condition if the regression is not consistent. SPSS offers a test of the homogeneity of regression. This simply means that the regression slope is constant for each condition of the independent variable.

Covariates that are unreliable can cause difficulty because ANCOVA assumes that all covariates are reliable. Of course, few psychological variables are reliable in the same sense that, say, a measure of age is. Estimates of the adjusted mean may be over-inflated if covariates are unreliable and it is likely that the test of significant is reduced in power.

22.4 Data requirements for ANCOVA

Generally any ANOVA model can be used as an ANCOVA. The covariates in ANCOVA should have a clear *linear* relationship with the dependent variable otherwise ANCOVA will not be helpful. Curvilinear relationships are inappropriate because of the way in which ANCOVA works. Avoid the use of non-continuous variables such as gender as covariates in ANCOVA. These could, however, potentially be used as an additional independent variable.

22.5 Problems in the use of ANCOVA

Conceptually be very wary when speaking of causality in relation to the analysis of covariance. Controlling for a covariate has no strong implication in relation to the issue of causality.

In general, it is fairly difficult to meet in full the requirements of data for ANCOVA, which should encourage extra caution where the results of an ANCOVA are marginal in terms of significance.

22.6 The data to be analysed

The analysis of covariance is much the same as the analysis of variance dealt with elsewhere but with one major difference. This is that the effects of additional variables (covariates) are taken away as part of the analysis. It is a bit like using partial correlation to get rid of the effects of a third variable on a correlation. We will illustrate the computation of ANCOVA with the data shown in Table 22.1 on page 205.

It could be that differences in depression prior to the treatment affect the outcome of the analysis. Essentially by adjusting the scores on the dependent variable to 'get rid' of these pre-existing differences, it is possible to disregard the possibility that these pre-existing differences are affecting the analysis. So, if (a) the pre-treatment or test scores are correlated with the post-treatment or test scores, and (b) the pre-test scores differ between the three treatments, then these pre-test differences can be statistically controlled by covarying them out of the analysis.

22.7 One-way ANCOVA

Step 1:

Enter the data. The 1st two columns
are the same as the data in
Chapters 17 and 20. The data for
the 3rd column are new.

Step 2:

Select 'Analyze',
'General Linear Model' and
'Univariate ...'.

22.8 Testing that the slope of the regression line within cells is similar

Step 1:

Select 'Posttest' and the ▶ button beside
the 'Dependent Variable:' box to put it there.

Select 'Condition' and the ▶ button beside
the 'Fixed Factor(s):' box to put it there.

Select 'Pretest' and the ▶ button beside the
'Covariate(s):' box to put it there.

Select 'Model ...'.

Step 2:

Select 'Custom'.

Select 'Condition(F)' and the ▶ button to put it
in the 'Model:' box. Do the same for 'Pretest(C)'.

Select both variables and the ▶ button to put
the interaction between them in the 'Model:' box.

Select 'Continue'.

Select 'OK' in the previous box.

22.9 Interpreting the output

Tests of Between-Subjects Effects

Dependent Variable: Posttest

Source	Type III Sum of Squares	df	Mean Square	F	Sig.
Corrected Model	82.722[a]	5	16.544	10.269	.042
Intercept	19.230	1	19.230	11.936	.041
Condition	24.333	2	12.167	7.552	.067
Pretest	.100	1	.100	.062	.819
Condition * Pretest	12.571	2	6.286	3.901	.146
Error	4.833	3	1.611		
Total	388.000	9			
Corrected Total	87.556	8			

a. R Squared = .945 (Adjusted R Squared = .853)

The interaction between the conditions and the covariate is not significant which means that the prerequisite that the slope of the regression line within the three conditions is similar is met.

22.10 Running ANCOVA

Step 1:

Select 'Full factorial'.

Select 'Continue'.

Step 2:

Select 'Options ...'.

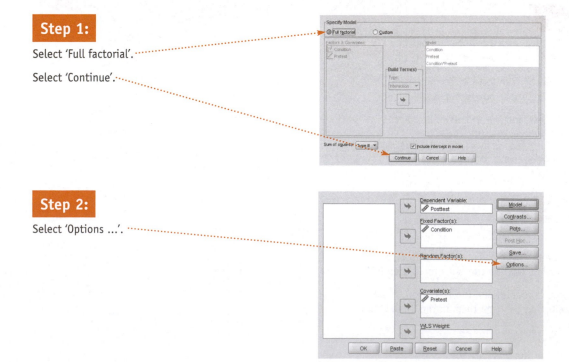

Step 3:

Select 'Condition' and the ▶ button to put it in the 'Display Means for:' box.

Select 'Descriptive statistics' and 'Estimates of effect size'.

Select 'Continue'.

Select 'OK' in the previous box.

22.11 Interpreting the output

The second table shows the unadjusted means for the three conditions.

Descriptive Statistics

Dependent Variable: Posttest

Condition	Mean	Std. Deviation	N
Hormone 1	9.67	2.082	3
Hormone 2	3.67	1.528	3
Placebo control	4.00	1.732	3
Total	5.78	3.308	9

This table simply gives the means for the three conditions at the post-test. Total is the average post-test score in the original data.

The fourth and last table shows the adjusted means for these three conditions. The adjusted means of the three treatments are what the means are when all groups are adjusted to be identical on the covariate (in this case pre-treatment depression scores).

The means for the post-test given in this output table have been adjusted for the effect of the covariate on the three conditions. The effect of the covariate has effectively been removed from the data.

Condition

Dependent Variable: Posttest

Condition	Mean	Std. Error	95% Confidence Interval	
			Lower Bound	Upper Bound
Hormone 1	10.881[a]	1.955	5.856	15.906
Hormone 2	2.952[a]	1.443	−.756	6.661
Placebo control	3.500[a]	1.269	.237	6.763

a. Covariates appearing in the model are evaluated at the following values: Pretest = 3.11.

■ The adjusted mean is 10.881 for the first treatment, 2.952 for the second treatment and 3.500 for the third treatment.

■ We can see that these adjusted means seem to differ from the unadjusted means shown in the second table of the output. For the first treatment the adjusted mean is 10.88 and the unadjusted mean is 9.67. For the second treatment the adjusted mean is 2.95 and the unadjusted mean is 3.67, while for the third treatment the adjusted mean is 3.50 and the unadjusted mean is 4.00.

The third table shows the F-ratio for the analysis of covariance.

Tests of Between-Subjects Effects

Dependent Variable: Posttest

Source	Type III Sum of Squares	df	Mean Square	F	Sig.	Partial Eta Squared
Corrected Model	70.151[a]	3	23.384	6.718	.033	.801
Intercept	27.684	1	27.684	7.953	.037	.614
Pretest	1.929	1	1.929	.554	.490	.100
Condition	26.425	2	13.213	3.796	.099	.603
Error	17.405	5	3.481			
Total	388.000	9				
Corrected Total	87.556	8				

a. R Squared = .801 (Adjusted R Squared = .682)

Following removal of the effects of the covariate, there is not a significant difference between the means of the three conditions as the significance is .099 which is not statistically signficant.

Partial eta squared is .603.

■ The F-ratio for the main effect is 3.796 (13.213/3.481 = 3.796).

■ The probability of this F-ratio is 0.099. In other words, it is greater than the 0.05 critical value and so is not statistically significant.

Reporting the output

We could report the results of the output as follows: 'A one-way ANCOVA showed that when pre-test depression was covaried out, the main effect of treatment on post-test depression was not significant ($F_{2,5} = 3.80$, $p = 0.099$, partial $\eta^2 = 0.60$). We would normally also report the changes to the means once the covariate has been removed.

In addition, we would normally give an ANCOVA summary table as in Table 22.2.

Table 22.2   ANCOVA summary table for effects of treatments on depression controlling for pre-treatment depression

Source of variance	Sums of squares	Degrees of freedom	Mean square	*F*-ratio
Covariate (pre-treatment depression scores)	1.93	1	1.93	0.55*
Main effect (treatment)	26.43	2	13.21	3.80
Residual error	17.41	5	3.48	

* Significant at 5% level.

For further resources including data sets and questions, please refer to the CD accompanying this book.

23 Multivariate analysis of variance (MANOVA)

Overview

■ MANOVA is a variant of ANOVA that is applied when one wishes to analyse several dependent variables at the same time. These dependent variables should be *conceptually* related to the hypothesis and each other. They need to be score rather than categorical variables.

■ Essentially MANOVA computes a composite variable based on the several dependent variables and then tests to see whether the means of the groups on the combined dependent variables differ significantly.

■ MANOVA helps deal with the problems created by multiple significance tests being applied to the same data.

■ If MANOVA is statistically significant then it is appropriate to test the significance of the individual dependent variables using ANOVAs and also to explore the combination of variables used in the MANOVA using discriminant function analysis (see Chapter 24).

23.1 What is multivariate analysis of variance (MANOVA)?

Multivariate analysis of variance (MANOVA) is a test of the statistical significance of differences between several groups. It is different from ANOVA in that the means that are compared are a composite variable based on combining several score variables statistically. It is most commonly used by researchers using randomised experimental designs but, like ANOVA, not exclusively so. Read Chapter 17 on one-way ANOVA if you have not already done so as this forms the starting point for this chapter.

Table 23.1 summarises a study for which MANOVA may be the preferred test of significance (see *ISP*, Table 26.2). The study is of the effectiveness of different team building methods in sport. There are three groups (or conditions) – team building with a sports psychologist, team building with a sports coach, and a no team building control. The hypothesis is that team building has a positive influence on team cohesiveness. Three dependent variables were measured following this experimental manipulation. These are: (1) the difference between ratings of most and least liked team members; (2) the number

Table 23.1 Data suitable for a MANOVA analysis

Group (independent variable)								
Team building with sports psychologist Dependent variables			Team building with sports coach Dependent variables			No team building controls Dependent variables		
Like*	Gym*	Game*	Like	Gym	Game	Like	Gym	Game
9**	12	14	4	6	15	9	6	10
5	9	14	5	4	12	1	2	5
8	11	12	4	9	15	6	10	12
4	6	5	3	8	8	2	5	6
9	12	3	4	9	9	3	6	7
9	11	14	5	3	8	4	7	8
6	13	14	2	8	12	1	6	13
6	11	18	6	9	11	4	9	12
8	11	22	4	7	15	3	8	15
8	13	22	4	8	28	3	2	14
9	15	18	5	7	10	2	8	11
7	12	18	4	9	9	6	9	10
8	10	13	5	18	18	3	8	13
6	11	22	7	12	24	6	14	22

* Like = Difference between ratings of most and least liked team members, Gym = Number of gym sessions voluntarily attended, and Game = Number of games played.
** The scores are the scores on the three dependent variables.

of gym sessions voluntarily attended; and (3) the number of games played. The researchers considered that these were measures that would indicate the success of the team building sessions. There are other possibilities too, of course, and it is difficult to choose which one of the three should be used. After all, they are all measures of different aspects that might be expected of successful team building so why not use them all?

One could analyse the data in Table 23.1 by: (a) using separate ANOVA analyses for each of the three different dependent variables measured or (b) by combining the dependent variables in some way to give a composite variable mean score which is then analysed in a single analysis. The latter is the approach used in MANOVA. In fact, in the MANOVA procedure in SPSS both these approaches are taken though the ANOVAs are not considered unless the MANOVA is statistically significant. Why is this?

Researchers do not simply use MANOVA because it uses a composite measure of several dependent variables in combination. It has the major advantage that it deals with the problem of multiple tests of significance. If one carries out multiple tests of significance on any data (such as several ANOVAs in this case) there is an increased likelihood that at least one of the tests of significance will be statistically significant. All things being equal, the more tests of significance that are performed on any data the more likely it is that at least one test will be statistically significant by chance in any data analysis. By using a single combined dependent variable, MANOVA avoids the problem of multiple tests of significance.

Things are a little more complicated than this in practice:

■ If the MANOVA is statistically significant then it is legitimate to examine the results of ANOVAs performed on each of the several dependent variables that were combined for the MANOVA. (You will probably find that there is more MANOVA output on SPSS that refers to these individual ANOVAs than refers to MANOVA.)

■ You will notice that so far we have said nothing about how the dependent variables are combined in MANOVA. Just how are they combined to give the combined variable in MANOVA? Without this information it is not possible to interpret the meaning of the MANOVA precisely. The complication is that this requires a separate and distinct analysis using discriminant function analysis (described in Chapter 24). So, if you have a significant MANOVA, then you will probably wish to do a discriminant function analysis. (The separate ANOVAs do not tell you anything about the combined dependent variable for the simple reason that the several dependent variables will correlate to different extents with each other.)

All of this means that a MANOVA analysis actually involves several steps. These steps and some other essential features of a MANOVA analysis are summarised in Figure 23.1 which shows the important elements of a data analysis using MANOVA.

Figure 23.1   The basic steps of a MANOVA analysis

23.2 When to use MANOVA

MANOVA can be used when the researcher has employed a randomised experimental design in which there are several groups of participants but where several different variables have been measured to reflect different aspects of the dependent variable described in the hypothesis. There is no point (and a great deal to be lost) by simply trying to combine different variables together in MANOVA that have no *conceptual* relationship to each other and the hypothesis. MANOVA will indicate whether the means for the groups on the combined dependent variables differ significantly. Of course, it is possible to use MANOVA even in circumstances were participants were not randomly allocated to the different groups formed by the independent variable. In such a study, researchers would be less likely to refer to the causal influence of the independent variable on the dependent variable.

MANOVA is used when there are three or more different groups (just like one-way ANOVA). If there are just two groups (as in the unrelated *t*-test), then the analysis becomes Hotelling's *t*-test which is just the same as any other unrelated *t*-test conceptually but uses a combination of several different dependent variables. Hotelling's *t*-test can be calculated simply by carrying out the MANOVA procedure on SPSS.

23.3   When not to use MANOVA

If the dependent variables are very highly correlated with each other then there may be simpler ways of combining the variables (e.g. simply by adding up the scores of each participant over the several dependent variables and then carrying out an ANOVA on these summated scores). What is the advantage of this? One of the problems of using MANOVA is that degrees of freedom are lost due to the number of dependent variables in the analysis. This, effectively, reduces the statistical significance of MANOVA, which is not desirable if it can be avoided. So if there is an alternative but unproblematic way of combining the separate dependent variables then this can be employed to good effect. This will not work where some dependent variables correlate with each other highly while others do not since it is unclear how the dependent variables should be combined to give a combined score on the dependent variable. But these are the circumstances in which MANOVA is likely to be at its most effective and so would be the preferred approach.

We would not recommend the use of MANOVA if you have many dependent variables to combine. For example, if one has a lengthy questionnaire (say, ten or more questions) then it would not be helpful to treat answers to each question as a separate dependent variable as part of MANOVA as there are more informative ways of combining items to yield a small number of combined variables. It would be better, for example, to factor analyse (Chapter 26) the set of dependent variables. In this way, the structure of the items will be clarified. It is likely that a very small number of significant factors will emerge. Individuals may be given a score on each factor using the factor score procedure of SPSS which puts a score on each factor at the end of the SPSS spreadsheet (see page 240). These factor scores may be used as variables in ANOVA.

23.4   Data requirements for MANOVA

■ The independent variable (grouping variable) consists of three or more different categories for MANOVA (do not use score variables as the independent variable unless they have been recoded into a small number of categories).

■ Always try to ensure that the sample sizes of each group in the MANOVA are the same. This helps avoid problems in the analysis if assumptions related to something called the equality of the covariance matrices are not met.

■ The two sample equivalent to the *t*-test is known as the Hotelling's *t*-test but it would be calculated on SPSS using the MANOVA procedure.

■ There needs to be several dependent variables which take the form of numerical scores.

23.5 Problems in the use of MANOVA

It is possible to run before you can walk with MANOVA. Many of the features of SPSS MANOVA output require understanding of ANOVA – post hoc multiple comparisons tests and the like are discussed in the chapters on ANOVA and are not dealt with in this chapter for reasons of clarity. So it is best to have a grounding in ANOVA before moving on to MANOVA. If you need to cut corners then try a crash-course in ANOVA by studying Chapter 17 on one-way ANOVA and then trying out what you have learnt on your data by using just one dependent variable. Also study post hoc tests in Chapter 20.

You can find out more about MANOVA from Chapter 26 of Howitt, D. and Cramer, D. (2008) *Introduction to Statistics in Psychology*. Harlow: Pearson.

23.6 The data to be analysed

The data in Table 23.1 on page 213 are used as the example for SPSS analysis for MANOVA.

23.7 MANOVA

Step 1:

Enter the data.
'Group' is the independent variable.
These are the dependent variables.

	group	leastliked	gymnsessions	gamesplayed
1	1	9	13	14
2	2	4	6	15
3	3	9	6	10
4	1	5	9	14
5	2	5	4	12
6	3	1	2	5
7	1	8	11	12
8	2	4	9	15
9	3	6	10	12
10	1	4	6	5
11	2	3	8	8
12	3	2	5	6

Step 2:

Select 'Analyze', then 'General Linear Model' and then 'Multivariate ...'.

Step 3:

Move the dependent variables from the large left-hand panel to the small 'Dependent Variables:' box.

Move the grouping variable from the left to the 'Fixed Factor(s):' box.

Select 'Options'.

Buttons such as 'Post Hoc ...' allow the user to carry out pertinent statistical analyses that should be familiar from ANOVA. For simplicity, this valuable information is omitted here.

Step 4:

Move 'group' over to the right-hand 'Display Means for:' panel.

Select 'Descriptive statistics' and 'Estimates of effect size'.

Select 'Continue'.

Select 'OK' from the previous box.

23.8 Interpreting the output

The interpretation of the SPSS output from MANOVA is complicated when options are selected but there is only a small core of the SPSS output that contains the results of the MANOVA analysis. If this is significant then one would normally go on to examine other aspects of the output that deal with the individual dependent variables – and probably go on to do a discriminant function analysis as detailed in Chapter 24.

The SPSS output for MANOVA contains the results of separate ANOVA analyses for each separate dependent variable. These are considered when the overall MANOVA is

significant. However, the individual ANOVAs actually do not tell us about the combined dependent variable since we need to know the contribution of each dependent variable to the combined scores before we can know this. This is why it is usually recommended that a discriminant function analysis is carried out in addition.

This table merely identifies the groups based on the independent variable and gives the sample size involved. It is good that equal sample sizes were used as this helps avoid technical problems.

Between-Subjects Factors

		Value Label	N
group	1	teampsychologist	14
	2	teamcoach	14
	3	control	14

This gives the mean scores on the three dependent variables for each grouping variable.

Descriptive Statistics

	group	Mean	Std. Deviation	N
leastliked	teampsychologist	7.29	1.637	14
	teamcoach	4.43	1.222	14
	control	3.79	2.259	14
	Total	5.17	2.305	42
gymnsessions	teampsychologist	11.21	2.082	14
	teamcoach	8.36	3.565	14
	control	7.14	3.110	14
	Total	8.90	3.384	42
gamesplayed	teampsychologist	14.93	5.784	14
	teamcoach	13.86	6.011	14
	control	11.29	4.322	14
	Total	13.36	5.512	42

Multivariate Tests[c]

Effect		Value	F	Hypothesis df	Error df	Sig.	Partial Eta Squared
Intercept	Pillai's Trace	.937	184.710[a]	3.000	37.000	.000	.937
	Wilks' Lambda	.063	184.710[a]	3.000	37.000	.000	.937
	Hotelling's Trace	14.976	184.710[a]	3.000	37.000	.000	.937
	Roy's Largest Root	14.976	184.710[a]	3.000	37.000	.000	.937
group	Pillai's Trace	.490	4.109	6.000	76.000	.001	.245
	Wilks' Lambda	.522	4.733[a]	6.000	74.000	.000	.277
	Hotelling's Trace	.892	5.349	6.000	72.000	.000	.308
	Roy's Largest Root	.865	10.953[b]	3.000	38.000	.000	.464

a. Exact statistic
b. The statistic is an upper bound on F that yields a lower bound on the significance level.
c. Design: Intercept+group

This contains the MANOVA analysis. There are several multivariate tests that are very similar. Use the Pillai's trace as using all four is cumbersome. The MANOVA is significant at the .001 level. Thus the group means on the composite dependent variable differ significantly at the .001 level. Therefore the hypothesis is supported.

Tests of Between-Subjects Effects

Source	Dependent Variable	Type III Sum of Squares	df	Mean Square	F	Sig.	Partial Eta Squared
Corrected Model	leastliked	97.190[a]	2	48.595	15.709	.000	.446
	gymnsessions	122.333[b]	2	61.167	6.869	.003	.260
	gamesplayed	98.143[c]	2	49.071	1.668	.202	.079
Intercept	leastliked	1121.167	1	1121.167	362.438	.000	.903
	gymnsessions	3330.381	1	3330.381	374.000	.000	.906
	gamesplayed	7493.357	1	7493.357	254.676	.000	.867
group	leastliked	97.190	2	48.595	15.709	.000	.446
	gymnsessions	122.333	2	61.167	6.869	.003	.260
	gamesplayed	98.143	2	49.071	1.668	.202	.079
Error	leastliked	120.643	39	3.093			
	gymnsessions	347.286	39	8.905			
	gamesplayed	1147.500	39	29.423			
Total	leastliked	1339.000	42				
	gymnsessions	3800.000	42				
	gamesplayed	8739.000	42				
Corrected Total	leastliked	217.833	41				
	gymnsessions	469.619	41				
	gamesplayed	1245.643	41				

a. R Squared = .446 (Adjusted R Squared = .418)
b. R Squared = .260 (Adjusted R Squared = .223)
c. R Squared = .079 (Adjusted R Squared = .032)

This gives the significance of the individual ANOVAs applied to the three dependent variables separately. As can be seen, two of the dependent variables differ significantly according to the group. However, the dependent variable 'number of games played' does not produce significant results.

Estimated marginal means

group

Dependent Variable	group	Mean	Std. Error	95% Confidence Interval Lower Bound	Upper Bound
leastliked	teampsychologist	7.286	.470	6.335	8.237
	teamcoach	4.429	.470	3.478	5.379
	control	3.786	.470	2.835	4.737
gymnsessions	teampsychologist	11.214	.798	9.601	12.827
	teamcoach	8.357	.798	6.744	9.970
	control	7.143	.798	5.530	8.756
gamesplayed	teampsychologist	14.929	1.450	11.996	17.861
	teamcoach	13.857	1.450	10.925	16.789
	control	11.286	1.450	8.353	14.218

This shows the means of the three dependent variables for the three groups. Which means differ for each dependent variable needs to be determined with further SPSS analyses (see Chapter 20).

Reporting the output

In circumstances in which the MANOVA is not significant then we could briefly report this (inserting your own values as appropriate) as follows: 'The hypothesis that team work training improves team training was tested using MANOVA. However, the null hypothesis was supported by the data (Pillai's trace = , df = , ns, partial η^2 =).'

In the example, the findings were significant and we might report: 'MANOVA showed there was a significant multivariate effect of team building on the three dependent variables (Pillai's $F_{6,76} = 4.12$, $p < 0.01$, partial $\eta^2 = 0.25$). Each dependent variable was subjected to a further ANOVA in order to show whether this trend is the same for each of the separate dependent variables. For the measure of the difference between favourite and least favourite team member, an ANOVA showed there was an overall significant difference between the means ($F_{2,39} = 15.71$, $p = 0.001$, partial $\eta^2 = 0.45$). Similar, the mean number of gym sessions attended was different according to group ($F_{2,39} = 61.17$, $p = 0.03$, partial $\eta^2 = 0.26$). However, the number of games played failed to reach statistical significance ($F_{2,39} = 49.07$, ns, partial $\eta^2 = 0.08$).'

Note that had we selected post hoc tests during the analysis, it would be possible to specify exactly which groups differed significantly from each other on each dependent variable. We would recommend that you routinely do this as explained in Chapter 20.

Furthermore, if the findings for MANOVA are significant, you are likely to wish to carry out a discriminant function analysis as described in the next chapter.

For further resources including data sets and questions, please refer to the CD accompanying this book.

24 Discriminant function analysis (for MANOVA)

Overview

- Discriminant function analysis has its major application in a better understanding of the meaning of a significant MANOVA (see Chapter 23). It can be used alone as a way of assessing whether a set of predictor (independent) score variables effectively distinguishes different categories or groups of participants. However, logistic regression (Chapters 31 and 32) does a far better job of this.

- A discriminant function is basically a computed variable that combines several score variables. It is computed in such a way that the differences between the groups of participants on the means (centroids) of the discriminant function are maximised.

- There may be several discriminant functions obtained in an analysis. The number depends on the characteristics of the data especially the number of independent variables. Each discriminant function is uncorrelated with the others.

- Discriminant function analysis and MANOVA are mathematically similar.

- Discriminant function analysis can help understand the meaning of a significant MANOVA analysis since it identifies the combination of score variables that led to the significant MANOVA.

- Discriminant function analysis produces a classification table that indicates the accuracy of the group membership predications based on the independent variables.

- Confusingly, the independent variables and dependent variables are reversed for discriminant function analysis compared to MANOVA. That is, the independent variable in MANOVA is the dependent variable in discriminant function analysis.

24.1 What is discriminant function analysis?

Discriminant function analysis is a way of assessing whether members of different groups can be identified on the basis of their scores on a set of variables. It is sometimes used as a final stage of MANOVA (see Chapter 23) where it indicates which of a set of scores had been used by MANOVA as the 'combined' dependent variable. In discriminant function analysis a mathematical function (or functions) is calculated based on weighted combination of variables. This function is calculated in such a way that the group differences on the function are maximised. This is probably best understood in terms of an example and all of the hard work of analysis is done by SPSS – you just need to understand what it all means.

Table 24.1 summarises a study for which MANOVA may be the preferred test of significance. It should be familiar to you as it is more or less the same data that was used to illustrate MANOVA in the previous chapter (Chapter 23). Eagle-eyed readers may notice that there is a difference. The grouping variable (team building) has been labelled the dependent variable whereas the score variables have been labelled the independent variables. This is exactly the reverse of how the variables were labelled for MANOVA. This reversal of labelling is the consequence of MANOVA being a test of differences between means and discriminant function analysis being a form of regression. Essentially, what we are trying to do when using discriminant function analysis is to use the scores

Table 24.1 Data suitable for a discriminant function analysis

GROUP (dependent variable)								
Team building with sports psychologist Independent variables			Team building with sports coach Independent variables			No team building controls Independent variables		
Like*	Gym*	Game*	Like	Gym	Game	Like	Gym	Game
9**	12	14	4	6	15	9	6	10
5	9	14	5	4	12	1	2	5
8	11	12	4	9	15	6	10	12
4	6	5	3	8	8	2	5	6
9	12	3	4	9	9	3	6	7
9	11	14	5	3	8	4	7	8
6	13	14	2	8	12	1	6	13
6	11	18	6	9	11	4	9	12
8	11	22	4	7	15	3	8	15
8	13	22	4	8	28	3	2	14
9	15	18	5	7	10	2	8	11
7	12	18	4	9	9	6	9	10
8	10	13	5	18	18	3	8	13
6	11	22	7	12	24	6	14	22

* Like = Difference between ratings of most and least liked team members, Gym = Number of gym sessions voluntarily attended, and Game = Number of games played.
** The scores are the scores on the three independent variables.

on the three score variables (the difference between ratings of most and least liked team members, the number of gym sessions voluntarily attended and the number of games played) to discriminate participants in terms of the group that they belong to (the team building with a sports psychologist group or the team building with a sports coach group or the no team building controls group).

A discriminant function is a weighted combination of variables. In this example, the discriminant function would be based on a weighted combination of the independent variables like Gym and Game that are the independent variables in the table. Just to illustrate the general idea, the formula for the discriminant function might include the following weights applied to scores on each variable:

Discriminant function = (2 × like) + (1 × gym) + (3 × games)

For example, 'like' is weighted twice as much (2 ×) as 'gym'. To calculate this discriminant function we would apply the above formula for the scores of every participant in the study. Then we can calculate the means of each of the groups of participants on the resulting discriminant function. A group mean on a discriminant function is called a centroid.

A discriminant function can be regarded as a derived variable based on a particular combination of other variables.

Of course, the problem is that there are many different discriminant functions possible. Each would have its own pattern of weightings. So which discriminant function or pattern of weightings do we choose? Since we wish to discriminate between the groups of participants in our research we choose the discriminant function that has the maximum difference between the groups in terms of the group means (or centroids). There is only one discriminant function that meets this requirement and that is the one we use. Fortunately the SPSS calculation of the discriminant function analysis does all of this work of identifying this one discriminant function for us.

It is, however, a little misleading to talk of a single discriminant function emerging from an analysis since there may be several discriminant functions depending on the data – and especially the number of variables. Discriminant functions are independent of each other – that is they are not correlated. This ensures that the discriminant functions have the maximum possible power to differentiate between the groups of participants.

The steps involved in discriminant function analysis are summarised in Figure 24.1.

Figure 24.1   The steps of a discriminant function analysis

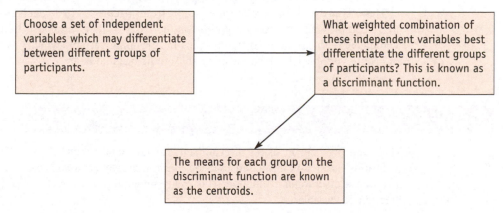

Choose a set of independent variables which may differentiate between different groups of participants.

What weighted combination of these independent variables best differentiate the different groups of participants? This is known as a discriminant function.

The means for each group on the discriminant function are known as the centroids.

24.2 When to use discriminant function analysis

If you carry out a MANOVA and find that it is statistically significant (Chapter 23), a discriminant function analysis may be used to explore the nature of the weighted combination of variables that was calculated as part of this analysis. Mathematically MANOVA and discriminant function analysis have much in common. The discriminant functions identified in discriminant function analysis are the basis of the combination of variables used in MANOVA.

It is possible to use discriminant function analysis in any circumstance in which you wish to use a set of score variables to predict membership of groups of participants. It can thus be regarded as a form of regression in which score variables are used to predict membership of groups (as opposed to scores on a dependent variable). This use of discriminant function analysis is suggested in a number of popular SPSS texts but should be regarded as superseded by logistic regression (Chapters 31 and 32).

24.3 When not to use discriminant function analysis

As indicated above, discriminant function analysis has no advantages over the more powerful and flexible logistic regression methods (Chapters 31 and 32). It is built on a less adequate mathematical model than logistic regression and does not have the latter's flexibility. For example, logistic regression can be used with both score variables and nominal (category) variables as predictors. Binary logistic regression is capable of producing quite complex models of one's data. Basically, discriminant function analysis should only be used in support of MANOVA analyses. Why not use logistic regression in relation to MANOVA? Unfortunately this is not appropriate as the underlying statistical model is different in logistic regression whereas the statistical models underlying MANOVA and discriminant function analysis are essentially the same.

24.4 Data requirements for discriminant function analysis

Discriminant function analysis requires a set of score variables and a single nominal (category) variable which defines the groups used. Cases can only be in one of the groups.

There is no point in deriving the groups from a score variable such as by classifying high, medium and low scoring groups on the basis of that variable. Multiple regression would handle this situation better by using the grouping variable which has been measured as a score variable (the dependent variable) in its original form.

24.5 Problems in the use of discriminant function analysis

The main problem in using discriminant function analysis is its use of the concept of 'centroids', which is not a self-evident concept. However, a centroid is merely a group mean on a discriminant function so is easily understood as a mean of a particular combination of variables.

Another problem is that the meaning of a discriminant function lies in the variables that were used to derive the discriminant function. Some of the variables will be strongly related to the discriminant function and others will relate to it poorly. So the variables that correlate with (or load on) a discriminant function are the ones that help you to identify what the discriminant function is.

 There is more about discriminant function analysis in Chapter 27 of Howitt, D. and Cramer, D. (2008) *Introduction to Statistics in Psychology*. Harlow: Pearson.

24.6   The data to be analysed

The data in Table 24.1 on page 222 is used as the example for the SPSS analysis for discriminant function analysis.

24.7   Discriminant function analysis

As you will be using discriminant function analysis as an adjunct to MANOVA you will already have entered the data into SPSS. Step 1 in Section 23.7 describes this.

Step 1:

Select 'Analyze', then 'Classify' then 'Discriminant'.

Step 2:

Move 'group' from the left-hand panel to the 'Grouping Variable:'panel.

Select 'Define Range'.

Step 3:

Enter the smallest numeric code ········
given to the grouping variable.

Enter the largest numeric code ········
given to the grouping variable.

Select 'Continue'. ···············

Step 4:

Move the independent variables (the
score variables) from the left-hand ········
panel to the 'Independents:' panel.

Select 'Classify'. ···············

Step 5:

Select 'Compute from group sizes'. ········

Select 'Summary table'. ···············

Select 'Continue'. ···············

Select 'Statistics ...' in previous box.

Step 6:

Select 'Means' and ···············
'Box's M'. ···············

Select 'Continue'. ···············

Then select 'OK' from the previous box.

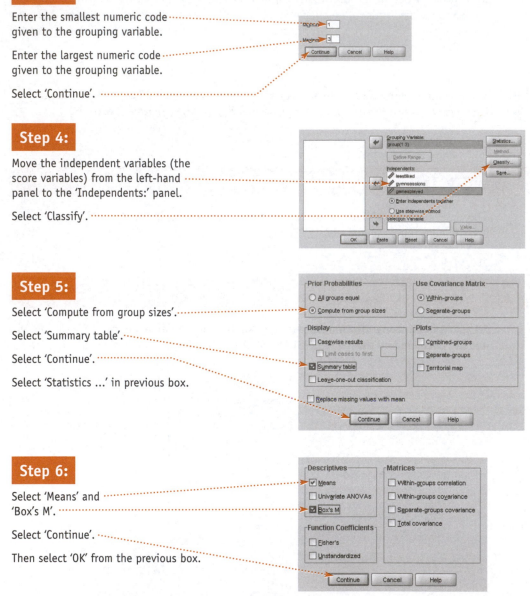

24.8 Interpreting the output

The interpretation of discriminant function analysis on SPSS is reasonably straightforward
if the appropriate options are chosen. The key thing to remember is that a discriminant
function is a sort of variable based on several measured variables. As such, in order
to understand what the discriminant function measures it is necessary to know how each
of the score variables that contribute to the discriminant function correlate with that discriminant function. This information is to be found in the structure matrix table.

This, taken in combination with the classification results table, gives a basic understanding of the output of the discrimination function analysis. If the classification results table is examined then it is apparent the extent to which the predicted classification on the basis of the predictor variables matches the known, actual classification of participants into the various groups.

There can be problems if the Box test is statistically significant but generally speaking, so long as the sample sizes of all of the groups are all equal, this can be ignored. However, if the sample sizes are very different from each other then be very cautious about your analysis. It is not possible to specify how much of a problem a significant Box test is in these circumstances.

Analysis Case Processing Summary

Unweighted	Cases	N	Percent
Valid		42	100.0
Excluded	Missing or out-of-range group codes	0	.0
	At least one missing discriminating variable	0	.0
	Both missing or out-of-range group codes and at least one missing discriminating variable	0	.0
	Total	0	.0
Total		42	100.0

It is useful to check this table to make sure that the data analysed are what you expect. For example, you may have entered the wrong codes for the groups earlier.

Group Statistics

group		Mean	Std. Deviation	Valid N (listwise) Unweighted	Valid N (listwise) Weighted
teampsychologist	leastliked	7.29	1.637	14	14.000
	gymnsessions	11.21	2.082	14	14.000
	gamesplayed	14.93	5.784	14	14.000
teamcoach	leastliked	4.43	1.222	14	14.000
	gymnsessions	8.36	3.565	14	14.000
	gamesplayed	13.86	6.011	14	14.000
control	leastliked	3.79	2.259	14	14.000
	gymnsessions	7.14	3.110	14	14.000
	gamesplayed	11.29	4.322	14	14.000
Total	leastliked	5.17	2.305	42	42.000
	gymnsessions	8.90	3.384	42	42.000
	gamesplayed	13.36	5.512	42	42.000

This table gives basic descriptive statistics for each group on the dependent variables. It is clear in this case that the means for the team psychologist group are consistently higher than for the team coach group whose mean scores are consistently higher than for the control condition, when each variable is considered in turn. This is in perfect agreement with the hypothesis.

Analysis 1
Box's test of equality of covariance matrices

Log Determinants

group	Rank	Log Determinant
teampsychologist	3	5.093
teamcoach	3	6.274
control	3	6.021
Pooled within-groups	3	6.275

The ranks and natural logarithms of determinants printed are those of the group covariance matrices.

Test Results

Box's M		18.700
F	Approx.	1.383
	df1	12
	df2	7371.000
	Sig.	.166

Tests null hypothesis of equal population covariance matrices.

The Box test basically assesses whether the variances of the different dependent variables are similar. If the test is significant then there may be problems. However, in this case it is not significant so there is no problem.

However, if it is significant and the group sizes are equal then once again there is no major problem. Only when it is significant and the group sizes are very different should you be cautious about proceeding.

Summary of Canonical Discriminant Functions

Eigenvalues

Function	Eigenvalue	% of Variance	Cumulative %	Canonical Correlation
1	.865[a]	97.0	97.0	.681
2	.027[a]	3.0	100.0	.162

a. First 2 canonical discriminant functions were used in the analysis.

Two discriminant functions have been identified. One is substantial as it accounts for 97% of the reliable variance whereas the other is quite small in comparison as it explains only 3.0%.

Wilks' Lambda

Test of Function(s)	Wilks' Lambda	Chi-square	df	Sig.
1 through 2	.522	24.685	6	.000
2	.974	1.007	2	.605

Wilks' lambda indicates that the two discriminant functions are statistically significant though discriminant function 2 is not statistically significant alone.

Standardized Canonical Discriminant Function Coefficients

	Function	
	1	2
leastliked	.848	−.305
gymnsessions	.302	.047
gamesplayed	−.037	.996

This is not a very useful table when independent variables are measured on dissimilar scales so it is best ignored.

Structure Matrix

	Function	
	1	2
leastliked	.965*	−.093
gymnsessions	.635*	.378
gamesplayed	.265	.958*

These numbers are the correlations of each independent variable with the first discriminant function.

It is clear that the difference between ratings of most and least liked team members is the biggest contributor to the Function 1 and number of games played is the biggest contributor to Function 2.

Pooled within-groups correlations between discriminating variables and standardized canonical discriminant functions
Variables ordered by absolute size of correlation within function.
  *. Largest absolute correlation between each variable and
     any discriminant function.

Functions at Group Centroids

	Function	
group	1	2
teampsychologist	1.244	−.042
teamcoach	−.415	.211
control	−.830	−.169

Unstandardized canonical discriminant functions
evaluated at group means

Classification statistics

Classification Processing Summary

Processed		42
Excluded	Missing or out-of-range group codes	0
	At least one missing discriminating variable	0
Used in Output		42

Prior Probabilities for Groups

		Cases Used in Analysis	
group	Prior	Unweighted	Weighted
teampsychologist	.333	14	14.000
teamcoach	.333	14	14.000
control	.333	14	14.000
Total	1.000	42	42.000

Classification Results[a]

		group	team psychologist	teamcoach	control	Total
			Predicted Group Membership			
Original	Count	teampsychologist	11	2	1	14
		teamcoach	3	4	7	14
		control	4	2	8	14
	%	teampsychologist	78.6	14.3	7.1	100.0
		teamcoach	21.4	28.6	50.0	100.0
		control	28.6	14.3	57.1	100.0

a. 54.8% of original grouped cases correctly classified.

This table gives the accuracy of the classification based on the independent variables. Team building by the psychologist is the most accurately predicted (78.6%) whereas team building by the coach is the least accurately predicted (28.6%) which is less than the chance level of 33.3%.

Reporting the output

The results of this discriminant function analysis could be reported as follows: 'A discriminant analysis was carried out using the three predictors: (1) the difference between the most and least liked team member, (2) the number of gym sessions voluntarily attended and (3) the number of games played. The grouping variable was team building which consisted of three different conditions: (1) team building with a sports psychologist, (2) team building with a sports coach and (3) the no team building controls. Two discriminant functions differentiated membership of these conditions effectively and accounted for 97% and 3% of the variance respectively. Wilks' lambda was statistically significant for the combined functions ($\chi^2_6 = 24.69$, $p < 0.001$) but was not significant when the first function was removed ($\chi^2_2 = 1.01$, p ns). The first discriminant function differentiated the psychologist teamwork building group from the other two groups. The variable "the difference between the most and least liked team member" correlated with the discriminant function at 0.96. The variable "number of gym sessions attended" also correlated but at the lower level of 0.64. The second discriminant function maximally distinguished the sports coach's team work group from the other two groups and loaded most strongly with the number of games played (0.96). Classification based on the discriminant functions was good with about 80% of the cases correctly classified compared with the 33% chance accuracy. Approximately 79% of the psychologist's team group were correctly identified with 14% misclassified as belonging to the coach's team building group. Of the control group 57% were correctly identified with 29% misclassified in the psychologist's team building group. Of the coach's team building group 29% were correctly identified with 50% misclassified as the control team members.'

For further resources including data sets and questions, please refer to the CD accompanying this book.

Part 5 More advanced correlational statistics

25 Partial correlation

Overview

- If you suspect that a correlation between two variables is affected by their correlations with yet another variable, it is possible to adjust for the effects of this additional variable by using the partial correlation procedure.

- The correlation between two variables (before partialling) is known as the zero-order correlation.

- Using SPSS, it is also possible to simultaneously control for several variables that may be affecting the correlation coefficient.

- If the variable to be controlled for consists of a small number of nominal categories, it is useful to explore the correlations for separate sets of cases based on the control variable. For example, if gender is to be controlled, then separate your sample into a male subsample and then a female subsample. Explore what the correlations between your main variables are for these two groups. Often this clarifies the effect of partialling in unanticipated ways.

25.1 What is partial correlation?

We know that variables correlate with each other. Height correlates with weight, age correlates with general knowledge, experiencing violence in childhood correlates with being violent as an adult, and so on. But it is not simply that pairs of variables correlate but that pairs of variables correlate with other variables. The patterns are, of course, complex. Partial correlation takes a correlation between two variables and adjusts that correlation for the fact that they correlate with a third variable. Essentially it calculates what the correlation would be if the two variables did not correlate with this third variable.

Table 25.1 gives some data which illustrate what is meant. The basic data consist of two variables – one is scores on a measure of numerical intelligence and the other variable is scores on a measure of verbal intelligence. These two variables correlate highly with a Pearson correlation of 0.97. But the table also contains a third variable – age. There is a correlation between verbal intelligence and age of 0.85 and a correlation between numerical intelligence and age of 0.80. In other words, part of the correlation between verbal

Table 25.1 Numerical and verbal intelligence test scores and age

Numerical scores	Verbal scores	Age
90	90	13
100	95	15
95	95	15
105	105	16
100	100	17

intelligence and numerical intelligence is associated with age. Partial correlation tells us what the correlation between verbal intelligence and numerical intelligence would be *if* their association with age were removed. That is, what the correlation would be if the correlations with age were zero. Usually researchers would refer to age (the variable being removed) as the third-variable. As can be seen in Figure 25.1, the correlation becomes 0.91.

This is a relatively simple calculation but SPSS also allows you to control for several third variables at the same time with scarcely any additional effort. A partial correlation in which one variable is partialled out is called a first order partial correlation, if two variables are partialled out it is called a second order partial correlation, and so on. You will see the main correlation (before partialling) referred to as the zero-order partial correlation.

The change in the size of the correlation between verbal intelligence and numerical intelligence following partialling is not at all great in this case. There is an important lesson here since it is all too easy to believe that a third variable if it has strong correlations with the two main variables will produce a massive change in interpretation when partialled out. This is not always the case, as can be seen. Also be aware that it is possible to have any pattern of change following partialling – a positive correlation can become a negative one, a zero correlation can become substantial and a large correlation can become smaller – and quite what will happen is not easily predictable especially by inexperienced researchers.

Figure 25.1 The correlations between the three variables before partialling

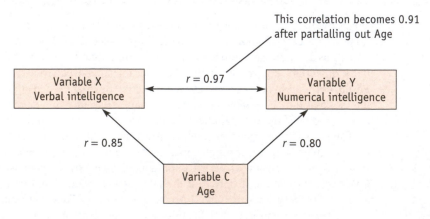

25.2 When to use partial correlation

Partial correlation is built on the assumption that the relationships between the variables in question are linear. That is, if plotted on a scattergram the points are best represented by a straight line. Where the relationships depart from linearity then partial correlation may be misleading.

This aside, the partial correlation can be a useful technique for estimating the influence of a third variable on any correlation coefficient.

25.3 When not to use partial correlation

Many techniques in statistics can do a similar job to partial correlation – that is, control for the influences of third variables: for example, analysis of covariance and multiple regression. If you are using these, then it is sensible to partial out influences of third variables using these techniques rather than carry out an additional partial correlation analysis.

25.4 Data requirements for partial correlation

At a minimum, partial correlation requires three score variables, each of which should ideally be normally distributed. There can be any number of third variables partialled at the same time though it is recommended that the ones to include are carefully planned to be the minimum needed.

25.5 Problems in the use of partial correlation

The main problem when using partial correlation is that some researchers try to make too strong claims about what they can achieve. In particular, it should be understood that partial correlation is not about establishing causality by removing the spurious influence of third variables. They may take away the influence of a variable which may be influencing the relationship between the two key variables but that does not mean that the remaining partialled correlation is a causal one. There may be any number of other third variables that need to be removed before any confidence can be gained about the relationship being a causal one. It is the research design that enables causality to be assessed (such as randomised experiments) and not the statistical analysis.

 You can find out more about partial correlation in Chapter 29 of Howitt, D. and Cramer, D. (2008) *Introduction to Statistics in Psychology*. Harlow: Pearson.

25.6 The data to be analysed

We will illustrate the computation of partial correlations with the raw scores in Table 25.1 on page 234, which represent a numerical intelligence test score, a verbal intelligence test score and age in years. We will correlate the two test scores partialling out age.

25.7 Partial correlation

Step 1:

In 'Variable View' of the 'Data Editor' name the 3 variables 'Num_IQ', 'Verb_IQ' and 'Age'.

Remove the 2 decimal places by setting number to 0.

Step 2:

In 'Data View' of the 'Data Editor' enter the numerical IQ scores in the 1st column, the verbal IQ scores in the 2nd column and age in the 3rd column.

Step 3:

Select 'Analyze', 'Correlate' and 'Partial ...'.

Step 4:

Select 'Num_IQ' and 'Verb_IQ' and the ▶ button to put these 2 variables into the 'Variables:' box.

Select 'Age' and the ▶ button to put it into the 'Controlling for:' box.

Select 'OK'.

25.8 Interpreting the output

Correlations

Control Variables			Num_IQ	Verb_IQ
Age	Num_IQ	Correlation	1.000	.776
		Significance (2-tailed)	.	.224
		df	0	2
	Verb_IQ	Correlation	.776	1.000
		Significance (2-tailed)	.224	.
		df	2	0

The partial correlation between numerical and verbal IQ controlling for age is .776.

This cell gives the same information.

The two-tailed significance is .224 which is not significant. There are 2 degrees of freedom.

Reporting the output

We need to mention the original correlation between numerical and verbal intelligence which is 0.92. So we could report the results as follows: 'The correlation between numerical and verbal intelligence is 0.92 ($df = 3$, two-tailed $p = 0.025$). However, the correlation between numerical and verbal intelligence controlling for age declines to 0.78, which is not significant (two-tailed $p = 0.224$). In other words, there is no significant relationship between numerical and verbal intelligence when age is controlled.'

For further resources including data sets and questions, please refer to the CD accompanying this book.

26 Factor analysis

Overview

- There are two types of factor analysis: exploratory and confirmatory factor analysis. SPSS does not compute confirmatory factor analysis directly. Exploratory factor analysis is probably the more important and SPSS has a very extensive package of options for this.

- (Exploratory) factor analysis allows one to make sense of a complex set of variables by reducing them to a smaller number of factors (or supervariables) which account for many of the original variables. Although it is possible to obtain valuable insights from a matrix of correlations between several variables, the sheer size of the matrix may make this difficult even with a relatively small number of variables.

- Factor analysis is commonly used when trying to understand the pattern of responses of people completing closed-ended questionnaires. The items measuring similar things can be identified through factor analysis and, consequently, the structure of replies to the questionnaire.

- Factor analysis, however, includes a variety of techniques and approaches that can be bewildering. We provide a 'standard' approach that will serve the purposes of most researchers well.

- Factor analysis requires a degree of judgement, especially on the matter of the number of factors to extract. The speed of computer factor analyses means that more than one approach may be tried even within quite a short analysis session. It is a useful exercise to explore the effects of varying the method of analysis in order to assess the effect of this on one's conclusions.

26.1 What is factor analysis?

Factor analysis is a different sort of statistical technique from those in previous chapters. It is one of a number of statistical procedures that can be used to try to identify patterns in fairly large sets of data with substantial numbers of variables. There are other techniques such as cluster analysis that do a similar thing. One of the commonest uses of factor analysis is where one has written a number of questions (items) to measure things like attitudes, personality, and so on. Such questionnaires tend to be fairly lengthy and there is little to be done with them using the statistical techniques so far covered in this book. One could, perhaps, produce a correlation matrix of answers to all of the items on the measure but, say, if you have 20 items then this results in a 20×20 correlation matrix of every item correlated with every other item. This is a table containing 400 correlation coefficients that would not even fit on a page of SPSS output. Consequently it is not simply mentally difficult to handle but it is physically virtually unmanageable too.

Factor analysis is usually based on such a correlation matrix. The matrix is produced by SPSS as part of doing the factor analysis so it does not have to be produced separately. Table 26.1 contains a very simplified set of data that in many ways would be suitable for a factor analysis. It contains performance scores on six variables (batting, crosswords, darts, Scrabble, juggling and spelling) from nine participants for the purposes of illustration. In truth, one would not normally do a factor analysis on data from so few cases but we should emphasise that this is for purposes of illustration only, not to be emulated directly.

A correlation matrix for all of these variables is shown in Table 26.2. Because a correlation matrix is symmetrical around the top left to bottom right diagonal, we have left out some of the correlations for clarity's sake. The diagonal contains correlations of 1 because the correlation of a set of scores with itself is a perfect correlation. What can be made of this correlation matrix? Well it is quite a simple one and deliberately highly structured so you may be able to work out patterns, but this would be difficult in many cases.

Table 26.1 Scores of nine individuals on six variables

Individual	Batting	Crosswords	Darts	Scrabble	Juggling	Spelling
1	10	15	8	26	15	8
2	6	16	5	25	12	9
3	2	11	1	22	7	6
4	5	16	3	28	11	9
5	7	15	4	24	12	7
6	8	13	4	23	14	6
7	6	17	3	29	10	9
8	2	18	1	28	8	8
9	5	14	2	25	10	6

Table 26.2 Correlation matrix of the six variables

	Batting	Crosswords	Darts	Scrabble	Juggling	Spelling
Batting	1	0.00	0.91	−0.05	0.96	0.10
Crosswords		1	0.08	0.88	0.02	0.80
Darts			1	−0.01	0.90	0.29
Scrabble				1	−0.08	0.79
Juggling					1	0.11
Spelling						1

If we subject this correlation matrix to a factor analysis we get a factor loading matrix such as that in Table 26.3 on page 248. Each of the six variables is listed and there are columns headed 'Factor One' and 'Factor Two'. There are also a lot of numbers. The numbers are known as 'factor loadings' but they are nothing other than correlation coefficients. The new idea in this is the factors. Factors are empirically derived variables based on the data in the correlation matrix. They are made up of combinations of variables that tend to correlate together. So the factor loadings are the correlations of variables with an empirically derived 'combined variable' or factor.

The researcher's task is to make sense of each of these factors. This is done by looking at which set of variables correlates highly with the factor. For Factor One these are batting, darts and juggling. What do these variables have in common? They seem to reflect sensory-motor skills and Factor One could be labelled with this phrase. Factor Two has its high correlations with crosswords, Scrabble and spelling. These all seem to reflect verbal skills and Factor Two could be given that name. Of course, the naming of the factors requires some creativity and insight.

That is basically what factor analysis produces but there are a number of other issues that need to be considered:

■ What sort of factor analysis? There are many sorts but for most psychological data we would recommend principal axes analysis or, failing that, principal components analysis which is more suitable if the typical correlations are large. With some data, principal axes analysis simply fails to work properly on SPSS. This is not a fault in SPSS.

■ How many factors? A factor analysis will produce as many factors as variables in the analysis. This is not helpful as many of the factors are simply nonsensical error. At the very minimum, a factor should have an eigenvalue of 1.00 or greater. The eigenvalue is simply the sum of the squared factor loadings on a particular factor. As such it is a measure of the amount of variance associated with that factor. You will also see it referred to as the latent root. However, in order to estimate the number of factors to use it is more helpful to use the scree test. This produces a graph and where the graph of the eigenvalue of each of the factors levels off (i.e. becomes virtually a straight line) then this is the number of factors that should be used.

■ Rotation: if you choose rotation in factor analysis then you are more likely to get a factor matrix that is readily interpretable. We would recommend that you use some method of rotation though this sometimes only changes things a little.

■ It is often desirable to get factor scores for each factor. These are essentially a score for each participant on each factor so factors can be treated just like any other variable. SPSS saves them as an additional column(s) on the SPSS data spreadsheet. You will see a button on the SPSS Factor Analysis window labelled 'Scores' that will allow you to save the factors as variables. Factor scores look odd on the spreadsheet because they are standardised around a mean of zero just like z-scores of which they are a sort of variant.

SPSS describes factor analysis as a data reduction procedure. This is because it takes a number of variables and condenses them into a number of factors that are still variables and can be used as any other score variable can be. Figure 26.1 gives a schematic presentation of a factor analysis.

Figure 26.1 Steps in factor analysis

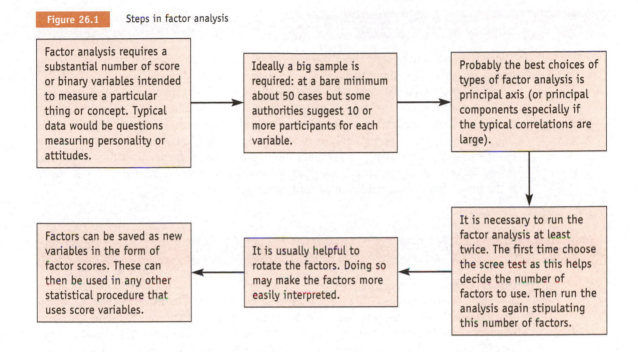

Factor analysis requires a substantial number of score or binary variables intended to measure a particular thing or concept. Typical data would be questions measuring personality or attitudes.

Ideally a big sample is required: at a bare minimum about 50 cases but some authorities suggest 10 or more participants for each variable.

Probably the best choices of types of factor analysis is principal axis (or principal components especially if the typical correlations are large).

It is necessary to run the factor analysis at least twice. The first time choose the scree test as this helps decide the number of factors to use. Then run the analysis again stipulating this number of factors.

It is usually helpful to rotate the factors. Doing so may make the factors more easily interpreted.

Factors can be saved as new variables in the form of factor scores. These can then be used in any other statistical procedure that uses score variables.

26.2   When to use factor analysis

Factor analysis can be used whenever you have a set of score variables (or it can be used with binary (yes–no) variables). It identifies patterns in the correlations between these variables. However, it is not desirable to put every variable that meets these criteria into your factor analysis since the output will be somewhat meaningless. It is better to confine your factor analysis to a set of variables that is relatively coherent in the first place. So if you have a number of items intended to measure 'strength of religious feeling', say, then do not throw into the analysis other variables such as gender, age and number of marathons run in a year as what you get may not make too much sense at all. But this would be advice that should generally be applied to statistical analysis: aim to have a coherent set of data that address the questions that you are interested in; avoid simply collecting data because you can; and avoid statistically analysing data simply because it is there.

26.3   When not to use factor analysis

Factor analysis merely identifies patterns in data and it is not, for example, a test of significance. Neither does it have independent and dependent variables. So if either of these is in your mind then you do not need factor analysis.

Also it makes little sense to carry out a factor analysis if one has less than a handful of variables. So it is unlikely that you would wish to do a factor analysis where say you had five or fewer variables.

26.4 Data requirements for factor analysis

There is some controversy about the number of participants required for a study using factor analysis. The suggestions vary widely according to different sources. Generally speaking, you would not carry out a factor analysis with fewer than about 50 participants. Of course, for student work a smaller sample than this would be common and in this context probably acceptable as part of learning and assessment. However, one also finds suggestions that for a factor analysis to be stable one should have a minimum of about ten participants per variable. Sometimes the figure given is greater than this. Basically, the more participants the better, though factor analysis may be illuminating even if one is at the lower end of acceptable numbers of participants.

26.5 Problems in the use of factor analysis

Our experience is that beginners have the greatest difficult with the least statistical of the aspects of factor analysis – that is the interpretation of factors. Partly this is because many statistical techniques seem to require little special input from the user but factor analysis requires some inductive reasoning and is not merely a rule-following task. However, the task is really relatively straightforward since it merely involves explaining why a number of variables should be closely related. Usually, and this is a rule-of-thumb, we recommend that the variables that have a factor loading of about 0.5 on a particular factor should be considered when trying to name the factor. Of course, −0.5 and bigger negative values also count.

Of course, factor analysis is a somewhat abstract procedure so it can take a little while to grasp the core ideas. But persevere since it is the first step towards a variety of procedures that help you explore complex data rather than simply test significance.

 You can find out more about factor analysis in Chapter 30 of Howitt, D. and Cramer, D. (2008) *Introduction to Statistics in Psychology*. Harlow: Pearson.

26.6 The data to be analysed

The computation of a principal components analysis is illustrated with the data in Table 26.1 on page 239, which consist of scores on six variables for nine individuals. This is only for illustrative purposes; it would be considered a ludicrously small number of cases to perform a factor analysis on. Normally, you should think of having at least two or three times as many cases as you have variables. The following is a standard factor analysis that is adequate for most situations. However, SPSS has many options for factor analysis.

26.7 Principal components analysis with orthogonal rotation

Step 1:

In 'Variable View' of the 'Data Editor' name the 6 variables 'Batting', 'Crosswords' and so on.

Remove the 2 decimal places by setting number to 0.

	Name	Type	Width	Decimals
1	Batting	Numeric	8	0
2	Crosswords	Numeric	8	0
3	Darts	Numeric	8	0
4	Scrabble	Numeric	8	0
5	Juggling	Numeric	8	0
6	Spelling	Numeric	8	0

Step 2:

In 'Data View' of the 'Data Editor' enter the values.

	Batting	Crosswords	Darts	Scrabble	Juggling	Spelling
1	10	15	8	26	15	8
2	6	16	5	25	12	9
3	2	11	1	22	7	6
4	5	16	3	28	11	9
5	7	15	4	24	12	7
6	8	13	4	23	14	6
7	6	17	3	29	10	9
8	2	18	1	28	8	8
9	5	14	2	25	10	6

Step 3:

Select 'Analyze', 'Data Reduction' and 'Factor ...'.

Step 4:

Select the 6 variables either individually or together and the ▶ button to put them in the 'Variables:' box.

Select 'Descriptives ...'.

Step 5:

Select 'Univariate descriptives' and 'Coefficients'.

Select 'Continue'.

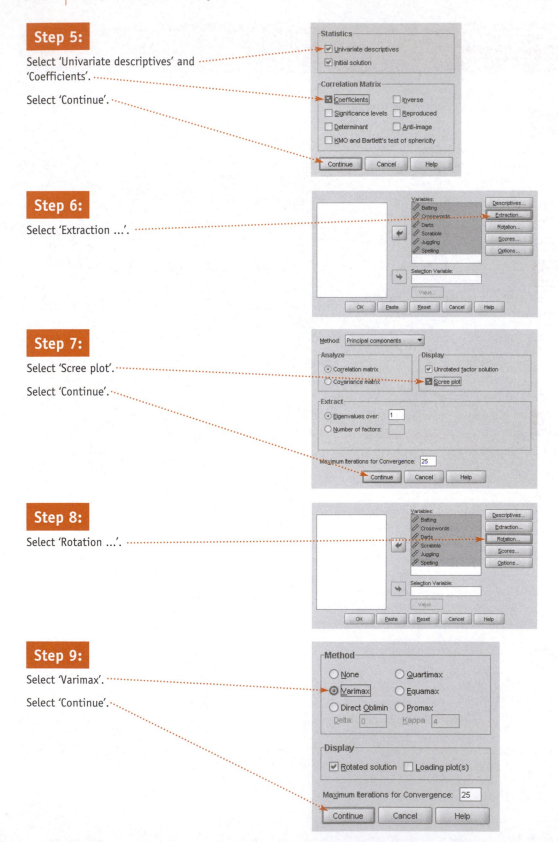

Step 6:

Select 'Extraction ...'.

Step 7:

Select 'Scree plot'.

Select 'Continue'.

Step 8:

Select 'Rotation ...'.

Step 9:

Select 'Varimax'.

Select 'Continue'.

Step 10:

Select 'Options ...'.

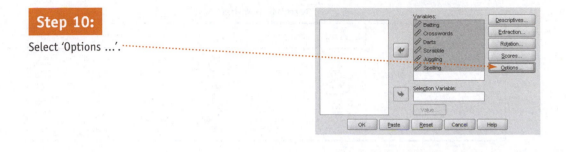

Step 11:

Select 'Sorted by size'.

Select 'Continue'.

Select 'OK' in the initial box.

26.8 Interpreting the output

The first table gives the mean, standard deviation and number of cases for each variable.

Descriptive Statistics

	Mean	Std. Deviation	Analysis N
Batting	5.67	2.598	9
Crosswords	15.00	2.121	9
Darts	3.44	2.186	9
Scrabble	25.56	2.404	9
Juggling	11.00	2.598	9
Spelling	7.56	1.333	9

N shows the number of cases on which your analysis is based. This information is essential particularly if you have missing data.

The second table presents the correlation matrix. From this it appears that there are two groups of variables that are strongly intercorrelated. One consists of batting, juggling and darts, and the other of crosswords, Scrabble and spelling. These have been indicated – but remember that as a correlation matrix is symmetrical only the lower half below the diagonal has been marked. Normally in factor analysis the correlation matrix is much more difficult to decipher than this. Our data are highly stylised.

Correlation Matrix

		Batting	Crosswords	Darts	Scrabble	Juggling	Spelling
Correlation	Batting	1.000	.000	.910	−.047	.963	.096
	Crosswords	.000	1.000	.081	.883	.023	.795
	Darts	.910	.081	1.000	−.005	.902	.291
	Scrabble	−.047	.883	−.005	1.000	−.080	.789
	Juggling	.963	.023	.902	−.080	1.000	.108
	Spelling	.096	.795	.291	.789	.108	1.000

The largest correlations are enclosed in ovals for the first group of variables and in rectangles for the second group. Because factor analysis usually involves a lot of variables and there is a limit to what can be got onto a computer screen, normally the correlation matrix is difficult to see in its entirety.

The third table shows that two principal components were initially extracted in this case. The computer ignores factors with an eigenvalue of less than 1.00. This is because such factors consist of uninterpretable error variation. Of course, your analysis may have even more (or fewer) factors.

Total Variance Explained

Component	Initial Eigenvalues			Extraction Sums of Squared Loadings			Rotation Sums of Squared Loadings		
	Total	% of Variance	Cumulative %	Total	% of Variance	Cumulative %	Total	% of Variance	Cumulative %
1	2.951	49.186	49.186	2.951	49.186	49.186	2.876	47.931	47.931
2	2.579	42.981	92.167	2.579	42.981	92.167	2.654	44.236	92.167
3	.264	4.401	96.567						
4	.124	2.062	98.630						
5	.058	.974	99.604						
6	.024	.396	100.000						

Extraction Method: Principal Component Analysis.

The first two factors (components) will be analysed further by the computer as their eigenvalues are larger that 1.00.

The scree plot also shows that a break in the size of eigenvalues for the factors occurs after the second factor: the curve is fairly flat after the second factor. Since it is important in factor analysis to ensure that you do not have too many factors, you may wish to do your factor analysis and rotation stipulating the number of factors once you have the results of the scree test. (This can be done by inserting the number in the 'Number of factors:' in the 'Factor Analysis: Extraction' subdialog box.) In the case of our data this does not need to be done since the computer has used the first two factors and ignored the others because of the minimum eigenvalue requirement of 1.00. It is not unusual for a component analysis to be recomputed in the light of the pattern that emerges.

Scree Plot

These two components are then orthogonally rotated and the loadings of the six variables on these two factors are shown in the fourth table entitled 'Rotated Component Matrix'.

Rotated Component Matrix[a]

	Component	
	1	2
Batting	.980	−.012
Juggling	.979	−.011
Darts	.962	.104
Crosswords	.006	.951
Scrabble	−.078	.951
Spelling	.153	.914

These numbers are called factor loadings and are essentially correlation coefficients.

Extraction Method: Principal Component Analysis.
Rotation Method: Varimax with Kaiser Normalization.
  a. Rotation converged in 3 iterations.

The variables are ordered or sorted according to their loading on the first factor from those with the highest loadings to those with the lowest loadings. This helps interpretation of the factor since the high loading items are the ones that primarily help you decide what the factor is.

- On the first factor, 'Batting' and 'Scrabble' have has the highest loading (.980) followed by 'Juggling' (.979) and 'Darts' (.962).

- On the second factor, 'Crosswords' and 'Scrabble' have the highest loading (.951) followed by 'Spelling' (.914). The apparent lack of difference in size of loading of 'Crosswords' and 'Scrabble' is due to rounding. This can be seen if you double click on the rotated component matrix table and then double click on these two loadings in turn.

■ We would interpret the meaning of these factors in terms of the content of the variables that loaded most highly on them.

■ The percentage of variance that each of the orthogonally rotated factors accounts for is given in the third table under '% of variance' in the 'Rotation Sums of Squared Loadings' columns. It is 47.931 for the first factor and 44.236 for the second factor.

Reporting the output

It would be usual to tabulate the factors and variables, space permitting. Since the data in our example are on various tests of skill, the factor analysis table might be as in Table 26.3. The figures have been given to two decimal places.

The exact way of reporting the results of a factor analysis will depend on the purpose of the analysis. One way of describing the results would be as follows: 'A principal components analysis was conducted on the correlations of the six variables. Two factors were initially extracted with eigenvalues equal to or greater than 1.00. Orthogonal rotation of the factors yielded the factor structure given in Table 26.3. The first factor accounted for 48% of the variance and the second factor 44%. The first factor seems to be hand–eye coordination and the second factor seems to be verbal flexibility.' With factor analysis, since the factors have to be interpreted, differences in interpretation may occur.

Table 26.3 Orthogonal factor loading matrix for six skills

Variable	Factor 1	Factor 2
Skill at Batting	0.98	−0.01
Skill at Crosswords	0.01	0.95
Skill at Darts	0.96	0.10
Skill at Scrabble	−0.08	0.95
Skill at Juggling	0.98	−0.01
Skill at Spelling	0.15	0.91

For further resources including data sets and questions, please refer to the CD accompanying this book.

27 Item reliability and inter-rater agreement

Overview

- Reliability is a complex matter, as the term refers to a range of very different concepts and measures that can easily be confused.

- Item alpha reliability and split-half reliability assess the internal consistency of the items in a questionnaire – that is, do the items tend to be measuring much the same thing?

- Split-half reliability on SPSS refers to the correlation between scores based on the first half of items you list for inclusion and the second half of the items. This correlation can be adjusted statistically to maintain the original questionnaire length.

- Coefficient alpha is merely the average of all possible split-half reliabilities for the questionnaire and so may be preferred, as it is not dependent on how the items are ordered. Coefficient alpha can be used as a means of shortening a questionnaire while maintaining or improving its internal reliability.

- Inter-rater reliability (here assessed by kappa) is essentially a measure of agreement between the ratings of two different raters. Thus it is particularly useful for assessing codings or ratings by 'experts' of aspects of open-ended data; in other words, the quantification of qualitative data. It involves the extent of exact agreement between raters on their ratings compared with the agreement that would be expected by chance. Note then that it is different from the correlation between raters, which does not require *exact* agreement to achieve high correlations but merely that the ratings agree relatively for both raters.

- Other forms of reliability, such as the consistency of a measure taken at two different points in time (test–retest reliability), could be assessed simply using the correlation coefficient (Chapter 7).

27.1 What are item reliability and inter-rater agreement?

■ **Alpha and split-half reliability**

The concept of reliability is one of the most important in psychological methodology alongside that of validity. Both of these concepts are applied to psychological test scores and other measures. The concept of reliability covered in this chapter is primarily to do with the construction of psychological tests and scales. There are two important and very different meanings of reliability:

1. External reliability, which considers the stability of scores on psychological tests and other measures over time. This is typically known as test–retest reliability and essentially consists of the correlation between measures taken at different points in time.

2. Internal reliability, which considers the internal consistency of a test or scale. Alpha and split-half reliabilities are both examples of measures of internal consistency.

Psychological tests and scales consist of a number of items intended to measure a psychological concept such as self-esteem, locus of control, personality characteristics, and so on. A lot of items are used simply because it is believed that a single item is not powerful enough to adequately measure the concept. So the assumption is that all of the items on the scale are measuring aspects of the psychological concept in question. This has several implications – one of which is that the items will all correlate with each other over a sample of participants. (Factor analysis could be used to explore this pattern, of course.) Another implication is that any subset or subgroup of items on the test or scale should show a good correlation with any other subset of items on the test or scale. This is essentially because all of the items are assumed to be measuring the same thing.

Table 27.1 contains data illustrative of the situation. There are data from ten participants for a four-item questionnaire. Normally, to score such a scale one would simply sum the scores on the four individual items to give a total score for each participant on the four-item scale. So do these items form an internally consistent (i.e. reliable) scale? The approach of split-half reliability is simply to split the items into two halves and sum the total for each half. So Item 1 + Item 2 would be the score of each participant on the first half of the items and Item 3 + Item 4 would be the score of each participant on the second half of the items.

Table 27.1 Data for ten cases from a four-item questionnaire

Cases	Item 1	Item 2	Item 3	Item 4
1	1	3	5	6
2	2	1	1	2
3	1	1	1	1
4	5	2	4	2
5	6	4	3	2
6	5	4	5	6
7	4	5	3	2
8	2	1	2	1
9	1	2	1	1
10	1	1	2	2

Essentially, the split-half reliability for these data would be the correlation between the sum of the first half of items with the sum of the second half of these items. One would expect a good correlation between the two if the items on the scale are internally consistent. There is one slight problem with this. We have so far calculated the reliability of just halves of the scale and not the total scale. So an adjustment is made to the split-half reliability to estimate the reliability of the full-length scale. This is an easy computation but SPSS does it for you automatically so no further action is needed on your part.

Alpha reliability (or Cronbach's coefficient alpha) is conceptually much the same as split-half reliability but deals with an obvious problem with split-half reliability. How one splits a scale into two halves will affect the size of the reliability. If Item 1 and Item 3 are summed and Item 2 and Item 4 summed then this will give a different answer from summing the first two and last two items. This is a little less than satisfactory. Alpha reliability gets around this problem by calculating the average of all possible split half reliabilities based on a scale. That is, it works out all possible ways of choosing two different halves of the set of items. In other words, alpha reliability is based on more information in the data and, consequently, is a better estimate of the internal reliability.

■ Inter-rater agreement

This is used in a quite different set of circumstances. Self-evidently, it would be used when the data are from raters who are making assessments of the characteristics of individuals, for example. Imagine that the study is comparing the ratings of a forensic psychologist and a psychiatrist of the risk posed to the public by sex offenders, a rating of 3 being the highest risk level. This situation is illustrated in Table 27.2. At first sight, one might assume that the reliability of these ratings could be assessed by correlating the ratings of the forensic psychologist with those of the psychiatrist. There is a problem with this which is due to the fact that correlation coefficients actually assess covariation in data and do not reflect agreement on the actual scores. So, for example, if a number such as 7 were added to each of the ratings made by the psychiatrist, this would make no difference to the size of the correlation coefficient between the two sets of ratings but would make a big difference to the mean score.

The kappa coefficient is a measure of the extent to which the actual ratings of the forensic psychologist and the psychiatrist are identical. We could take the data set in Table 27.2

Table 27.2   Ratings of risk by two professionals of 12 offenders

Sex offenders	Forensic psychologist	Psychiatrist
1	3	3
2	3	3
3	3	3
4	1	1
5	1	2
6	3	3
7	2	3
8	3	3
9	2	3
10	3	3
11	3	3
12	3	3

Table 27.3 Agreements and disagreements between the forensic psychologist and the psychiatrist on ratings of sex offenders with marginal totals added

		Psychiatrist		
		1	2	3
Psychologist	1	1	1	0
	2	0	0	2
	3	0	0	8

and recast it into a table that shows the frequency of agreements and disagreements between the two (see Table 27.3). It is probably obvious that the agreement is largely due to the high number of high ratings (extremely dangerous) made since there is little agreement at the lower rating levels. The kappa coefficient makes allowance for this sort of tendency by adjusting for the chance level of agreement based on the data.

27.2 When to use item reliability and inter-rater agreement

Item reliability should be used whenever you have a group of items that you intend to combine into a total score. You may wish to employ factor analysis too in these circumstances. If you are using a ready-made scale (e.g. a commercial test) then it may be appropriate to assess its reliability on the sample you are researching as reliability is not totally a feature of a test but may be affected by the nature of the sample and the circumstances of the research.

Inter-rater agreement in the form of the kappa coefficient can be used in any circumstances where independent ratings are being used. Do not forget, however, that the chances of agreement are reduced if there are many rating categories. So consider the extent to which you might wish to combine rating categories for the purposes of the analysis should you have more than a few categories.

27.3 When not to use item reliability and inter-rater agreement

Not all test and scale construction methods are built on the assumption that scores on individual items are intercorrelated and can be summed to give a total score. Be on the look out for such circumstances and consider carefully the applicability of item reliability methods. These exceptional circumstances are unlikely, however.

Inter-rater agreement is important in some circumstances but not in all circumstances. So low inter-rater agreement may be unimportant for research studies and having a good correlation between the two sets of ratings sufficient to indicate that the measure is reliable for the purposes of the research.

27.4 Data requirements for item reliability and inter-rater agreement

Item reliability can be used for response scales using Likert ratings as well as those using binary (yes–no) answer formats. It cannot be used for responses that are on a three or more category nominal scale or where the responses are not entered into SPSS in the form of scores.

Inter-rater agreement requires two separate raters making ratings on a small number of categories.

27.5 Problems in the use of item reliability and inter-rater agreement

Item analysis does not generally cause any problems. However, compared with factor analysis it performs a very limited task. Although the higher the item reliability the better (alphas of 0.8 are considered satisfactory), really the reliability has to be assessed in terms of the purposes of the measurement. Scales for research purposes may have lower reliabilities than scales that are being used, say, by a clinician to make decisions about the future of an individual.

Inter-rater agreement is what it says with one proviso – that is, it is agreement adjusted for the chance level of agreement. So it is possible that where raters agree in percentage terms very accurately the value of kappa is low simply because both raters are using a particular category very frequently.

 You can find out more about item reliability and inter-rater agreement in Chapter 36 of Howitt, D. and Cramer, D. (2008) *Introduction to Statistics in Psychology.* Harlow: Pearson.

27.6 The data to be analysed: item alpha reliability

The answers of ten people to the four items of a questionnaire are shown in Table 27.1 on page 250. These data will be used to illustrate two measures of item reliability known as alpha reliability and split-half reliability.

Step 1:

Enter the data.

	Batting	Crosswords	Darts	Scrabble	Juggling	Spelling
1	10	15	8	26	15	8
2	8	16	5	25	12	9
3	2	11	1	22	7	6
4	5	16	3	28	11	9
5	7	15	4	24	12	7
6	8	13	4	23	14	6
7	6	17	3	29	10	9
8	2	18	1	28	8	8
9	6	14	2	25	10	8

Step 2:

Select 'Analyze',
'Scale'
and 'Reliability Analysis ...'.

Step 3:

Select the 4 items singly or
together and the ▶ button to put
them in the 'Items:' box.

Select 'Statistics ...'.

Step 4:

Select 'Scale if item deleted'.

Select 'Continue'.

Select 'OK' in the
previous box.

27.7 Interpreting the output

Case Processing Summary

		N	%
Cases	Valid	10	100.0
	Excluded[a]	0	.0
	Total	10	100.0

The 1st table shows the number
of cases on which the analysis is
based, which is 10.

a. Listwise deletion based on all variables in the
   procedure.

The 2nd table shows the alpha reliability of the four items and is .811, which rounded to 2 decimal places is .81.

Reliability Statistics

Cronbach's Alpha	N of Items
.811	4

This is the alpha reliability of the scale with one of the items dropped. From this column we can see that if we remove the first item ('Item1'), the alpha reliability of the remaining three items of the scale increases slightly to .840 from .811. Since this is a very small change, Item 1 is probably best retained.

Item-Total Statistics

	Scale Mean if Item Deleted	Scale Variance if Item Deleted	Corrected Item-Total Correlation	Cronbach's Alpha if Item Deleted
Item1	7.60	18.933	.490	.840
Item2	8.00	19.556	.718	.731
Item3	7.70	17.789	.842	.671
Item4	7.90	18.767	.547	.806

Reporting the output

One way of reporting the results of this analysis is as follows: 'The alpha reliability of the four-item scale was 0.81, indicating that the scale had good reliability.' An alpha of 0.70 or above is considered satisfactory.

27.8 Split-half reliability

The previous data are reused for this analysis.

Select the ▼ button in the 'Model:' window and 'Split-half'.

Select 'OK' (which is hidden by the drop-down menu, see Step 3 in section 27.1).

(Deselect 'Scale if item deleted' in 'Statistics ...' if you wish.)

27.9 Interpreting the output

The last line of the second table shows the (Guttman) split reliability of the four items as 0.646, which rounded to two decimal places is 0.65.

Reliability Statistics

Cronbach's Alpha	Part 1	Value	.777
		N of Items	2[a]
	Part 2	Value	.904
		N of Items	2[b]
	Total N of Items		4
Correlation Between Forms			.477
Spearman-Brown Coefficient	Equal Length		.646
	Unequal Length		.646
Guttman Split-Half Coefficient			.646

a. The items are: Item1, Item2.
b. The items are: Item3, Item4.

Reporting the output

One way of reporting the results of this analysis is as follows: 'The split-half reliability of the four-item scale was 0.65, indicating that the scale had only moderate reliability.'

27.10 Inter-rater agreement (kappa)

Kappa is used to measure the agreement between two raters, taking into account the amount of agreement that would be expected by chance. We will illustrate its computation for the data in Table 27.2, which shows the ratings by a forensic psychologist and a psychiatrist of 12 sex offenders in terms of the offenders being no risk (1), a moderate risk (2) or a high risk (3) to the public.

Step 1:

Enter the data. ┄┄┄┄┄┄┄┄┄┄┄┄┄┄➤

	Psychologist	Psychiatrist
1	3	3
2	3	3
3	3	3
4	1	1
5	1	2
6	3	3
7	2	3
8	3	3
9	2	3
10	3	3
11	3	3
12	3	3

Step 2:

Select 'Analyze', 'Descriptive Statistics' and 'Crosstabs ...'.

Step 3:

Select 'Psychologist' and the ▶ button beside 'Row(s):' to put it there.

Select 'Psychiatrist' and the ▶ button beside 'Column(s):' to put it there.

Select 'Statistics ...'.

Step 4:

Select 'Kappa'.

Select 'Continue'.

Select 'OK' in the previous box.

27.11 Interpreting the output

In the 2nd table of the output the data have been arranged in a 2 × 2 contingency format. The numbers of cases on which the forensic psychologist and the psychiatrist agree are shown in the diagonal cells of this table. They are 1 for the rating of 1, 0 for the rating of 2, and 8 for the rating of 3.

Psychologist * Psychiatrist Crosstabulation

Count

		Psychiatrist			
		1	2	3	Total
Psychologist	1	1	1	0	2
	2	0	0	2	2
	3	0	0	8	8
Total		1	1	10	12

In the 3rd table kappa is shown as .400. Although kappa is statistically significant with $p = .046$, it indicates only moderate agreement.

Symmetric Measures

	Value	Asymp. Std. Error[a]	Approx. T[b]	Approx. Sig.
Measure of Agreement Kappa	.400	.219	2.000	.046
N of Valid Cases	12			

a. Not assuming the null hypothesis.
b. Using the asymptotic standard error assuming the null hypothesis.

Note that kappa allows for raters tending to use the same ratings most of the time. It is *not* a measure of percentage agreement.

Reporting the output

One way of reporting the results of this analysis is as follows: 'Kappa for the agreement between the ratings of the forensic psychologist and the psychiatrist was 0.40, which indicates only moderate agreement.'

For further resources including data sets and questions, please refer to the CD accompanying this book.

28 Stepwise multiple regression

Overview

- Stepwise multiple regression is a way of choosing predictors of a particular dependent variable on the basis of statistical criteria.

- Essentially the statistical procedure decides which independent variable is the best predictor, the second best predictor, etc.

- The emphasis is on finding the best predictors at each stage. When predictors are highly correlated with each other and with the dependent variable, often one variable becomes listed as a predictor and the other variable is not listed. This does not mean that the latter variable is *not* a predictor, merely that it adds nothing to the prediction that the first predictor has not already done. Sometimes the best predictor is only marginally better than the second predictor and minor variations in the procedures may affect which of the two is chosen as the predictor.

- There are a number of multiple regression variants. Stepwise is usually a good choice though one can enter all variables simultaneously as an alternative. Similarly, one can enter all of the variables simultaneously and gradually eliminate predictors one by one if elimination does little to change the overall prediction.

- It is possible to enter variables as different groups for analysis. This is called hierarchical multiple regression and can, for example, be selected alongside stepwise procedures. The use of blocks is discussed in the next chapter.

28.1 What is stepwise multiple regression?

Multiple regression is like simple or bivariate regression (Chapter 8) except that there is more than one predictor variable. Multiple regression is used when the variables are generally normally distributed. In other words, it is used when the criterion is a quantitative or score variable. In stepwise multiple regression the predictor variables are entered one variable at a time or step according to particular statistical criteria.

The first predictor to be considered for entry on the first step is the predictor that has the highest correlation with the criterion (Chapter 7). This predictor on its own will explain the most variance in the criterion. This correlation has to be statistically significant for it to be entered. If it is not significant, the analysis stops here with no predictors being entered.

The second predictor to be considered for entry on the second step is the one that explains the second highest proportion of the variance after its relation with the first predictor and the criterion is taken into account. In other words it is the predictor that has the highest part correlation with the criterion after the first predictor has been removed. Once again, this first-order part correlation has to be statistically significant for it to be entered. If it is not significant, the analysis stops after the first predictor has been entered.

The third predictor to be considered for entry on the third step is the predictor that has the highest part correlation after its association with the first two predictors and the criterion is taken into account. This second-order part correlation has to be statistically significant for it to be entered. If it is not significant, the analysis stops after the second step and does not proceed any further. If it is significant, then it is entered. At this stage, the second-order part correlations of the first two predictors with the criterion is examined. It is possible that one or both of these second-order part correlations are not significant. If this is the case, then the predictor with the non-significant second-order part correlation will be dropped from the analysis. The process continues until no other predictor explains a significant proportion of the variance in the criterion.

We will illustrate a stepwise multiple regression with the data in Table 28.1, which shows the scores of six children on the four variables of educational achievement, intellectual ability, school motivation and parental interest. We would not normally use such a small sample to carry out a stepwise multiple correlation as it is unlikely that any of the correlations would be significant. So what we have done to make the correlations significant is to weight or multiply these six cases by 20 times so that we have a sample of 120, which is a reasonable number for a multiple regression.

The correlations between these four variables is shown in Table 28.2 (see also Chapter 7). We can see that the predictor with the highest correlation is ability which is 0.70 and which is statistically significant. So ability is the first predictor to be entered into the stepwise multiple regression.

The two first-order part correlations of achievement with motivation and interest controlling for ability are 0.16 and 0.05 respectively. As the first-order part correlation for motivation is higher than that for interest and is statistically significant it is entered in the second step. The second-order part correlation for interest is 0.00 and is not significant. Consequently the analysis stops after the second step.

Table 28.1 Data for stepwise multiple regression

Educational achievement	Intellectual ability	School motivation	Parental interest
1	2	1	2
2	2	3	1
2	2	3	3
3	4	3	2
3	3	4	3
4	3	2	2

Table 28.2   A correlation matrix for the four variables

	1 Achievement	2 Ability	3 Motivation	4 Interest
1 Achievement				
2 Ability	0.70			
3 Motivation	0.37	0.32		
4 Interest	0.13	0.11	0.34	

The proportion of variance explained by the first predictor is simply the square of its correlation with achievement which is 0.70^2 or about 0.49 or 49.0%. The values can be found in the SPSS regression in the Model Summary table which we illustrate on page 265. You will find Model 1 and Model 2 referred to. The first model includes just the first variable selected for inclusion in the regression, the second model includes the first and second variables selected for inclusion, and so forth. However, it may be helpful to understand that the proportion of the variance explained by the first two predictors, for example, is their squared multiple correlation (R^2) which is calculated by multiplying the standardised partial beta regression coefficient by the correlation coefficient for each predictor and the criterion and summing these products. The standardised partial regression coefficient is normally referred to as the standardised regression coefficient. It is 0.649 for ability and 0.164 for motivation. Consequently the squared multiple correlation is about 0.515 [$(0.649 \times 0.70) + (0.164 \times 0.37)$]. In other words, the two predictors taken together explain about 51.5% of the variance in achievement. As ability explains about 49.0% of the variance, motivation explains about a further 2.5%.

You can use nominal (category) variables as predictors (independent variables) in regression using what is known as dummy coding. This is discussed at length in Chapters 31 and 32 on logistic regression. Basically it involves creating a variable for each category of the nominal (category) variable. If the categories are oranges, apples and bananas then one could create three dummy variables – oranges or not orranges, apples or not apples, and bananas or not bananas. These variables would only have two coding categories, obviously, and so can be used in correlations and hence in regression. You would have to create the dummy variables using Recode (Chapter 35). You must also understand that one of the dummy variables will *not* be used in the regression analysis because it contains the same information as the other two dummy variables. It does not matter which dummy variable you choose to omit.

28.2   When to use stepwise multiple regression

Stepwise multiple regression should be used when you want to find out what are the smallest number of predictors that you need which make a significant contribution in explaining the maximum amount of variance in the criterion variable, what these predictors are and how much of the variance of the criterion variable they explain. It may be helpful to use stepwise multiple regression when you have a large number of predictor variables and you want to get a quick impression of which of these explain most of the variance in the criterion variable.

28.3   When not to use stepwise multiple regression

Ideally it is better to use theoretical criteria rather than purely statistical ones in determining how you think your predictor variables are related to your criterion variable. This may be done by looking at particular variables or groups of variables at a time as is done in simple path analysis or by putting the variables in a multiple regression in a particular order. Hierarchical regression (which is dealt with in Chapter 29) is the procedure used for entering predictor variables in a particular sequence. Stepwise multiple regression would not generally be used when one or more of the predictor variables are nominal (category) variables involving three or more categories as these have to be converted into dummy variables. The dummy variables are best entered in a single step as a block to see what contribution this predictor variable makes to the criterion. This is done using hierarchical multiple regression.

28.4   Data requirements for stepwise multiple regression

Although multiple regression can handle categorical variables when they have been turned into dummy variables, a basic requirement for any form of simple or multiple regression is that the scatterplot of the relation between a predictor variable and the criterion should show homoscedasticity, which means that the plot of the data points around the points of the line of best fit should be similar. This can be roughly assessed by plotting the line of best fit in a scatterplot and seeing if this assumption seems to have been met for each of the predictor variables (Chapter 8). It is important the criterion or dependent variable should be a continuous score which is normally distributed. If the criterion is a binomial variable, then it is far better to use binomial logistic regression (Chapter 32). If it is a multinomial varaible, then multinomial logistic regression should be used (Chapter 31).

28.5   Problems in the use of stepwise multiple regression

Care needs to be taken in interpreting the results of a stepwise multiple regression. If two predictor variables show multicollinearity in that they are highly correlated, then the predictor variable which has the higher relation with the criterion variable will be entered first even if this relation is minutely bigger than that with the other predictor variable. As both variables are strongly related to each other, it is likely that the other variable may not be entered as a significant predictor in the multiple regression even though it may be an equally strong candidate. As the relation between each predictor and the criterion is similar, the results for this analysis may not be very reliable in the sense that the other predictor may have the higher relation with the criterion in a second sample. Consequently it is important to look at the zero-order and the partial correlations of these variables to see whether the difference in the size of their relation can be considered small.

You can find out more about stepwise multiple regression in Chapter 31 of Howitt, D. and Cramer, D. (2008) *Introduction to Statistics in Psychology*. Harlow: Pearson.

28.6   The data to be analysed

We will illustrate the computation of a stepwise multiple regression analysis with the data shown in Table 28.1 on page 260, which consist of scores for six individuals on the four variables of educational achievement, intellectual ability, school motivation and parental interest respectively.

Because this is for illustrative purposes and to save space, we are going to enter these data 20 times to give us a respectable amount of data to work with. Obviously you would *not* do this if your data were real. It is important to use quite a lot of research participants or cases for multiple regression. Ten or 15 times your number of variables would be reasonably generous. Of course, you can use less for data exploration purposes.

28.7   Stepwise multiple regression analysis

Step 1:

Enter the data.
The 'Freq' variable is for weighting these 6 cases 20 times using the 'Weight Cases ...' procedure (see section 6.8 or 13.7). Save this data file to use in Chapter 29.

	Achievement	Ability	Motivation	Interest	Freq
1	1	2	1	2	20
2	2	2	3	1	20
3	2	2	3	3	20
4	3	4	3	2	20
5	3	3	4	3	20
6	4	3	2	2	20

Step 2:

Select 'Analyze',
'Regression' and
'Linear ...'.

Step 3:

Select 'Achievement' and the ▶ button beside the 'Dependent:' box to put it there.

Select 'Ability', 'Motivation' and 'Interest' and the ▶ button beside the 'Independent(s):' box to put them there.

Select the ▼ button beside 'Method:' and select 'Stepwise'.

Select 'Statistics ...'.

Step 4:

Select 'Confidence intervals',
'R squared change', 'Descriptives'
and 'Part and partial correlations'.

Select 'Continue'.

Select 'OK' in the previous
box which reappears.

28.8 Interpreting the output

■ There is a great deal of information in the output. Multiple regression is a complex area and needs further study in order to understand all of its ramifications. In interpreting the results of this analysis we shall restrict ourselves to commenting on the following statistics: multiple R, R square, adjusted R square, B, beta, R square change and part correlations. Most of these are dealt with in a simple fashion in *ISP* Chapter 31.

■ In stepwise multiple regression, each new step is discussed as a model. In this example, two significant steps were involved. The first step (Model 1) uses the predictor Ability. The second step (Model 2) is built on this predictor with the addition of a second predictor Motivation. Generally, it is reasonable to concentrate on the highest numbered model.

■ Notice how badly the first table in particular is laid out. If you double click on a table it will be enclosed in a rectangle. To move any but the first line, move the cursor to that line. When it changes to a double arrow ($\leftrightarrow$), click the left button of the mouse and, holding the left button down, move the line to the position you want before releasing the button. By dragging the column dividers in this way you should be able to obtain a better and more easily read table.

Variables Entered/Removed[a]

Model	Variables Entered	Variables Removed	Method
1	Ability	.	Stepwise (Criteria: Probability-of-F-to-enter <= .050, Probability-of-F-to-remove >= .100).
2	Motivation	.	Stepwise (Criteria: Probability-of- F-to-enter <= .050, Probability-of-F-to-remove >= .100).

a. Dependent Variable: Achievement

■ The second table of the output 'Model Summary' gives the values of multiple R, R square and adjusted R square for the two steps (models). This is really a table of the multiple correlation coefficients between the models and the criterion. It also includes statistics indicating the improvement of fit of the models with the data. Each model in this example gives an improvement in fit. This can be seen from the final figures where the change in fit is significant for both Model 1 and Model 2. (The regression weights (B and beta) are to be found in the fourth table of the output entitled 'Coefficients'.)

The most important thing is that the Sig. F change indicates the improvement in fit for the two models is significant.

Model Summary

Model	R	R Square	Adjusted R Square	Std. Error of the Estimate	Change Statistics				
					R Square Change	F Change	df1	df2	Sig. F Change
1	.701[a]	.491	.487	.689	.491	113.786	1	118	.000
2	.718[b]	.515	.507	.675	.024	5.850	1	117	.017

a. Predictors: (Constant), Ability
b. Predictors: (Constant), Ability, Motivation

- The predictor that is entered on the first step of the stepwise analysis (Model 1) is the predictor that has the highest correlation with the criterion. In this example this predictor is 'Ability'. (Note 'a' immediately underneath the Model Summary table indicates this.)

- As there is only one predictor in the regression equation on the first step, Multiple R is the same as the correlation between Ability and Achievement (the dependent or criterion variable). In this case it is 0.701 or 0.70 to two decimal places.

- R square is simply the multiple correlation coefficient squared, which in this instance is 0.491 or 0.49 to two decimal places. This indicates that 49% of the variance in the criterion is shared with or 'explained by' the first predictor.

- Adjusted R square is R square which has been adjusted for the size of the sample and the number of predictors in the equation. The effect of this adjustment is to reduce the size of R square, so adjusted R square is 0.487 or 0.49 to two decimal places.

- The variable that is entered second in the regression equation is the predictor which generally explains the second greatest significant proportion of the variance in the criterion. In this example, this variable is 'Motivation'.

- The multiple R, R square and adjusted R square for Model 2 are 0.718, 0.515 and 0.507 respectively which, rounded to two decimal places, are 0.72, 0.52 and 0.51. As might be expected, these values are bigger than the corresponding figures for Model 1. This is to be expected because there is an additional predictor contributing to a better prediction.

- In Model 2, then, two variables ('Ability' and 'Motivation') explain or account for 51% of the variance in the criterion.

- R square change presented under 'Change Statistics' in the second table shows the increase in the proportion of the variance in the criterion variable ('Achievement') by predictors that have been entered after the first predictor ('Ability'). In this case there is only one other predictor ('Motivation'). This predictor explains a further 2.4% of the variance in the criterion.

- Examine the table headed 'Coefficients'. Find the column headed Beta in the table. The first entry is 0.701 for Model 1. This is exactly the same as the value of the multiple correlation above for Model 1. That is because beta is the standardised regression coefficient, which is the same as the correlation when there is only one predictor. It is as if all your scores had been transformed to z-scores before the analysis began.

Coefficients[a]

Model		Unstandardized Coefficients		Standardized Coefficients	t	Sig.	95% Confidence Interval for B		Correlations		
		B	Std. Error	Beta			Lower Bound	Upper Bound	Zero-order	Partial	Part
1	(Constant)	.100	.234		.428	.669	−.363	.563			
	Ability	.900	.084	.701	10.667	.000	.733	1.067	.701	.701	.701
2	(Constant)	−.167	.254		−.656	.513	−.670	.337			
	Ability	.833	.087	.649	9.561	.000	.661	1.006	.701	.622	.615
	Motivation	.167	.069	.164	2.419	.017	.030	.303	.369	.218	.156

a. Dependent Variable: Achievement

> The quickest way to access the output from multiple regression is to concentrate on the final model's output in the table labelled Coefficients. Ignore the row for constants, then concentrate on the remaining rows. These give the important predictors of the dependent variable. These are clearly Ability and Motivation, both of which contribute significantly. B weights are hard to interpret since they are dependent on the scale of measurement involved. Beta weights are analogous to correlation coefficients. Both Beta weights are positive so there is a positive relation between each predictor and the dependent variable. Ability has a correlation of .649 with Achievement and Motivation contributes an additional independent correlation of .164 with Achievement. The t values plus their corresponding Sig. Values indicates that the two independent variables contribute significantly to the prediction. The part correlation of Ability and Ability are .615 and .156 respectively so they explain about 38% and 2% of the variance in Achievement when not taking account of the variance they share together.

- For Model 2 Beta is 0.649 for the first predictor ('Ability') and 0.164 for the second predictor ('Motivation').

- The analysis stops at this point, as the third predictor ('Interest') does not explain a further significant proportion of the criterion variance. Notice that in the final table of the output entitled 'Excluded Variables', 'Interest' has a *t* value of 0.000 and a significance level of 1.0000. This tells us that 'Interest' is a non-significant predictor of the criterion ('Achievement').

- The part correlation for Ability and Motivation are 0.615 and 0.156 respectively, which when squared means that they explain about 37.8% and 2.4% of the variance in Achievement when not taking account of the variance they share together. As the total percentage of variance these two variables explain is about 51.5% this means that the percentage of variance they share is about 11.3% (51.5 − 40.2).

Reporting the output

There are various ways of reporting the results of a stepwise multiple regression analysis. In such a report we should include the following kind of statement: 'In the stepwise multiple regression, intellectual ability was entered first and explained 49% of the variance in educational achievement ($F_{1,118} = 113.76$, $p < 0.001$). School motivation was entered second and explained a further 2% ($F_{1,117} = 5.85$, $p = 0.017$). Greater educational attainment was associated with greater intellectual ability and school motivation.'

A table is sometimes presented. There is no standard way of doing this but Table 28.3 is probably as clear as most.

Table 28.3 Stepwise multiple regression of predictors of educational achievement (only significant predictors are included)

Variable	Multiple R	B	Standard error b	Beta	t	Significance of t
Intellectual ability	0.70	0.83	0.09	0.65	9.56	0.001
School motivation	0.72	0.17	0.07	0.16	2.42	0.05

For further resources including data sets and questions, please refer to the CD accompanying this book.

29 Hierarchical multiple regression

Overview

- Hierarchical multiple regression allows the researcher to decide which order to use for a list of predictors.

- This is achieved by putting the predictors or groups of predictors into blocks of variables. The computer will carry out the regression taking each block in the order that it was entered into SPSS. So it provides a way of forcing the variables to be considered in the sequence chosen by the researcher. Rather than let the computer decide on statistical criteria as in the previous chapter, the researcher decides which should be the first predictor, the second predictor, and so forth.

- A block may be a single predictor but it may be a group of predictors. If it is a group of predictors then it is sensible to instruct the computer how to select the order within the blocks. If this is not done, the computer merely takes the variables in the block and includes them in the analysis in the order that the researcher entered them into the block.

- This order of the blocks is likely to be chosen on theoretical grounds. One common procedure is to put variables that need to be statistically controlled in the first block. The consequence of this is that the control variables are partialled out before the rest of the blocks are analysed.

- Since the researcher is trying to produce models of the data, the multiple regression may be varied to examine the effects of, say, entering the blocks in a different order.

- Hierarchical mutliple regression is used to calculate the path coefficients in a simple path analysis.

29.1 What is hierarchical multiple regression?

Hierarchical multiple regression is used to determine how much variance in the criterion, dependent or outcome variable is explained by predictors (independent variables) when they are entered in a particular sequence. The more variance that a predictor explains the potentially more important that variable may be. The variables may be entered in a particular sequence on practical or theoretical grounds. An example of a practical situation is where we are interested in trying to predict how good someone might be at their job. We could collect a number of variables that we think might be related to how good they might be. This might include how well they did at school, how many outside interests they have, how many positions of responsibility they hold, how well they performed in interview and so on. Now some of these variables might be easy and cheap to obtain such as finding out how well they did at school or how many outside interests they have while other variables might be more costly to obtain such as how well they performed at interview. We may be interested in whether using these more costly variables enable us to make much better predictions about how likely someone is to be good at their job than the cheaper ones. If they do not add much to how well we are able to predict job competence, then it might be better not to use them. So we could add the cheaper variables in the first step of our hierarchical multiple regression and see how much of the variance in job competence is generally explained. We could then add the more costly variables in the second step to see how much more of the variance in job competence these variables explain.

Turning to a more theoretical situation, we may be interested in trying to explain how much different variables or types of variables explain some criterion such as educational achievement. We may arrange the variables in a particular sequence. We may be interested first in how much basic demographic variables explain, such as social class and age. Next we may wish to consider whether going to pre-school made any difference to explaining educational achievement beyond social class and age. Third, we may wish to look at the effects of intellectual ability on educational achievement. And finally, we may want to examine the effects of other variables such as how motivated children are to do well at school and how interested their parents are in how well they do at school. Entering these variables in a sequence like this will enable us to see how much each group or block of variables adds to how well we can predict educational achievement.

Hierarchical multiple regression will be illustrated with the same data as we used in Chapter 28 except that we will add another variable, that of social class. These data are shown in Table 29.1. We will enter social class in the first step of the analysis, ability in the second step and motivation and interest in the third step.

To work out the proportion of variance in educational achievement that is explained at each step we calculate the squared multiple correlation (R^2) which is derived by multiplying the standardised (partial) beta regression coefficient by the correlation coefficient for each predictor and the criterion in that step and summing their products. The correlations between educational achievement and ability, motivation, interest and class are about 0.70,

Table 29.1 Data for hierarchical multiple regression

Educational achievement	Intellectual ability	School motivation	Parental interest	Social class
1	2	1	2	2
2	2	3	1	1
2	2	3	3	5
3	4	3	2	4
3	3	4	3	3
4	3	2	2	2

0.37, 0.13 and 0.07 respectively. The standardised regression coefficient for class in the first step is its correlation which is 0.07. Consequently class explains about 0.5% ($0.07 \times 0.07 \times 100$) of the variance in educational achievement, which is effectively none. The standardised regression coefficients for class and ability in the second step are about -0.14 and 0.74 respectively. So the variance explained by both class and ability is about 51% $\{[(0.07 \times -0.14) + (0.70 \times 0.74)] \times 100\}$. If we subtract the per cent of variance in the first step from that in the second step we see that ability explains about a further 50.5%. Finally the standardised regression coefficients for class, ability, motivation and interest is about -0.439, 0.730, 0.185 and 0.314 respectively. Thus the variance explained by all four of these predictors in the third step is about 59% $\{[(0.07 \times -0.439) + (0.70 \times 0.730) + (0.37 \times 0.185) + (0.13 \times 0.314)] \times 100\}$. If we subtract the per cent of variance in the second step from that in the third step we see that motivation and interest explain about a further 8.5%. We can see that ability explains the most variance in educational achievement even when social class is taken into account. There is no reason to calculate these yourself as they can be found under Model Summary in the SPSS output discussed later in this chapter.

29.2 When to use hierarchical multiple regression

Hierarchical multiple regression should be used when you want to enter the predictor variables in a particular sequence as described above. It is also used to determine whether there is a significant interaction between your predictor variables and the criterion. The interaction term is created by multiplying the predictor variables together and entering this term in a subsequent step in the multiple regression after the predictor variables have been entered. If the interaction term explains a significant proportion of the variance in the criterion, this implies that there is an interaction between these predictor variables. The nature of this interaction needs to be determined.

29.3 When not to use hierarchical multiple regression

Hierarchical multiple regression should not be used when there is no reason why the predictor variables should be entered in a particular order. If there are no good grounds for prioritising the variables, then it is better to enter them in a single block or step. This is known as a standard multiple regression.

29.4 Data requirements for hierarchical multiple regression

The data requirements for hierarchical multiple regression are the same as those for stepwise multiple regression which are outlined in Chapter 28. The criterion variable should be a quantitative variable which is normally distributed. The relation between each predictor and the criterion should show homoscedasticity in the sense that the plot of the data points around the best-fitting regression line should be similar at each point along the regression line. A rough idea of whether this is the case can be obtained by producing a scatterplot with a line of best fit between each predictor and the criterion as shown in Chapter 8.

29.5 Problems in the use of hierarchical multiple regression

As in all regression and correlation analyses, it is important to look at the mean and standard deviation of the variables. If the mean is very low or high then this suggests that the variation in the variable may not be well spread. A variable that has a smaller standard deviation indicates that it has a smaller variance which means that the relation between this variable and the criterion may be smaller than a predictor that has a larger variance when all other things are equal.

 You can find out more about hierarchical multiple regression in Chapter 32 of Howitt, D. and Cramer, D. (2008) *Introduction to Statistics in Psychology*. Harlow: Pearson.

29.6 The data to be analysed

We will illustrate the computation of a hierarchical multiple regression analysis with the data shown in Table 29.1 on page 269, which consist of scores for six individuals on the four variables of educational achievement, intellectual ability, school motivation and parental interest.

We have added a further variable, social class, which is on a scale of 1 to 5, with 5 being the highest social class. Hierarchical analysis is used when variables are entered in an order predetermined by the researcher on a 'rational' basis rather than in terms of statistical criteria. This is done by ordering the independent variables in terms of blocks of the independent variables, called Block 1, Block 2, etc. A block may consist of just one independent variable or several. In this particular analysis, we will make Block 1 social class ('Class'), which is essentially a demographic variable we would like to control for. Block 2 will be intellectual ability ('Ability'). Block 3 will be school motivation ('Motivation') and parental interest ('Interest'). The dependent variable or criterion to be explained is educational achievement ('Achievement').

In our example, the model essentially is that educational achievement is affected by intellectual ability and motivational factors such as school motivation and parental interest. Social class is being controlled for in this model since we are not regarding it as a psychological factor.

When doing a path analysis, it is necessary to do several hierarchical multiple regressions. One redoes the hierarchical multiple regression using different blocks and in different orders so that various models of the interrelationships can be explored.

29.7 Hierarchical multiple regression analysis

Step 1:

Select the data file if you saved it. Otherwise enter the data. A 5th variable, 'Class' has been put in the 6th column.

	Achievement	Ability	Motivation	Interest	Freq....	Class
1	1	2	1	2	20	2
2	2	2	3	1	20	1
3	2	2	3	3	20	5
4	3	4	3	2	20	4
5	3	3	4	3	20	3
6	4	3	2	2	20	2

Step 2:

Select 'Analyze',
'Regression'
and 'Linear ...'.

Step 3:

Select 'Achievement' and the ▶ button
beside the 'Dependent:' box to put it
there.

Select 'Class' and the ▶ button beside
the 'Independent(s):' box to put it
there.

Select 'Next'.

Step 4:

Select 'Ability' and the ▶ button
beside the 'Independent(s):' box to
put it there.

Note this is 'Block 2 of 2'.

Select 'Next'.

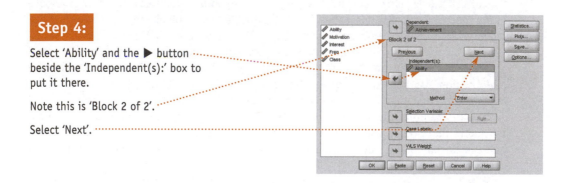

Step 5:

Select 'Motivation' and 'Interest'
and the ▶ button beside the
'Independent(s):' box to put them
there.

Select 'Statistics'.

Step 6:

Select 'Confidence intervals', 'R squared change', 'Descriptives' and 'Part and partial correlations'.

Select 'Continue'.

Select 'OK' in the previous box which reappears.

29.8 Interpreting the output

- As summarised in the second table of the output entitled 'Model Summary', the variable entered on the first block is 'Class' (social class). The R square for this block is effectively 0.0 (0.004), which means that social class explains 0% of the variance of educational achievement.

Model Summary

Model	R	R Square	Adjusted R Square	Std. Error of the Estimate	Change Statistics R Square Change	F Change	df1	df2	Sig. F Change
1	.065ᵃ	.004	−.004	.963	.004	.497	1	118	.482
2	.714ᵇ	.509	.501	.679	.505	120.333	1	117	.000
3	.769ᶜ	.591	.577	.626	.082	11.500	2	115	.000

a. Predictors: (Constant), Class
b. Predictors: (Constant), Class, Ability
c. Predictors: (Constant), Class, Ability, Motivation, Interest

- The statistical significance of the F-ratio of 0.497 for this block or model is 0.482. As this value is above the critical value of 0.05, this means that the regression equation at this first stage does not explain a significant proportion of the variance in educational achievement.

- The variable entered on the second block is 'Ability' (intellectual ability). The adjusted R square for this block or model is 0.501, which means that intellectual ability together with social class explains 50.1% of the variance of educational achievement.

- The statistical significance of the F-ratio for this block is 0.000 which means that it is less than 0.001. As this value is much lower than the critical value of 0.05, the first two steps of the regression equation explain a significant proportion of the variance in educational achievement.

- The variables entered on the third and final block are 'Motivation' (school motivation) and 'Interest' (parental interest). The adjusted R square for this block is 0.557, which means that all four variables explain 55.7% of the variance of educational achievement.

- The *F*-ratio for this block is 0.000. As this value is much lower than the critical value of 0.05, the first three steps in the regression equation explain a significant proportion of the variance in educational achievement.

- The simplest interpretation of the output comes from examining the fourth table entitled 'Coefficients' of the output. Especially useful are the Beta column and the Sig. (of *t*) column. These tell us that the correlation (beta) between 'Class' (social class) and 'Achievement' (educational achievement) is −0.439 when the other predictors are taken into account. This correlation is significant at the 0.000 level which means that it is less than 0.001. This coefficient is now significant because the two variables of 'Ability' and 'Interest' suppress the zero-order coefficient between 'Class' and 'Achievement'. Having controlled for social class in Block 1, the correlation between 'Ability' (intellectual ability) and 'Achievement' (educational achievement) is 0.730. This is also significant at the 0.000 level. Finally, having controlled for 'Class' (social class) and 'Ability' (intellectual ability), the correlations for each of the variables in Block 3 (school motivation and parental interest) with educational achievement ('Achievement') are given separately.

- The Part correlations for Class, Motivation, Ability and Interest were −0.275, 0.667, 0.165 and 0.201 respectively which when squared means that they account for about 7.6%, 44.5%, 2.7% and 4.0% of the variance in Achievement not taking into account the variance that they share between them. As the total percentage of variance these four variables explain is about 59.1% this means that the percentage of variance they share together is 0.3% (59.1 − 58.8).

Coefficients[a]

Model		Unstandardized Coefficients B	Std. Error	Standardized Coefficients Beta	t	Sig.	95% Confidence Interval for B Lower Bound	Upper Bound	Correlations Zero-order	Partial	Part
1	(Constant)	2.369	.205	.065	11.543	.000	1.963	2.776			
	Class	.046	.065		.705	.482	−.083	.176	.065	.065	.065
2	(Constant)	.250	.241		1.036	.302	−.228	.728			
	Class	−.100	.048	−.140	−2.082	.040	−.195	−.005	.065	−.189	−.135
	Ability	.950	.087	.740	10.970	.000	.778	1.122	.701	.712	.711
3	(Constant)	−.563	.284		−1.984	.050	−1.124	−.001			
	Class	−.313	.068	−.439	−4.615	.000	−.447	−.178	.065	−.395	−.275
	Ability	.938	.084	.730	11.180	.000	.771	1.104	.701	.722	.667
	Motivation	.188	.068	.185	2.769	.007	.053	.322	.369	.250	.165
	Interest	.438	.130	.314	3.374	.001	.181	.694	.127	.300	.201

a. Dependent Variable: Achievement

The quickest way to access the output is to concentrate on the third model in the above output. The output indicates that when Class, Ability, Motivation and Interest are all entered that each has a significant association with the dependent variable Achievement. Class has a negative relationship whereas the others have a positive one.

Reporting the output

■ There are various ways of reporting the results of a hierarchical multiple regression analysis. In such a report we would normally describe the percentage of variance explained by each set or block of predictors (from the value of the R square).

■ One way of reporting these results is to state that: 'In a hierarchical multiple regression, potential predictors of Achievement were entered in blocks. Social class was entered first, then Intellectual ability was added in the second block, and School motivation and Parental interest were added in the final block. The final model indicated that social class was a negative predictor ($B = 0.31$), intellectual ability was a positive predictor $B = 0.94$), and school motivation and parental interest were also positive predictors ($B = 0.19$ and 0.44). All predictors were significant at the 1% level.'

■ One would also need to summarise the regression equation as in Table 29.2.

Table 29.2   Hierarchical multiple regression of predictors of educational achievement

Blocks	B	Standard error B	Beta
Block 1:			
Social class	−0.31	0.07	−0.44*
Block 2:			
Intellectual ability	0.94	0.08	0.73*
Block 3:			
School motivation	0.19	0.07	0.19*
Parental interest	0.44	0.13	0.31*

* Significant at 0.01.

For further resources including data sets and questions, please refer to the CD accompanying this book.

Part 6 Advanced qualitative or nominal techniques

30 Log-linear analysis

Overview

- Log-linear analysis is used to analyse frequency tables (contingency or cross-tabulation) consisting of three or more variables. It can therefore be regarded as an extension of the chi-square test discussed in Chapter 13.

- Its purpose is to determine which of the variables and their interactions best explain (or reproduce) the observed frequencies in the table.

- Variables and their interactions on their own and in combination are known as models in log-linear analysis.

- Goodness-of-fit test statistics are used to assess the degree of correspondence between the model and the data. Statistical significance when comparing the model with the data indicates that the model fails to account totally for the observed frequencies. Statistical non-significance means that the model being analysed fits the observed frequencies. If more than one model fits the data well, the model having the fewer or fewest variables and interactions is the simplest one and may be the preferred model.

- Hierarchical log-linear analysis described in this chapter begins with the saturated model (which includes all possible main effects and interactions) and examines the effect of removing these in steps. If a main effect or interaction is removed then the question is whether this affects the statistical fit of the model to the data. If its removal produces a significant change (reduction) in fit then the main effect or interaction should be reinstated in the model as it is having an important influence.

- Generally, main effects are unimportant in interpreting the model since they merely reflect different proportions of cases in each category.

- Likelihood ratio chi-square is employed as the test statistic in log-linear analysis.

30.1 What is log-linear analysis?

Log-linear analysis can be regarded as being simply an extension of chi-square (see Chapter 13). However, rather than being limited to two nominal (category) independent variables as in the case of chi-square, log-linear analysis allows the researcher to study the associations between several variables. Chi-square can only deal with a two-way contingency (cross-tabulation) table whereas log-linear can deal with three-way, four-way, etc. tables. Contingency (or cross-tabulation) tables record the frequencies in each of the categories produced by the various independent variables. An example is shown in Table 30.1.

The table shows the relationship between having been sexual abused, physically abused and gender in a sample of psychiatric hospital patients. Of course, this table is more difficult to interpret than the two-way examples we saw in the chi-square chapter (Chapter 13). This is not simply because of the extra variable, it is also because we would not expect equal numbers in the cells if there was no relationship between the three variables since the categories of the independent variables do not have equal sample sizes, for one reason. But it becomes an even more complex situation in reality because, for example, two of the three independent variables may have an association that is different from the association between all three of the independent variables. There is no intuitively obvious way of working out the expected frequencies in these circumstances. Actually, we are faced with a mathematically extremely complex situation compared to the two-way chi-square we studied earlier. Without computers, the analysis is not possible.

Log-linear analysis does use chi-square but it is a slightly different form from the Pearson chi-square used in Chapter 13. This is known as the likelihood ratio chi-square. Log-linear analysis also uses natural logarithms (Napierian logarithms) which give the log-linear method its name. Neither of these are particularly helpful in understanding log-linear output from SPSS.

Log-linear analysis involves things called interactions that are not dissimilar from interactions in ANOVA. They are simply aspects of the data that cannot be accounted for on the basis of the independent variables acting independently (or the influence of lower-level interactions). In a sense, particular combinations of categories from two or more independent variables tend to result in relatively high or low cell frequencies in the data table. The number of interactions depends on the number of independent variables. If the analysis has three independent variables then there will be three main effects – one for each of the independent variables acting alone. But, in addition, there are interactions between two or more of the independent variables. If we call the independent variables (and so also the main effects) A, B and C, the interactions are A*B, B*C, A*C and A*B*C. That is, there are three two-way interactions and one three-way interaction. The three-way interaction

Table 30.1   A three-way contingency table showing the relationship between sex, sexual abuse and physical abuse in a sample of psychiatric hospital patients

Sexual abuse	Physical abuse	Sex		Margin totals
		Female	Male	
Sexually abused	Physical abuse	20	30	50
	No physical abuse	40	25	65
Not sexually abused	Physical abuse	35	55	90
	No physical abuse	45	50	95
Margin totals		140	160	300

is what cannot be accounted for by the main effects and the three two-way interactions. Step up a notch to four independent variables and there are 11 interactions.

Actually the chi-square itself (Chapter 13) works on interactions but nobody refers to them as such. When we discussed the two-way chi-square, we investigated the frequencies on the basis of the independent variables acting alone. What was left over after taking away the influences of these was used to calculate chi-square. This is another way of saying that chi-square assesses the interaction of the two independent variables.

In log-linear analysis there is a great deal of emphasis on models. A model is simply an attempt to explain the empirical data that we obtain on the basis of the influence of the independent variables. In log-linear analysis we try to explain the frequencies obtained in the research on the basis of the independent variables and their interactions. Goodness-of-fit is another commonly used term in log-linear analysis. It simply refers to the extent to which the observed frequencies are modelled (or predicted) by the variables in the model.

It is common in log-linear analysis to start with what is known as the saturated model and work backwards. This is the method that we demonstrate in this chapter. The saturated model is the one that perfectly fits the data so it includes all of the independent variables plus all of their interactions. Of course, some of these may have absolutely no influence on the data we obtain. So what happens next is that aspects of the model are removed one at a time to see whether removing them actually makes a significant difference to the model's fit to the data. If taking away a main effect or an interaction does not change the fit of the model to the actual data, then this main effect or interaction is doing nothing in the model – that is, it is making no contribution since when it is removed it makes no difference to the model.

It is only the interactions that are of interest since the main effects simply indicate whether the proportions of the sample in each category of the main effect differ. Does it matter, for example, whether the genders differ from each other in terms of numbers in the sample? The answer is almost certainly not, except in the unusual circumstances where there has been proper random sampling from the population. It is more important to know if there is an interaction between gender and being physically abused.

So, in the analysis we carry out on Table 30.1, basically we begin with all possible main effects and interactions and then discard any that make no difference to the fit of the model to the data. The way in which such main effects and interactions are identified is to examine the size of the likelihood-ratio chi-square when that component is removed. If the likelihood-ratio chi-square is statistically significant then this means that removing that component (main effect or interaction) makes a significant difference to the fit of the model to the data. Hence, that component should be retained in the data. Where removing a component results in a non-significant change in the fit of the model to the data then that component can be discarded from the analysis. This is done a step at a time. The final model consists of the original (saturated or full) model minus any component that makes no significant difference if it is removed.

In a sense, log-linear analysis is very much like three-way ANOVAs, etc. (see Chapter 21). The big difference is that it deals with frequencies in cells of a contingency table rather than the means of the scores in the cells.

30.2 When to use log-linear analysis

Log-linear analysis is used in exactly the same circumstances as a two-way chi-square to deal with the situation where the researcher has three or more nominal (category) independent variables which may be associated in some way. Many psychologists prefer to collect data primarily in the form of scores so may never need log-linear analysis. Score data cannot be used in log-linear analysis.

Of course, it is tempting to think that nominal (category) data are simpler data than score data. This may encourage the less numerate novice researcher to employ nominal (category) data and thus snare themselves into the trap of needing log-linear analysis which is among the more difficult statistical techniques to understand.

30.3 When not to use log-linear analysis

If any of your variables are score variables then they are not suitable for log-linear analysis.

Be careful to consider quite what you need out of a log-linear analysis which could not be obtained by some other form of statistical analysis. For example, in the case of the study described in this chapter does the researcher really want to know whether there is a difference between males and females in terms of their histories of physical and sexual abuse? If this were the case, then binomial logistic regression or multinomial logistic regression (Chapters 32 and 31) might be capable of supplying the analysis required. One could even mix score and nominal variables in this instance. It is possible to use interactions with some forms of logistic regression.

30.4 Data requirements for log-linear analysis

Three or more nominal (category) variables are required – score variables may not be used. Be parsimonious in terms of the number of variables you include as each additional one adds significantly more complexity to the output.

30.5 Problems in the use of log-linear analysis

Log-linear analysis is not the simplest statistic to understand because of the variety of new and difficult concepts it introduces. It is probably unsuitable for total novices. So we would suggest that you do not contemplate using it until you have a more advanced level of statistical skill and experience in deciphering SPSS output. Only choose it when there is no alternative analysis that would do an equally good job.

 You can find out more about log-linear analysis in Chapter 38 of Howitt, D. and Cramer, D. (2008) *Introduction to Statistics in Psychology*. Harlow: Pearson.

30.6 The data to be analysed

The computation of a log-linear analysis is illustrated with the data in Table 30.1 on page 280. This table shows the frequency of sexual and physical abuse in 140 female and 160 male psychiatric patients. To analyse a table of data like this one with SPSS we first have to input the data into the Data Editor and weight the cells by the frequencies of cases in them.

30.7   Log-linear analysis

Step 1:

Enter the data.
Weight the cases by 'Freq'
(see section 6.8 or 13.7).

Step 2:

Select 'Analyze',
'Loglinear' and
'Model Selection ...'.

Step 3:

Select singly or together 'Sexual',
'Physical' and 'Sex' and the ▶ button
beside the 'Factor(s):' box to put
them there.

Select 'Define Range'. As all 3
variables have the same range, they
can be defined at the same time.

Step 4:

Type '1' in the 'Minimum:' box.

Type '2' in the 'Maximum' box.

Select 'Continue'.

Select 'OK' in the previous box.

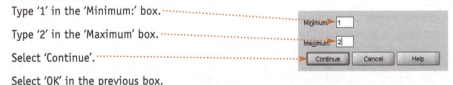

30.8   Interpreting the output

- The likelihood ratio chi-square for the saturated or full model is 0.00000 which has a probability of 1.000. In other words, the saturated model provides a perfect fit for the observed frequencies and so is non-significant. The saturated model in this case consists of the three main effects, three two-way interactions and one three-way interaction. In general, the saturated model includes all main effects and interactions.

- However, the saturated model includes *all* components whether or not they individually contribute to explaining the variation in the observed data. So it is necessary to eliminate components in turn to see whether this makes the model's fit worse. If it does, this component of the model is kept for the final model.

■ SPSS begins with the full model and eliminates each effect in turn to determine which effects make the least significant change in the likelihood ratio chi-square.

The likelihood ratio chi-square for the full or saturated model is zero and provides a perfect fit to the data.

Step Summary

Step[b]			Effects	Chi-Square[a]	df	Sig.	Number of Iterations
0	Generating Class[c]		Sexual* Physical* Sex	.000	0	.	
	Deleted Effect	1	Sexual* Physical* Sex	1.185	1	.276	3
1	Generating Class[c]		Sexual* Physical, Sexual* Sex, Physical* Sex	1.185	1	.276	
	Deleted Effect	1	Sexual* Physical	.454	1	.501	2
		2	Sexual* Sex	1.963	1	.161	2
		3	Physical* Sex	5.461	1	.019	2
2	Generating Class[c]		Sexual* Sex, Physical* Sex	1.639	2	.441	
	Deleted Effect	1	Sexual* Sex	2.272	1	.132	2
		2	Physical* Sex	5.770	1	.016	2
3	Generating Class[c]		Physical* Sex, Sexual	3.910	3	.271	
	Deleted Effect	1	Physical* Sex	5.770	1	.016	2
		2	Sexual	16.485	1	.000	2
4	Generating Class[c]		Physical* Sex, Sexual	3.910	3	.271	

a. For 'Deleted Effect', this is the change in the Chi-Square after the effect is deleted from the model.
b. At each step, the effect with the largest significance level for the Likelihood Ratio Change is deleted, provided the significance level is larger than .050.
c. Statistics are displayed for the best model at each step after step 0.

This is the best-fitting model. It has a likelihood ratio chi-square of 3.91, which is not significant.

■ The best-fitting model is presented last. In our example, this includes the interaction of physical abuse and sex and the main effect of sexual abuse. This model has a likelihood ratio chi-square of 3.91 (rounded to two decimal places), 2 degrees of freedom and a probability level of 0.271. In other words, it is not significant which means that the observed data can be reproduced with these two effects.

> These are the counts or frequencies for the data plus the expected frequencies under this model. The residuals are just the differences between the data and the data predicted by the model.

Cell Counts and Residuals

Sexual	Physical	Sex	Observed		Expected		Residuals	Std. Residuals
			Count	%	Count	%		
Sexually abused	Physically abused	Females	20.000	6.7%	21.083	7.0%	−1.083	−.236
		Males	30.000	10.0%	32.583	10.9%	−2.583	−.453
	Not physically abused	Females	40.000	13.3%	32.583	10.9%	7.417	1.299
		Males	25.000	8.3%	28.750	9.6%	−3.750	−.699
Not sexually abused	Physically abused	Females	35.000	11.7%	33.917	11.3%	1.083	.186
		Males	55.000	18.3%	52.417	17.5%	2.583	.357
	Not physically abused	Females	45.000	15.0%	52.417	17.5%	−7.417	−1.024
		Males	50.000	16.7%	46.250	15.4%	3.750	.551

> There are two statistics used to test the goodness-of-fit of the final model. These are the likelihood ratio chi-square and Pearson chi-square. The likelihood ratio chi-square is the test more commonly used because it has the advantage of being linear so chi-square values may be added or subtracted.

Goodness-of-Fit Tests

	Chi-Square	df	Sig.
Likelihood Ratio	3.910	3	.271
Pearson	3.953	3	.267

■ To interpret these two effects, we need to present the data in terms of a one-way table for sexual abuse and a two-way table for physical abuse and sex. We can do this using Chi-square ... for the one-way table (see section 13.13) and Crosstabs ... for the two-way table (see section 13.9). These two tables are shown in Table 30.2. The one-way table shows that more psychiatric patients have not been sexually abused than have been sexually abused. The two-way table indicates that males are more likely to be physically abused than females.

Table 30.2 Contingency tables for sexual abuse and the interaction of physical abuse and sex

Sexual abuse

	Observed N	Expected N	Residual
Sexually abused	115	150.0	−35.0
Not sexually abused	185	150.0	35.0
Total	300		

Physical abuse * Sex Cross-tabulation

			Sex		
			Females	Males	Total
Physical abuse	Physically abused	Count	55	85	140
		Expected count	65.3	74.7	140.0
		Residual	−10.3	10.3	
	Not physically abused	Count	85	75	160
		Expected count	74.7	85.3	160.0
		Residual	10.3	−10.3	
Total		Count	140	160	300
		Expected count	140.0	160.0	300.0

■ It is possible to see the contribution of each component to the final mode in the step just before the final step (step 4 in this example). These entries essentially indicate the change (reduction) in the goodness-of-fit chi-square if each component is taken away. Thus Physical*Sex has a likelihood ratio chi-square change of 5.770 which is significant (0.016). Sexual has a value of 16.485 which is very significant (0.000). Obviously these two effects cannot be eliminated from the model because of their significant contribution.

■ In a hierarchical model, components of an interaction may be significant. Since Physical*Sex has a significant contribution to the model, Physical and Sex may themselves be significant main effects. Select 'Model' in the 'Model Selection Loglinear Analysis' dialog box (Step 3 in section 30.7). The window that appears will allow you to test these main effects by stipulating models containing only these particular main effects.

Reporting the output

One way of describing the results found here is as follows: 'A three-way frequency analysis was performed to develop a hierarchical linear model of physical and sexual abuse in female and male psychiatric patients. Backward elimination produced a model that included the main effect of sexual abuse and the interaction effect of physical abuse and sex. The model had a likelihood ratio $\chi^2(3) = 3.91$, $p = 0.27$, indicating a good fit between the observed frequencies and the expected frequencies generated by the model. About 38% of the psychiatric patients had been sexually abused. About 53% of the males had been physically abused compared with about 39% of the females.'

For further resources including data sets and questions, please refer to the CD accompanying this book.

31 Multinomial logistic regression

Overview

- Logistic regression is a form of multiple regression (see Chapter 28). It identifies the variables that collectively distinguish cases belonging to different categories of a nominal (or category) variable. For example, it could be used to identify the differentiating characteristics of psychology, sociology and physics students.

- Put another way, logistic regression identifies groups of variables that accurately classify people according to their membership of the different categories of a nominal variable.

- Binomial logistic regression is used if there are just two categories of the variable to be predicted. This is dealt with in Chapter 32. Multinomial logistic regression is used if there are three or more categories.

- The predictors (i.e. the independent variables) may be score variables, nominal (category or categorical) variables, or a mixture of both.

- The best predictors of which category a case belongs to have significant *b*-weights (or regression weights). This is much the same as for the more familiar multiple regression procedures described in Chapter 28.

- The *b*-weights in logistic regression are actually applied to the natural logarithm of something termed the *odds ratio*, which is the ratio of the frequencies for two alternative outcomes. This logarithm is also known as the *logit*. Hence the term logistic regression. The odds ratio is simply the likelihood of being in one category rather than any of the other categories. There is little need for most researchers to calculate these values themselves so the logit is mainly of conceptual rather than practical importance.

- It is more important to understand the concept of *dummy variable*. This is a device by which a nominal variable may be dealt with numerically. If the nominal variable has just *two* categories then these may be coded numerically as 0 and 1.

- However, if the nominal category has *three* or more categories then the process is slightly more complex. Essentially, the data are coded for the presence or absence of each of the *three* (or more) categories. In effect, three (or more) new variables are created. So if the three categories are called A, B and C, three new variables are created:

The individual is in Category A (or not).
The individual is in Category B (or not).
The individual is in Category C (or not).

Each of these three variables is a different dummy variable.

■ However, one dummy variable from the set is always excluded from the analysis. It does not matter which one. The reason is that this dummy variable contains no new information that is not contained in the other dummy variables.

■ SPSS will generate dummy variables automatically for the dependent variable but needs to be informed which of the predictor variables are nominal (category) variables.

■ Classification tables are generated by SPSS and indicate the prediction of category membership based on the predictor variables. This is a good indication of how good the prediction is because the number of correct classifications is given in the table.

■ Logistic regression analyses contain numerous goodness-of-fit statistics based on chi-square. These serve a number of functions, but most importantly they indicate the improvement in fit of the predicted category membership to the actual category membership. A useful predictor should improve the fit of the predicted membership to the actual categories cases belong to.

■ Multinomial logistic regression must be used when there are three or more categories for the dependent (predicted or criterion) variable. If there are just *two* categories for the dependent variable, then binomial logistic regression is normally used (see Chapter 32).

31.1   What is multinomial logistic regression?

Multinomial regression is a form of regression analysis. However, unlike simple regression (Chapter 8) and multiple regression (Chapter 28) it does not use predictor (independent) variables in order to predict scores on a dependent variable. Instead it uses predictor variables to predict which groups individuals belong to. That is, it predicts which nominal category an individual belongs. Of course, the main function of regression is mostly to simply describe the relationship between a group of independent variables and a dependent variable – that is, to say what the significant predictors of the dependent variable are out of a set of predictors.

Multinomial logistic regression can use score variables as predictors but also nominal (category) variables too. Normally one would use a mixture of score variables and category variables but the technique is very flexible in this regard. One cannot easily do this with multiple regression but multinomial logistic regression makes this simple.

Multinomial logistic regression is so called firstly because the dependent variable consists of three or more nominal categories. There is also binomial logistic regression Chapter 32) that only handles nominal dependent variables which have just two categories. There is a greater range of options with binomial logistic regression, which actually makes it more complex to use on SPSS. So it is better, as a learning experience, to start with multinomial logistic regression.

As might be anticipated, logistic regression employs logarithms in the calculation. Actually, what one is predicting is something called the *logit*. The logit is the natural logarithm of something called the odds or odds ratio. This is closely related to probability but is expressed differently. If a sample consists of 30 men and 40 women then the odds of selecting a man by chance would be 30/40 = 0.75. In other words, there is 0.75 men for every woman in the sample. In truth, to carry out logistic regression on SPSS calls for absolutely no knowledge of logarithms or odds ratios. So if they are meaningless to you then do not worry too much.

Much more crucial in logistic regression is to understand the concept of *dummy variables*. These are needed when a nominal (category) variable has three or more categories. In order to analyse such data one has to create a new binary (yes–no) nominal variable for each category of the nominal (category) variable. (Actually one fewer but see later.) If you had three categories of the nominal variable colour consisting of red, yellow and blue then you would create three binary nominal variables from this: (1) red and not red, (2) yellow and not yellow, and (3) blue and not blue. These three categories contain as much information as was contained in the original three-category nominal variable. Actually, one of the categories is redundant since it contains no additional information. So if someone tells you that they are thinking of a colour which is red, yellow or blue then you only need to ask two questions to find out the colour. These questions might be 'Is it red?' and 'Is it blue?' If the person says no to both of these questions then you know that the colour they are thinking of is yellow. Actually, of course, it does not matter which two colours you ask about. For this reason, in multinomial logistic regression you will find that SPSS gives you one fewer dummy variable than it gives you score variables.

Table 31.1 contains data for which a multinomial logistic regression would be appropriate since the purpose of the research is to predict which type of sex offender a man is from six predictor variables. He can be a rapist, incest offender or a paedophile. The variable Type of offence is clearly a nominal (category) variable with three categories. This would be turned into two dummy variables by SPSS. These would be rapist versus non-rapist and incest offender versus non-incest offender possibly, but what two of the three dummy variables are used depends on how the data are coded and the options chosen in SPSS. It really makes no difference which of the three is omitted.

The predictor variables in this case are all binary nominal (category) variables in this example but score variables could have been used as predictors just as nominal (category) variables with three or more categories could be used. One has got to be sure that the dependent variable used is not a score.

The multinomial logistic regression analysis basically gives regression weights for the predictor variables which are much the same as the weights found in multiple regression. The difference is that in multinomial logistic regression the weights are used to predict group (category) membership on the dependent variable. There will be more than one dependent variable for the simple reason that the categories of the dependent variable will be converted to dummy variables by SPSS. So the output looks more complex than for a multiple regression. The Wald test is used to assess the statistical significance of the regression weight.

Table 31.1 Data for multinomial logistic regression

	Age	DAS*	Mother hostile	Father hostile	Children's home	Physical abuse	Sexual abuse	Type of offence
1	younger	low	high	low	no	yes	no	rapist
2	younger	low	high	low	no	yes	yes	rapist
3	older	low	high	low	no	yes	yes	rapist
4	older	high	high	high	yes	no	no	incest
5	older	high	high	high	yes	yes	yes	rapist
6	younger	low	high	low	no	no	no	rapist
7	older	high	low	high	no	yes	yes	rapist
8	older	high	low	high	yes	no	no	incest
9	younger	low	low	high	yes	no	yes	incest
10	older	high	high	low	no	yes	yes	incest
11	older	high	low	low	yes	no	yes	incest
12	younger	high	low	high	no	yes	no	rapist
13	older	high	low	high	yes	no	yes	incest
14	older	high	high	low	yes	yes	yes	incest
15	older	low	high	high	no	yes	yes	incest
16	younger	high	high	low	yes	no	no	paedophile
17	older	high	low	high	yes	no	yes	paedophile
18	older	low	high	high	no	no	yes	paedophile
19	younger	high	low	high	yes	yes	yes	paedophile
20	older	low	low	high	yes	no	no	paedophile
etc.								

* Depression Anxiety Stress scale.

All predictors which consist of three or more nominal categories are turned into dummy variable predictors by SPSS – except for the one which is left out because it is redundant. At first, unless you anticipate the production of these dummy variables it is easy to get confused so take care. There are two more important features of the multinomial logistic regression output that help the interpretation of the output:

1. Logistic regression produces pseudo *R*-square statistics analogous to the *R*-square statistics in multiple regression. They give an indication of how well the model (the predictor variables) fits the data.

2. Logistic regression produces a classification table that indicates the number of each group of the dependent variable which are accurately (and not) accurately predicted to be in their actual group (as well as those wrongly predicted to be in other groups). These tables give a concrete indication of what is happening in the analysis.

31.2 When to use multinomial logistic regression

Multinomial logistic regression is a very flexible regression procedure. The most important thing is that the dependent variable is a nominal (category) variable with three or more categories. It will work with a binomial dependent variable though it is probably better to use the binomial logistic regression that has more advanced features in SPSS for this. The predictor variables can be any mixture of score variables and nominal (category) variables. Multinomial logistic regression is useful when trying to differentiate a nominal (category) dependent variable's categories in terms of the predictor variables. In the present example, the question is what differentiates rapists, incest offenders and paedophiles?

31.3 When not to use multinomial logistic regression

There are few reasons not to use multinomial logistic regression where the dependent variable is a nominal (category) variable with three or more categories. The predictors used can be scores and nominal (category) variables so it is very flexible in this respect.

In circumstances where binomial logistic regression is appropriate then this should be used in preference simply because SPSS has more powerful procedures for the two-category case.

31.4 Data requirements for multinomial logistic regression

The dependent variable should consist of three or more nominal categories. We would not advise the use of dependent variables with more than say five or six categories simply because of the complexity of the output. SPSS will cope with more categories – though the researcher may not cope with the output.

The independent variables ideally should not correlate highly (as in any regression) and it is wise to examine the interrelationships between the independent variables when planning which of them to put into the logistic regression analysis.

31.5 Problems in the use of multinomial logistic regression

Multinomial logistic regression can produce a great deal of SPSS output. However, much of it is not necessary and a good interpretation can be based on a limited number of tables. We find it particularly helpful to keep an eye on the classification table as this is a simple and graphic summary of the analysis.

SPSS procedures for multinomial logistic regression and binomial logistic regression are rather different in terms of how one goes about the analysis. This can cause confusion. Even the terminology used is different.

The major problem in our experience centres around stipulating which are score variables and which are nominal (category) variables – or failing to differentiate between the two. The worst situation is where SPSS believes that a score variable is a nominal (category) variable. The problem is that each value of the score variable is regarded as a different nominal category so numerous dummy variables are created to the consternation of the researcher.

You can find out more about multinomial logistic regression in Chapter 39 of Howitt, D. and Cramer, D. (2008) *Introduction to Statistics in Psychology*. Harlow: Pearson.

31.6 The data to be analysed

The use of multinomial logistic regression can be illustrated using the data described in Table 31.1 (*ISP*, Table 39.2). These data are from a fictitious study of the differences between rapists, incestuous sex offenders and paedophiles. This means that the categories of offender equate to a nominal or category variable with three different values. In this example all of the predictor variables – age, DAS (depression, anxiety and stress scale), mother hostile, father hostile, children's home, physical abuse and sexual abuse – are nominal (category) variables with just two different values in each case. It must be stressed that any type of variable may be used as a predictor in multinomial logistic regression. However, the researcher needs to indicate which are score variables in the analysis.

31.7 Entering the data

These data are entered into SPSS in the usual way with each variable being represented by a column. For learning purposes, the data have been repeated ten times in order to have a realistic data set for the analysis, but to limit the labour of those who wish to reproduce the analysis exactly.

Enter the data.

Weight the cases with 'freq'
(see section 6.8 or 13.7).

	age	das	motherhs	fatherhs	childhom	physabus	sexualab	typoff	freq
1	1	1	2	1	2	1	2	1	10
2	1	1	2	1	2	1	1	1	10
3	2	1	2	1	2	1	1	1	10
4	2	2	2	2	1	2	2	2	10
5	2	2	2	2	1	1	1	1	10
6	1	1	2	1	2	2	2	1	10
7	2	2	1	2	2	1	1	1	10
8	2	2	1	2	1	2	2	2	10
9	1	1	1	2	1	2	1	2	10
10	2	2	2	1	2	1	1	2	10
11	2	2	1	1	1	2	1	2	10
12	1	2	1	2	2	1	2	1	10
13	2	2	1	2	1	2	1	2	10
14	2	2	2	1	1	1	1	2	10
15	2	1	2	2	2	1	1	2	10
16	1	2	2	1	1	2	2	3	10
17	2	2	1	2	1	2	1	3	10
18	2	1	2	2	2	2	1	3	10
19	1	2	1	2	1	1	1	3	10
20	2	1	1	2	1	2	2	3	10

In *all* multinomial logistic regression analyses, dummy variables are created by SPSS. This is always the case for the predicted variable (offence type in this case), but there may be also nominal (category) predictor variables with more than two categories. If this is the case, SPSS generates new variables (dummy variables) for inclusion in the analysis. So do not be surprised to find variables reported in the output which were not part of the data input. SPSS does not show the dummy variables that it creates in the data spreadsheet – they are referred to in the output, however. SPSS creates appropriate dummy variables for the dependent (criterion) variable automatically based on the number of different values (categories) of that variable. The predictor or independent variables are also dummy coded if they are defined by the researcher as being nominal (category or categorical) variables. Dummy variables are discussed in the overview and first section at the start of this chapter and also in the accompanying statistics text (*ISP*, Chapter 39).

Until Release 12 of SPSS, multinomial logistic regression was only available in a rather unsatisfactory number of options. However, from Release 12 onwards, SPSS includes a stepwise version in which variables are selected as predictors in order of their independent predictive powers. In this book we will analyse the data using stepwise multinomial logistic regression. The findings are slightly different in detail from those of the accompanying statistics text (*ISP*), but not substantially so.

31.8 Stepwise multinomial logistic regression

Step 1:

Select 'Analyze', 'Regression' and 'Multinomial Logistic …'.

Step 2:

Select 'typoff' and the ▶ button beside the 'Dependent:' box to put it there.

Select the other 7 variables either singly or together (excluding 'freq') and the ▶ button beside the 'Factor(s):' box to put them there.

Select 'Model:'.

Step 3:

Select 'Custom/Stepwise'.

Select each of the 7 variables in turn and the ▶ button beside 'Stepwise Terms:' to put them there.

Select 'Continue'.

Select 'Statistics …' in previous box.

Step 4:

Select 'Cell probabilities', 'Classification table' and 'Goodness-of-fit'.

Select 'Continue'.

Select 'OK' in the previous box.

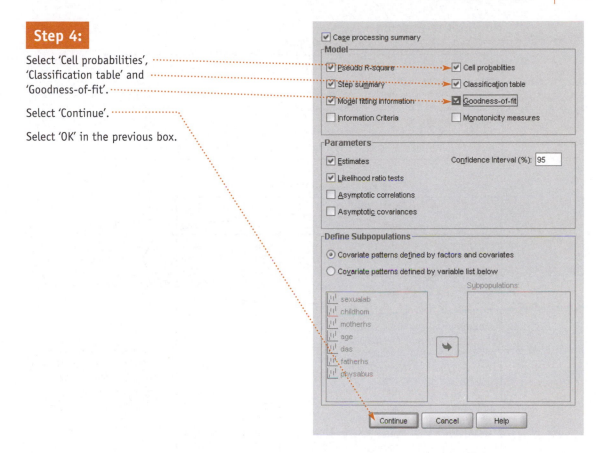

31.9   Interpreting the output

- The output for multinomial logistic regression is quite substantial. Of course, it is possible to reduce the amount of output but then the researcher needs to be clear just what aspects of the output are not necessary for their purposes. Since it is easier to ignore surplus tables than to redo the analysis it is better to err on the side of too much output.

- It is a useful reminder to examine the table labelled Case Processing Summary. This provides a reminder of the distributions of the categories of each of the variables in the analysis. In our example all of the variables simply have two categories so no dummy variables need to be created. However, the predictor variables may have three or more categories in which case SPSS will create appropriate dummy variables for all but one of the categories of that variable. (This does not apply to variables defined as a covariate which are treated as score variables.) There are, however, three different values of the criterion variable of offence type – rapists, incestuous offenders and paedophiles – and SPSS will create two dummy variables from these three categories.

Nominal regression

Warnings

There are 37 (64.9%) cells (i.e., dependent variable levels by subpopulations) with zero frequencies.

Unexpected singularities in the Hessian matrix are encountered. This indicates that either some predictor variables should be excluded or some categories should be merged.

The NOMREG procedure continues despite the above warning(s). Subsequent results shown are based on the last iteration. Validity of the model fit is uncertain.

Case Processing Summary

		N	Marginal Percentage
typoff	rapist	70	35.0%
	Incestuous child abuser	80	40.0%
age	paedophile	50	25.0%
	younger	70	35.0%
das	older	130	65.0%
	low score	80	40.0%
motherhs	high score	120	60.0%
	low hostility	90	45.0%
fatherhs	high hostility	110	55.0%
	low hostility	80	40.0%
childhom	yes	120	60.0%
	no	110	55.0%
physabus	yes	90	45.0%
	no	100	50.0%
sexualab	yes	100	50.0%
	no	130	65.0%
Valid		70	35.0%
Missing		200	100.0%
Total		0	
Subpopulation		200	
		19[a]	

This table shows the distribution for each of the variables in the analysis. The offence distribution is circled.

a. The dependent variable has only one value observed in 18 (94.7%) subpopulations.

■ The Step Summary table essentially gives the sequence of variables entered into the stepwise multiple regression.

■ Remember that in stepwise analyses the predictors are selected in terms of their (distinct) predictive power. So the best predictor is selected first, adjustments made, and the remaining best predictor selected second, and so forth. There is a Step 0 which contains only the intercept of the regression line. Steps 1 to 4 in this example add in the strongest predictors in turn. The variable 'childhom' (children's home) is added in Step 1, age in Step 2, 'physabus' (physical abuse) in Step 3 and 'sexualab' (sexual abuse) in Step 4. Each of these produces a significantly better fit of the predicted (modelled) data to the actual data. This can be seen from the lowering values of the −2 log-likelihood values (which are chi-square values) given in the table. Each of these changes is significant in this example meaning that none of the predictors may be dropped without worsening the accuracy of the classification.

The model at Step 0 has no predictor variables. At Step 1 the variable childhom is entered. It is the best predictor available.

This table gives the order in which the predictor variables were selected.

Step Summary

Model	Action	Effect(s)	Model Fitting Criteria −2 Log Likelihood	Effect Selection Tests Chi-Square[a]	df	Sig.
0	Entered	Intercept	407.957	.		
1	Entered	childhom	330.132	77.825	2	.000
2	Entered	age	300.651	29.481	2	.000
3	Entered	physabus	274.195	26.456	2	.000
4	Entered	sexualab	258.708	15.487	2	.000
5	Entered	fatherhs	250.102	8.606	2	.014

Stepwise Method: Forward Entry
a. The chi-square for entry is based on the likelihood ratio test.

Fatherhs is the last variable entered into the regression equation. The analysis proceeds no further after this in this example.

- The model fitting table gives the value of the −2 log-likelihood chi square for the fit of the model (i.e. the significant predictors plus the intercept). This value is significant in this case. It merely is an indication that the model (predictor variables) do not completely predict the actual data. In other words, the prediction is less than complete or partial. Clearly, there are other factors that need to be taken into account to achieve a perfect fit of the model to the data. This will normally be the case.

The Intercept Only model includes *none* of the predictor variables. The Final model is the one using the best set of predictors. Notice that there is a significant improvement in fit to the data by using the Final model.

Model Fitting Information

Model	Model Fitting Criteria −2 Log Likelihood	Likelihood Ratio Tests Chi-Square	df	Sig.
Intercept Only	407.957			
Final	250.102	157.856	10	.000

Goodness-of-Fit

	Chi-Square	df	Sig.
Pearson	230.126	26	.000
Deviance	246.629	26	.000

This table indicates how well the predicted data fit the actual data. There is a significant difference between the two – that is, the prediction is less than perfect.

■ The table of the pseudo *R*-square statistics merely confirms this. The *R*-square statistic gives the combined correlation of a set of predictors with the predicted variable for score data. The pseudo *R*-square is analogous to this in interpretation but is used when it is not possible to accurately compute the *R*-square statistic itself as in the case of logistic regression. As can be seen, there are three different methods of calculation used. They are all indicators of the combined relationship of the predictors to the category variable. A value of 0 means no multiple correlation, a value of 1.00 means a perfect multiple correlation. Values of around 0.5 are fairly satisfactory as they indicate an overall combined correlation of the predictor variables with the predicted variable of around 0.7. (This is obtained by taking the square root of 0.5.)

Pseudo R-Square ◄············

Cox and Snell	.546
Nagelkerke	.617
McFadden	.365

This table gives three estimates of the 'multiple correlation' between the predictor variables and sex offender category membership. It is interpreted like a squared correlation coefficient. The values in this case are moderate (1.00 would indicate a perfect classification), confirming that the prediction is less than perfect.

■ The table of the likelihood ratio tests tells us what happens to the model if we remove each of the predictor variables in turn. The model is merely the set of predictors that emerge in the analysis. In this case we have four predictors as already described. In each case there is a significant decrement in the fit of the predicted data to the actual data following the dropping of any of the predictors. In other words, each of the predictors is having a significant effect and normally should be retained. Of course, should the researcher have good reason then any predictor can be dropped, though it is recommended that inexperienced researchers do not do this.

This is a very important table that indicates whether removing each of the predictor variables from the prediction reduces significantly the fit of the prediction to the actual data. As can be seen, in this case removing any of the four predictors adversely affects the fit of the predicted data to the actual data.

Likelihood Ratio Tests

Effect	Model Fitting Criteria –2 Log Likelihood of Reduced Model	Likelihood Ratio Tests		
		Chi-Square	df	Sig.
Intercept	250.102[a]	.000	0	.
age	271.748	21.647	2	.000
fatherhs	258.708	8.606	2	.014
childhom	273.076	22.975	2	.000
physabus	291.381	41.280	2	.000
sexualab	264.656	14.555	2	.001

The chi-square statistic is the difference in –2 log-likelihoods between the final model and a reduced model. The reduced model is formed by omitting an effect from the final model. The null hypothesis is that all parameters of that effect are 0.

a. This reduced model is equivalent to the final model because omitting the effect does not increase the degrees of freedom.

■ The table of the parameter estimates basically gives the intercept and the regression weights for this multinomial regression analysis. The intercept value is clear at 0.88 for Rapists. But notice a number of things. The dependent variable (offence type) which has three categories has been turned into two dummy variables: Rapists (versus the other two groups) and Incestuous Child Molester (versus the other two groups).

> This table gives the B weights that the computer will use in making its predictions. The B weights are useful to report but the researcher would not need to actually do any calculations involving them.

Parameter Estimates

typoff[a]		B	Std. Error	Wald	df	Sig.	Exp(B)	95% Confidence Interval for Exp(B)	
								Lower Bound	Upper Bound
rapist	Intercept	.088	.787	.012	1	.911			
	[age=1]	−.160	.621	.066	1	.797	.852	.252	2.878
	[age=2]	0[b]	.	.	0	.	.	.	.
	[fatherhs=1]	1.024	.672	2.323	1	.127	2.783	.746	10.380
	[fatherhs=2]	0[b]	.	.	0	.	.	.	.
	[childhom=1]	−1.967	.606	10.535	1	.001	.140	.043	.459
	[childhom=2]	0[b]	.	.	0	.	.	.	.
	[physabus=1]	20.173	.654	951.829	1	.000	6E+008	160055390.3	2076804930
	[physabus=2]	0[b]	.	.	0	.	.	.	.
	[sexualab=1]	−18.398	.000	.	1	.	1.02E-008	1.02E-008	1.02E-008
	[sexualab=2]	0[b]	.	.	0	.	.	.	.
Incestuous child abuser	Intercept	−.206	.596	.119	1	.730			
	[age=1]	−1.955	.507	14.845	1	.000	.142	.052	.383
	[age=2]	0[b]	.	.	0	.	.	.	.
	[fatherhs=1]	1.481	.556	7.090	1	.008	4.399	1.478	13.087
	[fatherhs=2]	0[b]	.	.	0	.	.	.	.
	[childhom=1]	.380	.503	.572	1	.450	1.462	.546	3.917
	[childhom=2]	0[b]	.	.	0	.	.	.	.
	[physabus=1]	.613	.536	1.307	1	.253	1.846	.645	5.281
	[physabus=2]	0[b]	.	.	0	.	.	.	.
	[sexualab=1]	.488	.476	1.053	1	.305	1.629	.641	4.138
	[sexualab=2]	0[b]	.	.	0	.	.	.	.

a. The reference category is: paedophile.
b. This parameter is set to zero because it is redundant.

> When interpreting the output the values of the variable should be carefully checked. The B weight is −1.955 for the category 1.00 of the variable age – the other category is given a weight of 0.00. The value label 1.00 in this case means that the offender was younger. However, there is a negative value of B. This means that incestuous child abusers are partly distinguished from the other two groups by being older. This is a little confusing at first but is simply the way SPSS operates.

> The standard error is 0.00 so the Wald value would be infinitely large. No significance level can actually be computed although this variable is highly statistically significant.

■ Remember that the number of dummy variables is given by the number of categories minus one. There are three offender categories so two dummy variables. The dummy variables are created by taking one of the three offender categories and contrasting this with the remaining offender categories. In our example, we have Rapists versus Incestuous Child Molesters *and* Paedophiles, Incestuous Child Molesters versus Rapists *and* Paedophiles, and Paedophiles versus Rapists and Incestuous Child Molesters. The choice of which of the possible dummy variables to select is arbitrary and can be varied by selecting 'Custom/Stepwise' in Step 3. Also notice that the variables have been given two regression weights – a different one for each value. However, one of the pair is always 0 which essentially means that no contribution to the calculation is made by these values. The significance of each of these regression weights is given in one of the columns of the table. Significance is based on the Wald value, which is given in another column. Do not worry too much if you do not understand this too clearly as one does not need to do any actual calculations.

This is explained in more detail in Howitt, D. and Cramer, D. (2008) *Introduction to Statistics in Psychology*. Harlow: Pearson.

■ The classification table is very important and gives the accuracy of the predictions based on the parameter estimates. This cross-tabulation table indicates what predictions would be made on the basis of the significant predictor variables and how accurate these predictions are. As can be seen, the predictions are very accurate for Rape offenders and to a lesser degree for the Incestuous Child Molesters. However, the classification is poor for Paedophiles.

The classification table indicates in a simple form how good the prediction is. As can be seen, the predictors are very good at predicting rapists correctly (85.7% correct). The predictors do a poor job at predicting paedophiles (only 40% of paedophiles correctly identified).

Classification

Observed	Predicted			
	rapist	incestuous child abuser	paedophile	Percent Correct
rapist	60	10	0	85.7%
incestuous child abuser	20	50	10	62.5%
paedophile	0	30	10	40.0%
Overall Percentage	40.0%	45.0%	15.0%	65.0%

- The observed and predicted frequencies table is probably most useful to those who have a practical situation in which they wish to make the best prediction of the category based on the predictor variables. The table gives every possible pattern of the predictor variables (SPSS calls them covariates) and the actual classifications in the data for each pattern plus the most likely outcome as predicted from that pattern. In other words, the table could be used to make predictions for individual cases with known individual patterns.

> This gives all the possible combinations of the values of the predictor variables. As such, it can be used to trace the most likely predicted outcome for any combination of the predictor variables. That is, an individual offender's predictor pattern could be used to find the most likely prediction for that pattern.

Observed and Predicted Frequencies

sexualab	physabus	childhom	fatherhs	motherhs	das	age	typoff	Observed (Freq)	Predicted (Freq)	Pearson Residual	Observed (%)	Predicted (%)
yes	yes	yes	low hostility	high hostility	high score	older	rapist	0	1.302	−1.224	.0%	13.0%
							Incestuous child abuser	10	8.178	1.493	100.0%	81.8%
							paedophile	0	.519	−.740	.0%	5.2%
			high hostility	low hostility	high score	younger	rapist	0	3.375	−2.257	.0%	33.8%
							Incestuous child abuser	0	2.228	−1.693	.0%	22.3%
							paedophile	10	4.397	3.570	100.0%	44.0%
				high hostility	high score	older	rapist	10	1.644	7.130	100.0%	16.4%
							Incestuous child abuser	0	6.531	−4.339	.0%	65.3%
							paedophile	0	1.825	−1.494	.0%	18.2%
		no	low hostility	high hostility	low score	younger	rapist	10	8.581	1.286	100.0%	85.8%
							Incestuous child abuser	0	.857	−.968	.0%	8.6%
							paedophile	0	.562	−.772	.0%	5.6%
						older	rapist	10	6.036	2.563	100.0%	60.4%
							Incestuous child abuser	0	3.627	−2.386	.0%	36.3%
							paedophile	0	.337	−.590	.0%	3.4%
					high score	older	rapist	0	6.036	−3.902	.0%	60.4%
							Incestuous child abuser	10	3.627	4.192	100.0%	36.3%
							paedophile	0	.337	−.590	.0%	3.4%
			high hostility	low hostility	high score	older	rapist	10	6.512	2.314	100.0%	65.1%
							Incestuous child abuser	0	2.476	−1.814	.0%	24.8%
							paedophile	0	1.012	−1.061	.0%	10.1%
no	yes	no	low hostility	high hostility	low score	younger	rapist	10	10.000	.000	100.0%	100.0%
							Incestuous child abuser	0	.000	.000	.0%	.0%
							paedophile	0	.000	.000	.0%	.0%
			high hostility	low hostility	high score	younger	rapist	10	10.000	.000	100.0%	100.0%
							Incestuous child abuser	0	.000	.000	.0%	.0%
							paedophile	0	.000	.000	.0%	.0%
	no	yes	low hostility	high hostility	high score	younger	rapist	0	1.722	−1.443	.0%	17.2%
							Incestuous child abuser	0	3.524	−2.333	.0%	35.2%
							paedophile	10	4.754	3.322	100.0%	47.5%
			high hostility	low hostility	low score	older	rapist	0	.652	−.835	.0%	6.5%
							Incestuous child abuser	0	5.080	−3.213	.0%	50.8%
							paedophile	10	4.268	3.665	100.0%	42.7%
					high score	older	rapist	0	.652	−.835	.0%	6.5%
							Incestuous child abuser	10	5.080	3.112	100.0%	50.8%
							paedophile	0	4.268	−2.729	.0%	42.7%
				high hostility	high score	older	rapist	0	.652	−.835	.0%	6.5%
							Incestuous child abuser	10	5.080	3.112	100.0%	50.8%
							paedophile	0	4.268	−2.729	.0%	42.7%
		no	low hostility	high hostility	low score	younger	rapist	10	6.321	2.412	100.0%	63.2%
							Incestuous child abuser	0	1.237	−1.188	.0%	12.4%
							paedophile	0	2.441	−1.797	.0%	24.4%

The percentages are based on total observed frequencies in each subpopulation.

Reporting the output

There is no conventional method of reporting the findings succinctly for a multinomial logistic regression. If the technique has been used for previous studies in the chosen area of research then the reporting methods used in those studies might be adopted.

For the data analysed in this chapter, it is clear that there is a set of predictors that work fairly effectively in part. One way of reporting these findings would be as follows: 'Multinomial logistic regression was performed to establish what characteristics distinguish the three different types of offender. Out of the seven predictor variables included in the analysis, four were shown to distinguish the different types of offender to a degree. Rapists were correctly identified as such in 85.7% of cases, Incestuous child abusers were correctly identified in 62.5% of instances, but Paedophiles were correctly identified in only 40.0% of instances. Paedophiles tended to be misclassified as Incestuous child abusers very often. The predictors which distinguished Rapists from others the best were time spent in a children's home ($b = -1.967$), physical abuse ($b = 20.173$) and sexual abuse ($b = -18.398$). The latter is not reported as significant as such in the table. No significance is given. However, Paedophiles were best distinguished from the other two groups by age ($b = -1.955$) and father's hostility ($b = -1.481$).'

For further resources including data sets and questions, please refer to the CD accompanying this book.

32 Binomial logistic regression

Overview

- Binomial logistic regression may be regarded as a special case of multinomial logistic regression, which was described in Chapter 31. The major difference is that it differentiates the characteristics of people in just *two* different groups.

- SPSS has a much more extensive repertoire of regression techniques for binomial logistic regression although Releases 12 and onwards of SPSS have introduced a little more flexibility to its multinomial logistic regression procedures.

- Binomial logistic regression is a form of multiple regression. It identifies patterns of variables which can effectively differentiate between the members of two different categories. That is, binomial logistic regression predicts category membership as opposed to a score as in the case of multivariate regression (Chapter 28). For example, one could use it to examine the pattern of variables which best differentiates male from female participants in a study of reasons for seeking medical advice. There may be a different pattern of reasons why men go to a doctor from the pattern of reasons why women go to a doctor.

- Another way of putting this is that binomial logistic regression uses predictor variables to predict the most likely category of the dependent variable to which different individuals belong.

- The binomial logistic regression procedure calculates *b*-weights (or regression weights) much as in multiple regression (Chapter 28). The big difference is that in binomial logistic regression these *b*-weights are *not* applied to predict scores. Instead they are applied to something called the logit which is the natural logarithm of the odds ratio. The odds ratio is rather like a probability. It is simply the ratio of the numbers in one category to the number of cases in the other category. The logit (and natural logarithms for that matter) generally are not crucial to a researcher's use of binomial logistic regression so do not require detailed understanding.

- Although the categories are always a binomial (binary or two-value) category variable, the other variables in the analysis may be score variables, nominal (category or categorical) variables, or a mixture of both.

■ Any category variable which has more than two categories is automatically turned into a set of dummy variables by SPSS. Each dummy variable consists of one of the categories of the variable versus all of the rest of the categories. There are as many dummy variables as categories. For technical reasons, one of the possible dummy variables is arbitrarily omitted from the binomial logistic regression. This is because it contains no new information which is not already contained in the other dummy variables.

■ Binomial regression, for example, can proceed using stepwise procedures, forward entry of poor predictors, backward elimination of poor predictors and so forth. The choice of the type of model to use is often a rather subtle matter. Stepwise procedures gradually build up the model by selecting on a step-by-step basis variables which are good at differentiating between the members of the two categories of the dependent variable. Forward entry means that at each step the computer finds the best remaining variable for differentiating between the two categories. If it does not meet certain requirements in terms of predictive (or classificatory) power then it is not entered into the model. For many purposes, stepwise forward entry is a good choice in psychology.

■ Much of the binomial logistic regression output from SPSS consists of indicators of how well the modelled data (the category membership predicted by the predictor variables) fit the actual data (the actual category which the individual belongs to). These are based on chi-square for the most part. A useful predictor should improve the fit of the predicted membership to the actual categories cases belong to.

■ More directly understood are the classification tables generated by SPSS which indicate how well the predictions match the actual classifications.

32.1 What is binomial logistic regression?

Binomial logistic regression is more-or-less the same as multinomial logistic regression with the sole difference that the dependent variable consists of two nominal categories. Apart from that most things are identical – except for, unfortunately, the SPSS procedure which is frustratingly different for the two. Any type of variable – scores or nominal (category) – may be used as the predictor variables in binomial logistic regression. However, in our example in Table 32.1, we have used very simple variables such as age, previous imprisonment, treatment, contrition, marital status and whether or not the offender is a sex offender. We have also used a binomial variable as the dependent variable, of course. In this case it is where the offender goes on to be a repeat offender (i.e. recidivist). All of these are binomial nominal variables though they do not have to be except for the dependent variable. We can use score variables, which are defined as covariates in SPSS, as some or all of our predictor variables. We can also use nominal (category) variables with three or more different values (categories). In this case, SPSS recodes the variable into a number of dummy variables automatically as was the case with multinomial logistic

Table 32.1 Data for the study of recidivism – the data from 19 cases is reproduced five times to give realistic sample sizes but only to facilitate explanation

	Recidivism	Age	Previous prison	Treatment	Contrite	Married	Sex offender
1	yes	younger	yes	no	no	no	yes
2	yes	older	yes	no	no	no	yes
3	yes	older	yes	yes	no	no	yes
4	yes	older	yes	yes	no	yes	no
5	yes	younger	yes	no	no	no	no
6	yes	younger	no	yes	yes	no	no
7	yes	older	no	yes	yes	yes	yes
8	yes	younger	yes	no	no	no	yes
9	yes	younger	no	no	no	yes	yes
10	yes	older	no	no	no	no	no
11	no	younger	no	yes	yes	no	no
12	no	older	no	yes	yes	no	no
13	no	older	yes	yes	yes	yes	yes
14	no	younger	no	yes	yes	yes	yes
15	no	younger	no	yes	yes	no	yes
16	no	younger	no	no	yes	yes	no
17	no	older	no	no	no	yes	no
18	no	older	yes	yes	yes	no	no
19	no	older	yes	yes	yes	no	no
etc.	yes	younger	yes	no	no	no	yes

regression in the previous chapter. This means that the set of predictor variables is actually greater than the initial number of variables in the data. If we had a variable such as type of crime with the categories sex crime, violent crime and theft then, in theory, we could create three dummy variables. These would be:

Dummy variable 1 = sex crime or not
Dummy variable 2 = violent crime or not
Dummy variable 3 = theft or not.

It really is as simple as that to create dummy variables. There is just one complication to note what was discussed in the previous chapter. One of the dummy variables actually contains no new information if we know a person's values for the other two dummy variables. So, if we know that someone has not committed a sex crime and we know that they have not committed a violent crime then they must have committed a theft. Since they are *all* offenders, this is a simple logical assessment. Because one of the dummy variables is always repetitive and redundant, in logistic regression there is always one less than the maximum number of dummy variables. SPSS chooses this arbitrarily unless the user stipulates otherwise.

Table 32.2 demonstrates one way of coding the data ready for the computer analysis. It is best to enter data numerically into SPSS so each value of each variable is given a numerical code. 1s and 0s have been used in every case to indicate the presence or absence of a characteristic. The values would be given value labels in SPSS so as to make the output as clear as possible.

Table 32.2 Data from Table 32.1 coded in binary fashion as 0 and 1 for each variable

	Recidivism	Age	Previous prison	Treatment	Contrite	Married	Sex offender
1	1	0	1	0	0	0	1
2	1	1	1	0	0	0	1
3	1	1	1	1	0	0	1
4	1	1	1	1	0	1	0
5	1	0	1	0	0	0	0
6	1	0	0	1	1	0	0
7	1	1	0	1	1	1	1
8	1	0	1	0	0	0	1
9	1	0	0	0	0	1	1
10	1	1	0	0	0	0	0
11	0	0	0	1	1	0	0
12	0	1	0	1	1	0	0
13	0	1	1	1	1	1	1
14	0	0	0	1	1	1	1
15	0	0	0	1	1	0	1
16	0	0	0	0	1	1	0
17	0	1	0	0	0	1	0
18	0	1	1	1	1	0	0
19	0	1	1	1	1	0	0
etc.	1	0	1	0	0	0	1

Binomial logistic regression in SPSS has a good variety of analysis options, most of which are unavailable on multinomial logistic regression. Beginners will find the range a little bewildering and many of the options will be of no interest to many researchers. Choosing the appropriate options (what some would refer to as the appropriate model) depends very much on the purpose of one's analysis and only the researcher knows this. Generally speaking, if the sole purpose of the analysis is to obtain the best set of predictors to categorise people then it is sufficient to enter all of the predictors at the same time – SPSS merely takes the variables in the order they are listed. However, more typically the researcher is trying to build up a theoretical/conceptual explanation: for example, of why some offenders reoffend in this example. In these circumstances, the researcher may wish to give some variables priority in the analysis. This involves entering the predictors hierarchically in blocks. Furthermore, one needs to identify the best predictors. The variables may be entered in step-by-step form, in which the best predictor is taken first, then the next remaining best predictor entered second (allowing for correlations between predictors), and so forth until no significant improvement in prediction is achieved.

An alternative is to enter all of the predictors initially, then drop predictors one by one (backward elimination). If dropping the weakest predictor significantly reduces the accuracy of the prediction then it should be retained. However, it can be eliminated *if* dropping it makes no change to the accuracy of the prediction. The process goes on step-by-step by examining the effect of removing the weakest predictor in the remaining set. There is only one complication of note – that is eliminated predictors can actually return to the set of predictors if the elimination of another variable results in the previously eliminated variable increasing its independent predictive power.

Backward elimination is *not* better than other approaches: it largely does the job in a different way. It does not necessarily give exactly the same findings as other methods either – it is simply one reasonable and appropriate approach to the data.

Binary logistic regression produces weights for a set of predictor variables. The Wald test is the test of significance of these. The computer can also classify participants in terms of the accuracy of the predictions made as to which of the two categories of the dependent variable they belong to. You may find these categorisation tables very helpful in understanding what is happening in the analysis.

32.2 When to use binomial logistic regression

Binomial logistic regression helps the researcher decide which of a set of predictor variables best discriminates two groups of participants: for example, which of our variables best discriminates male and female participants. More generally, it can be regarded as an example of a regression procedure but designed for situations where the dependent variable simply has two categories.

32.3 When not to use binomial logistic regression

There are no major circumstances that would argue against the use of binomial logistic regression except where there is just a single predictor variable. Also your predictor variables should not be highly correlated with each other as in any regression. Avoid throwing every independent variable into the analysis without careful thought in advance. Usually it is better to be selective in the choice of predictors in any form of regression.

32.4 Data requirements for binomial logistic regression

The dependent variable should have just two nominal categories whereas the predictor variables can be any sort of variable including score variables. A participant may be only one category of the independent and dependent variable or contribute just a single score to score variables.

32.5 Problems in the use of binomial logistic regression

As with multinomial logistic regression, binomial logistic regression produces a great deal of SPSS output for most analyses, just a part of which may be useful to a researcher. Learning to identify the crucial aspects of the output is as essential here as with any other sort of SPSS analysis.

There is a confusing dissimilarity between how multinomial logistic regression and the binomial logistic regression are computed on SPSS and they do not use consistent terminology.

Score variables can cause problems if the researcher fails to tell SPSS that a particular variable is not a nominal (category) variable but it is a score. This is because SPSS will consider each different score mistakenly as a separate nominal category. Thus huge amounts of output may occur when the proper identification is not made.

 You can find out more about binomial logistic regression in Chapter 40 of Howitt, D. and Cramer, D. (2008) *Introduction to Statistics in Psychology*. Harlow: Pearson.

32.6 The data to be analysed

The example we will be working with is a study of the variables that might be used to help assess whether a prisoner is likely to reoffend or not reoffend after leaving prison. Reoffending is known as recidivism. The data from the study are shown in Table 32.2 on page 306 (*ISP*, Table 40.5). For pedagogical purposes and the convenience of those who wish to follow our steps on a computer, the 19 cases are reproduced five times. As can be seen, recidivism is a binomial category variable – in a given period of time, a prisoner either reoffends or does not. Since the purpose of our analysis is to find the pattern of variables that predict which of these two categories a prisoner will fall into then this is an obvious set of data for the binomial logistic regression.

32.7 Binomial logistic regression

Step 1:

Enter the data.
Weight the cases by 'freq'
(see section 6.8 or 13.7).

Step 2:

Select 'Analyze',
'Regression' and
'Binary Logistic …'.

Step 3:

Select 'recidivi' and the ▶ button beside the 'Dependent:' box to put it there.

Select the other 6 variables (excluding 'freq') and the ▶ button beside the 'Covariates:' box to put them there.

Select 'Categorical ...'.

Step 4:

Select all 6 variables (as they are nominal variables in this example) and the ▶ button beside the 'Categorical Covariates:' box to put them there.

Select 'Continue'.

Step 5:

Select the ▼ button in the 'Method:' box, move the scroll bar to show 'Backward: Conditional' and select it.

Select 'OK'.

32.8 Interpreting the output

Logistic Regression

Case Processing Summary

Unweighted Cases[a]		N	Percent
Selected Cases	Included in Analysis	19	100.0
	Missing Cases	0	.0
	Total	19	100.0
Unselected Cases		0	.0
Total		19	100.0

a. If weight is in effect, see classification table for the total number of cases.

Dependent Variable Encoding

Original Value	Internal Value
No	0
yes	1

Check this table – it makes clear just how the dependent variable has been coded by SPSS (the Internal Value). In this case they are the same as the values that we entered but it is well worth checking otherwise serious errors can be made.

Categorical Variables Codings

		Frequency	Parameter coding (1)
sexoff	sex offender	10	1.000
	not sex offender	9	.000
prepris	no previous	11	1.000
	previous prison	8	.000
treatmen	treated	11	1.000
	not treated	8	.000
contrite	Contrite	10	1.000
	not contrite	9	.000
married	married	7	1.000
	not married	12	.000
age	older (30 plus)	10	1.000
	younger	9	.000

This table breaks down each variable and gives numbers in each category. Thus there are 9 in the unweighted sample who are not sex offenders.

Block 0: Beginning Block

Block 0 is before any predictors have been taken into account. Generally you can skip this section.

Classification Table[a,b]

			Predicted		
			recidivist		Percentage Correct
	Observed		no	yes	
Step 0	recidivist	no	50	0	100.0
		yes	45	0	.0
	Overall Percentage				52.6

a. Constant is included in the model.
b. The cut value is .500

This table gives the actual numbers of recidivists and non-recidivists. There are 45 recidivists and 50 non-recidivists.

The constant is more or less the same as the intercept in multivariate regression.

Variables in the Equation

		B	S.E.	Wald	df	Sig.	Exp(B)
Step 0	Constant	−.105	.205	.263	1	.608	.900

No predictors have been included at this stage so there cannot be any in the regression equation.

Variables not in the Equation

			Score	df	Sig.
Step 0	Variables	age(1)	2.299	1	.129
		prepris(1)	21.159	1	.000
		treatmen(1)	6.345	1	.012
		contrite(1)	31.714	1	.000
		married(1)	.452	1	.501
		sexoff(1)	.293	1	.588
	Overall Statistics		50.804	6	.000

Block 1: Method = Backward Stepwise (Conditional)

Block 1 contains the key variables.

Omnibus Tests of Model Coefficients

		Chi-square	df	Sig.
Step 1	Step	70.953	6	.000
	Block	70.953	6	.000
	Model	70.953	6	.000
Step 2[a]	Step	−.210	1	.647
	Block	70.743	5	.000
	Model	70.743	5	.000

a. A negative Chi-squares value indicates that the Chi-squares value has decreased from the previous step.

Step 1 includes all of the predictors.

Step 2 and any later steps each involve the elimination of a variable – that is they are the backward elimination steps.

The Variables in the Equation table (see next page) indicate which predictors are in the model at each step.

Model Summary

Step	−2 Log likelihood	Cox & Snell R Square	Nagelkerke R Square
1	60.482[a]	.526	.702
2	60.692[a]	.525	.701

a. Estimation terminated at iteration number 20 because maximum iterations has been reached. Final solution cannot be found.

These are indexes of the fit of the model to the actual data. The nearer the two (pseudo) R-square measures are to 1.0 the better the fit of the model at that step to the data. The smaller the −2 log likelihood value the better the fit of the model to the data.

Notice that the final model (Step 2) shows an improved fit – a variable has been allowed to re-enter the regression equation.

Classification Table[a]

	Observed			Predicted		
				recidivist		Percentage Correct
				no	yes	
Step 1	recidivist	no		45	5	90.0
		yes		5	40	88.9
	Overall Percentage					89.5
Step 2	recidivist	no		45	5	90.0
		yes		5	40	88.9
	Overall Percentage					89.5

a. The cut value is .500

This table indicates the accuracy of the classification at each step. The overall accuracy remains constant throughout – what changes is the relative proportions of recidivists and non-recidivists correctly identified.

The least significant predictor in Step 1 is chosen for elimination in Step 2. Treatmen and sexoff both have significances of .998 but treatmen occurs first and is selected.

Variables in the Equation

		B	S.E.	Wald	df	Sig.	Exp(B)
Step 1[a]	age(1)	−2.726	.736	13.702	1	.000	.065
	prepris(1)	−1.086	.730	2.215	1	.137	.337
	treatmen(1)	19.362	8901.292	.000	1	.998	3E+008
	contrite(1)	−41.459	11325.913	.000	1	.997	.000
	married(1)	−.307	.674	.208	1	.648	.735
	sexoff(1)	−20.641	7003.092	.000	1	.998	.000
Step 2[a]	Constant	23.802	7003.092	.000	1	.997	2E+010
	age(1)	−2.699	.731	13.625	1	.000	.067
	prepris(1)	−1.153	.708	2.648	1	.104	.316
	treatmen(1)	19.428	8895.914	.000	1	.998	3E+008
	contrite(1)	−41.375	11337.365	.000	1	.997	.000
	sexoff(1)	−20.475	7028.411	.000	1	.998	.000
	Constant	23.542	7020.411	.000	1	.997	2E+010

a. Variable(s) entered on step 1: age, prepris, treatmen, contrite, married, sexoff.

It is important to note that the regression weights are only applied to the value of the category variable coded as 1. So the negative regression weight for sexoff(1) of −20.475 actually indicates that sex offenders are *less* likely to reoffend on release. Great care is needed to know what codings are given to the different values of variables. This is made worse because nominal variables not coded as 0 and 1 may be recoded by SPSS into those values.

Variables not in the Equation

			Score	df	Sig.
Step 2[a]	Variables	married(1)	.209	1	.648
	Overall Statistics		.209	1	.648

a. Variable(s) removed on step 2: married.

This table gives the significance of the variables not included in the model.

Reporting the output

One way of reporting the findings of this analysis is as follows: 'Using the conditional backward elimination model, characteristics differentiating prisoners who reoffend after release from those who do not reoffend were investigated. The final regression model indicated that younger offenders, those with a previous history of prison, those who were not contrite about their offences, and those who were not sex offenders, were more likely to reoffend. Age was a significant predictor at the 5% level. This Cox and Snell pseudo *R*-square was 0.53 indicating that the fit of the model to the data was only moderate. This model was almost equally accurate for reoffending (88.9% correct) as for non-reoffending (90.0%).'

For further resources including data sets and questions, please refer to the CD accompanying this book.

Part 7 Data handling procedures

33 Reading ASCII or text files into the Data Editor

Overview

■ Sometimes you have a computer file of data that you wish to use on SPSS. This chapter tells you how to use data not specifically entered into the SPSS Data Editor spreadsheet.

■ Although student work will rarely require the use of ASCII files, there are a number of data bases of archived data that researchers may wish to analyse.

■ It is worth noting that sometimes data from other spreadsheets can be entered into SPSS. For example, data from Excel spreadsheets can simply be cut and pasted into SPSS though not the spreadsheet in its entirety. SPSS data can be saved as an Excel file.

33.1 What is an ASCII file?

SPSS for Windows is obviously one of many different computer programs for analysing data. There are circumstances in which researchers might wish to take data sets which have been prepared for another computer and run those data through SPSS for Windows. It can be expensive in time and/or money to re-enter data, say, from a big survey into the Data Editor spreadsheet. Sometimes, the only form in which the data are available is as an archived electronic data file; the original questionnaires may have been thrown away. No matter the reason for using an imported data file, SPSS for Windows can accept files in other forms. In particular, data files are sometimes written as simple text or ASCII files, as these can be readily transferred from one type of computer to another. ASCII stands for American Standard Code for Information Interchange. To analyse an ASCII data file you first need to read it into the Data Editor.

Suppose, for example, that you had an ASCII data file called 'data.txt' consisting of the following numbers:

1118
2119
3218

Obviously you cannot sensibly use an ASCII file until you know exactly where the information for each variable is. However, we do know where and what the information is for this small file. The figures in the first column simply number the three different participants for whom we have data. The values in the second column contain the code for gender, with 1 representing females and 2 males. While the values in the third and fourth column indicate the age of the three people. We would carry out the following procedure to enter this ASCII data file into the Data Editor.

33.2 Reading an ASCII or text data file

Step 1:

Select 'File' and
'Read Text Data ...'.

Step 2:

Select the ▼ button of the 'Look in:'
box to find the data file (e.g. data).

Select the file.

Select 'Open'.

Step 3:

Select 'Next >'.

Step 4:

Select 'Next >'.

Step 5:

Select 'Next >'.

Step 6:

Click immediately after the 1st column as this column contains the number of the participant. Click after the 2nd column which holds the code for gender. The last 2 columns contain age.

Select 'Next >'.

Step 7:

Select 'Next >'.

Step 8:

Select 'Finish'.

Step 9:

The text data has now been entered into the 'Data Editor' and can be saved as an SPSS file.

	V1	V2	V3
1	1	1	18
2	2	1	19
3	3	2	18

For further resources including data sets and questions, please refer to the CD accompanying this book.

34 Missing values

Overview

- Sometimes in research, you may not have a complete set of data from each participant. Missing values tells the computer how to deal with such situations.

- Missing values can also be used to instruct the computer to ignore cases with a particular value(s) on particular variables.

- Typically, when coding the variables for entry into the SPSS spreadsheet, the researcher chooses a distinctive value to denote a missing value on that variable. This value needs to be outside of the possible range of actual values found in the data. Typically, numbers such as 9, 99 and 999 are used for missing values. It is possible to have more than one missing value for any variable. For example, the researcher may wish to distinguish between circumstances in which the participant refused to give an answer to a questionnaire and cases where the interviewer omitted the question for some reason.

- One needs to be very careful when using missing values on SPSS. If a value has not been identified as a missing value for a particular variable, the computer will analyse what the researcher intended as a missing value as a real piece of data. This can seriously and misleadingly distort the analysis.

- Missing values can be used in two main ways. In listwise deletion the case is deleted from the analysis if any missing values are detected for that case. This can rapidly deplete the number of participants in a study. The alternative is to simply delete the case from analyses involving pairs of variables for which there is a missing value (pairwise deletion).

- It is better to specify missing values as a value rather than type nothing under an entry. This is because typos made when typing in the data are too easily confused for an actual missing value.

34.1 What are missing values?

When collecting data, information for some of the cases on some of the variables may be missing. Take, for example, the data in Table 34.1, which consist of the music and mathematics scores of ten children with their code for gender and their age in years. There is no missing information for any of the four variables for any of the ten cases. But suppose that the first two children were away for the music test so that we had no scores for them. It would be a pity to discard all the data for these two cases because we have information on them for the other three variables of mathematics, gender and age. Consequently we would enter the data for these other variables. Although we could leave the music score cells empty for these two cases, what we usually do is to code missing data with a number that does not correspond to a possible value the variable could take. Suppose the scores for the music test can vary from 0 to 10. Any number other than 0 to 10, which are real scores, can be used to signify a missing value for the music test. We will use the number 11 as the code for a missing music score so that the values in the first two rows of the first column are 11. Additionally, it is assumed that the age for the third case is missing. The number 0 is the code for an age when the data are missing. Now we need to tell SPSS how we have coded missing data. If we do not do this, then it will read these codes as real numbers.

Missing values can also be used to tell the computer to ignore certain values of a variable that you wish to exclude from your analysis. So, for example, you could use missing values in relation to chi-square to get certain categories ignored. Leaving a cell blank in the Data Editor spreadsheet results in a full stop (.) being entered in the cell if it is part of the active matrix of entries. On the output these are identified as missing values but they are best regarded as omitted values. We would recommend that you do not use blank cells as a way of identifying missing values since this does not distinguish between truly missing values and keyboard errors. Normally, substantial numbers and distinctive numbers such as 99 or 999 are the best way of identifying a missing value.

There are two options for dealing with missing values. One, listwise, ignores all of the data for an individual participant if any of the variables in the particular analysis has a missing value. This is the more extreme version. Less extreme is pairwise deletion of missing data since the data are ignored only where absolutely necessary. So if a correlation matrix is being computed, the missing values are ignored only for the correlations involving the particular variables in question. There is a limit to the number of missing values that can be included for any variable on SPSS.

Table 34.1 Scores on musical ability and mathematical ability for ten children with their sex and age

Music score	Mathematics score	Sex	Age
2	8	1	10
6	3	1	9
4	9	2	12
5	7	1	8
7	2	2	11
7	3	2	13
2	9	2	7
3	8	1	10
5	6	2	9
4	7	1	11

34.2 Defining missing values

Step 1:

Select the file from Chapter 7 if you saved it. Enter the new data. Change the two 'Music' scores of cases 1 and 2 to '11'.

Change the 'Age' of case 3 to '0'.

	Music	Maths	Sex	Age
1	11	8	1	10
2	11	3	1	9
3	4	9	2	0
4	5	7	1	8
5	7	2	2	11
6	7	3	2	13
7	2	9	2	7
8	3	8	1	10
9	5	6	2	9
10	4	7	1	11

Step 2:

In 'Variable View' of the 'Data Editor' select the right side of the cell for 'Music' under 'Missing'. An ellipse of 3 dots appears.

Select 'Discrete missing values' and type '11' in the box below.

Select 'OK'.

'11' appears in the 'Missing' cell for 'Music'. Repeat this procedure for 'Age' but type in '0' instead of '11'.

pe	Width	Decimals	Label	Values	Missing
				None	None
				None	None
				None	None
				None	0

Missing Values

○ No missing values

● Discrete missing values

[11] [ ] [ ]

○ Range plus one optional discrete missing value

Low: [ ] High: [ ]

Discrete value: [ ]

[OK] [Cancel] [Help]

34.3 Pairwise and listwise options

We will illustrate some of the options available when you have missing data with the 'Correlate' procedure, although similar kinds of options are available with some of the other statistical procedures.

Step 1:

Select 'Analyze', 'Correlate' and 'Bivariate ...'.

Analyze	Graphs	Utilities	Add-ons	Window	Help

Reports ▶

Descriptive Statistics ▶ | Label

Tables ▶ | Nor

Compare Means ▶ | Nor

General Linear Model ▶ | Nor

Generalized Linear Models ▶ | Nor

Mixed Models ▶

Correlate ▶ | r_{12} Bivariate...

Regression ▶ | $r_{12·3}$ Partial...

Loglinear ▶ | δ Distances...

Step 2:

Select 'Music', 'Maths', 'Sex' and 'Age' and the ▶ button to put these 4 variables in the 'Variables:' box.

Select 'Options ...'.

Step 3:

Note that the default 'Missing Values' option is pairwise. The output for pairwise is presented below first. If you want listwise deletion, select 'Exclude cases listwise' and 'Continue'.

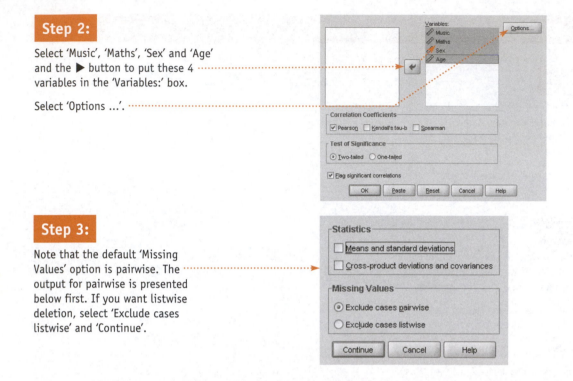

34.4 Sample output for pairwise deletion

Correlations

8 cases   7 cases

		Music	Maths	Sex	Age
Music	Pearson Correlation	1	−.923**	.293	.681
	Sig. (2-tailed)		.001	.482	.092
	N	8	8	8	7
Maths	Pearson Correlation	−.923**	1	−.161	−.550
	Sig. (2-tailed)	.001		.656	.125
	N	8	10	10	9
Sex	Pearson Correlation	.293	−.161	1	.118
	Sig. (2-tailed)	.482	.656		.762
	N	8	10	10	9
Age	Pearson Correlation	.681	−.550	.118	1
	Sig. (2-tailed)	.092	.125	.762	
	N	7	9	9	9

9 cases

10 cases

**. Correlation is significant at the 0.01 level (2-tailed).

Pairwise deletion means that a correlation will be computed for all cases that have non-missing values for any pair of variables. Since there are two missing values for the music test and no missing values for the mathematics test and gender, the number of cases on which these correlations will be based is 8. Since one value for age is missing for another case, the number of cases on which the correlation between music scores and gender is based is 7. As there are no missing values for the mathematics test and gender, the number of cases on which this correlation is based is 10. Finally, the number of cases on which the correlation between the mathematics score and age is 9, since there is one missing value for age and none for mathematics.

Notice that the number of cases varies for pairwise deletion of missing values.

34.5 Sample output for listwise deletion

Correlations[a]

		Music	Maths	Sex	Age
Music	Pearson Correlation	1	−.956**	.354	.681
	Sig. (2-tailed)		.001	.437	.092
Maths	Pearson Correlation	−.956**	1	−.483	−.729
	Sig. (2-tailed)	.001		.272	.063
Sex	Pearson Correlation	.354	−.483	1	.088
	Sig. (2-tailed)	.437	.272		.852
Age	Pearson Correlation	.681	−.729	.088	1
	Sig. (2-tailed)	.092	.063	.852	

**. Correlation is significant at the 0.01 level (2-tailed).
a. Listwise N = 7

All cases are 7

In Listwise deletion correlations are computed for all cases that have no missing values on the variables selected for this procedure. In this example, the number of cases that have no missing values on any of the four variables selected is 7.

Notice that the number of cases does not vary in listwise deletion of missing values.

34.6 Interpreting the output

There is little in the output which has not been discussed in other chapters. The only thing to bear in mind is that the statistics are based on a reduced number of cases.

Reporting the output

Remember to report the actual sample sizes (or degrees of freedom) used in reporting each statistical analysis rather than the number of cases overall.

For further resources including data sets and questions, please refer to the CD accompanying this book.

35 Recoding values

Overview

- From time to time researchers need to alter how certain values of a variable are recorded by the computer; perhaps several different values need to be combined into one.

- The recoding values procedure allows you considerable flexibility to quickly and easily modify how any value has been coded numerically.

- Because SPSS can quickly and easily recode values, it is good practice to enter as much data as possible in its original form. This leaves the researcher with the greatest freedom to recode the data. If data have been recoded by the researcher prior to entry into the SPSS data spreadsheet, it is not possible to try an alternative coding of the original data. For example, if all of the scores are entered for a measure of extraversion for each participant, SPSS can be used to recode the entries (such as reversing the scoring of an item) or to compute a total based on all or some of the extraversion items. If the researcher calculates a score on extraversion manually before entering this into SPSS, it is not possible to rescore the questionnaire in a different way without adding the original scores.

- It is usually best to keep your original data intact. So always make sure that you create a brand new variable (new column) for the recoded variable. Do *not* use the original variables unless you are absolutely certain that you wish to change the original data forever.

35.1 What is recoding values?

Sometimes we need to recode values for a particular variable in our data. There can be many reasons for this, including:

- To put together several categories of a nominal variable which otherwise has very few cases. This is commonly employed in statistics such as chi-square.
- To place score variables into ranges of scores.
- To recode items needing to be scored in the reverse way (see Chapter 36).

Table 35.1 Scores on musical ability and mathematical ability for ten children with their sex and age

Music score	Mathematics score	Sex	Age
2	8	1	10
6	3	1	9
4	9	2	12
5	7	1	8
7	2	2	11
7	3	2	13
2	9	2	7
3	8	1	10
5	6	2	9
4	7	1	11

We may wish to categorise our sample into two or more groups according to some variable such as age or intelligence. The recoding of cases can be illustrated using the data in Table 35.1 which shows the music and mathematics scores of ten children together with their code for gender and their age in years. These values are the same as those previously presented in Table 34.1. Suppose that we wanted to compute the correlation between the music and mathematics scores for the younger and older children. To do this, it would first be necessary to decide how many age groups we wanted. Since there are only ten children then one might settle for two groups. Next the cutoff point in age which divide the two groups has to be decided. As it would be good to have the two groups of similar size, age 10 would make a good cutoff point with children younger than 10 falling into one group and children aged 10 or more into the other group. SPSS can be used to recode age in this way.

35.2 Recoding values

Step 1:

Select the file from Chapter 34 if you saved it. Enter the new data.

	Music	Maths	Sex	Age
1	2	8	1	10
2	6	3	1	9
3	4	9	2	12
4	5	7	1	8
5	7	2	2	11
6	7	3	2	13
7	2	9	2	7
8	3	8	1	10
9	5	6	2	9
10	4	7	1	11

Step 2:

Select 'Transform' and
'Recode into Different Variables …'.

Step 3:

Select 'Age' and the ▶ button to put 'Age'
into the 'Numeric Variable –> Output
Variable:' box.

Type in the name of the new variable
(e.g. 'AgeRec') in the 'Name:' box.

Select 'Change' to add this new name to the
'Numeric Variable –> Output Variable:' box.

Select 'Old and New Values …'.

Step 4:

Select 'Range, LOWEST through value:'
and type '9' in the box beside it.

Select 'Value:' under 'New Value' and
type '1' in the box beside it.

Select 'Add' to put 'Lowest thru 9
--> 1' into the 'Old --> New:' box.

Step 5:

Select 'Range, value through HIGHEST:'
and type '10' in the box beside it.

Select 'Value:' under 'New Value'
and type '2' in the box beside it.

Select 'Add' to put '10 thru Highest
--> 2' into the 'Old --> New:' box.

Select 'Continue'.

Select 'OK' in the previous box.

Step 6:

The new variable and its values are shown in 'Data View'. Check that these values are what you needed.

Age	AgeRec
10	2.00
9	1.00
12	2.00
8	1.00
11	2.00
13	2.00
7	1.00
10	2.00
9	1.00
11	2.00
8	1.00
11	2.00
9	1.00

Step 7:

If the recoded data are not immediately next to the original data, it may be better to select 'Analyze', 'Reports' and 'Case Summaries ...'.

Step 8:

Select 'Age' and 'AgeRec' and the ▶ button to put these 2 variables in the 'Variables:' box.

If you have a large sample, you could look at only, say, the first 10 rather than 100 cases by changing 100 to 10 in the 'Limit cases to first' box.

Select 'OK'.

Case Summaries[a]

The cases are listed in the 1st column according to their row number.
The 2nd column has the original values.
The 3rd column has the recoded values.

	Age	AgeRec
1	10	2.00
2	9	1.00
3	12	2.00
4	8	1.00
5	11	2.00
6	13	2.00
7	7	1.00
8	10	2.00
9	9	1.00
10	11	2.00
Total N	10	10

a. Limited to first 10 cases.

With a complex set of data it is very easy to forget precisely what you have done to your data. Recoding can radically alter the output from a computer analysis. You need to carefully check the implications of any recodes before reporting them.

35.3 Recoding missing values

Note that if there are missing values (as for 'age' in Section 34.2, Step 2) it is necessary to code these by selecting 'System- or user-missing' in the 'Old Value' section of the 'Recode into Different Variables: Old and New Values' sub-dialog box and selecting 'System-missing' in the 'New Value' section.

Always check that your recoding has worked as you intended by comparing the old and new values in the Data Editor for each new value for one or more cases.

35.4 Saving the Recode procedure as a syntax file

You need to keep a note of how any new variables were created. The simplest way to do this is to write it down. Another way is to save what you have done as a syntax command by using the 'Paste' option in the main box of the procedure. The output for this procedure is shown below.

A syntax command. ┈┈┈┈┈┈┈┈┈┈┈┈┈┈┈┈┈┈┈┈┈➤

```
File  Edit  View  Data  Transform  Analyze  Graphs  Utilities  Run

RECODE Age (Lowest thru 9=1) (10 thru Highest=2) INTO AgeRec.
EXECUTE.
```

Save this command as a file. You could use this file to carry out this procedure on data subsequently added to this file or on new data with the same variables and variable names. Before Windows was developed SPSS commands were carried out with this kind of syntax command.

To check out this procedure select the column in 'Data View' containing recoded age and delete it. Then select the Syntax window, select the whole of the command in it and run it with the ▶ button on the toolbar shown above.

35.5 Adding some new data to Table 35.1

Add the values of these 3 new
cases to this file. ┈┈┈┈┈┈┈┈┈┈┈┈┈┈┈┈┈➤

10	4	7	1	11	2.00
11	5	4	1	8	
12	6	7	2	11	
13	8	4	1	9	

35.6 Running the Recode syntax command

Step 1:

Select 'Run' and 'All' to run this syntax command.

Alternatively, highlight the command and select the ▶ button.

Step 2:

Here are the recoded values for the 3 new cases.

10	4	7	1	11	2.00
11	5	4	1	8	1.00
12	6	7	2	11	2.00
13	8	4	1	9	1.00

For further resources including data sets and questions, please refer to the CD accompanying this book.

36 Computing new variables with no values missing

Overview

■ Computing new variables allows you to add, subtract, etc. scores on several variables to give you a new variable. For example, you might wish to add together several questions on a questionnaire to give an overall index of what the questionnaire is measuring.

■ One of the few disadvantages of SPSS for Windows is that no record is kept as to how the new variable was calculated in the first place. One can either keep a detailed written record of the formula used to compute the new variable or, if it is simple enough, then the variable label could be used to describe what it is.

■ When computing new variables, it is generally a wise precaution to do a few hand checks of cases. It is easy to inadvertently enter an incorrect formula that then gives a new variable which is not the one that you think you are creating.

36.1 What is computing new variables with no values missing?

When analysing data we may want to form a new variable out of one or more old ones. For example, when measuring psychological variables, several questions are often used to measure more or less the same thing, such as the following which assess satisfaction with life:

(a) I generally enjoy life
(b) Some days things just seem to get me down
(c) Life often seems pretty dull
(d) The future looks hopeful.

Participants are asked to state how much they agree with each of these statements on the following four-point scale:

1: Strongly agree   2: Agree   3: Disagree   4: Strongly disagree

These items could be used to determine how satisfied people are with their lives by adding up each participant's responses to all four of them.

Notice a problem that frequently occurs when dealing with questionnaires: if you answer 'Strongly agree' to the first and fourth items you indicate that you enjoy life, whereas if you answer 'Strongly agree' to the second and third items you imply that you are dissatisfied with life. We want higher scores to denote greater life satisfaction. Consequently, we will reverse the scoring for the *first* and *fourth* items as follows:

1: Strongly disagree   2: Disagree   3: Agree   4: Strongly agree

The 'Recode' procedure described in Chapter 35 can be used to recode the values for the first and fourth items.

The data in Table 36.1 show the answers to the four statements by three individuals, and the way in which the answers to the first and fourth items have to be recoded. We will use these data to illustrate the SPSS procedure for adding together the answers to the four statements to form an index of life satisfaction.

Table 36.1   Life satisfaction scores of three respondents

	(a) Enjoy life (recode)	(b) Gets me down (no recode)	(c) Dull (no recode)	(d) Hopeful (recode)
Respondent 1	Agree (2 recoded as 3)	Agree (2)	St. disagree (4)	Agree (2 recoded as 3)
Respondent 2	Disagree (3 recoded as 2)	Disagree (3)	Agree (2)	St. disagree (4 recoded as 1)
Respondent 3	St. agree (1 recoded as 4)	Disagree (3)	Disagree (3)	Disagree (3 recoded as 2)

36.2 Computing a new variable with no values missing

Step 1:

Enter the (recoded) data, having named the variables as shown and removed the 2 decimal places.

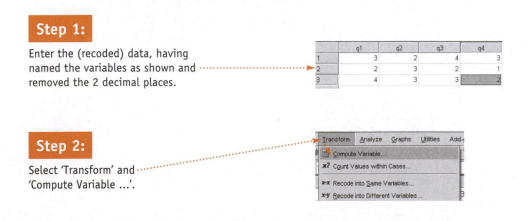

Step 2:

Select 'Transform' and 'Compute Variable ...'.

Step 3:

Type a name for the new variable
in the box under 'Target Variable:'
(e.g. 'LifeSat').

Either type in or select the terms
of the expression in the 'Numeric
Expression:' box.

Select 'OK'.

Select 'Paste' to save this procedure
as a syntax command.

Step 4:

An alternative 'Numeric Expression'
is to use the keyword 'sum'
followed by the variables in
brackets.

Step 5:

The new variable and its values is
entered into the 'Data Editor'.
Check that the values are what they
should be for a few cases. Save the
file if you want to use it again.

	q1	q2	q3	q4	LifeSat
1	3	2	4	3	12.00
2	2	3	2	1	8.00
3	4	3	3	2	12.00

Step 6:

If the recoded data are not
immediately next to the original
data, it may be better to select
'Analyze', 'Reports' and 'Case
Summaries ...'.

Step 7:

Select 'q1' to 'q4' and 'LifeSat' and the ▶ button to put these 5 variables in the 'Variables:' box.

If you have a large sample, you could look at only, say, the first 10 rather than 100 cases by changing 100 to 10 in the 'Limit cases to first' box.

Select 'OK'.

The cases are listed in the 1st column according to their row number.

The 2nd to 5th columns have the original values.

Case Summaries[a]

	q1	q2	q3	q4	LifeSat
1	3	2	4	3	12.00
2	2	3	2	1	8.00
3	4	3	3	2	12.00
Total N	3	3	3	3	3

a. Limited to first 10 cases

The 6th column has the values for the new computed variables.

36.3 Saving the Compute procedure as a syntax file

To save this procedure as a syntax file, select 'Paste' in the main box. This syntax command appears in the Syntax window. (See Step 7.)

```
COMPUTE LifeSat=q1 + q2 + q3 + q4.
EXECUTE.
```

36.4 Adding some new data to Table 36.1

Add the values of these 3 new cases to this file.

36.5 Running the Compute syntax command

Step 1:

Select 'Run' and 'All' to run this syntax command. Alternatively, highlight the command and select the ▶ button.

Step 2:

Here are the computed values for the 3 new cases. They are added as a new variable at the end of the data spreadsheet. Once created, the new variable may be used in the same way as other variables in SPSS.

3	4	3	3	2	12.00
4	1	2	1	3	7.00
5	2	2	3	2	9.00
6	3	2	3	2	10.00

For further resources including data sets and questions, please refer to the CD accompanying this book.

37 Computing new variables with some values missing

Overview

- Some of the data that go to make up a variable such as the score for an attitude or personality scale may be missing or unclear for some of your participants. For example, a few participants may have accidentally ticked or marked two of the Likert responses for the same item and not ticked an answer for the next item. In a situation like this, we would have to code the answers for these two items as missing (see Chapter 34) as we do not know what they are.

- If a large amount of data like these were missing for a participant, then it is better to discard the data for this participant. However, if only a small amount of data like these were missing it would be better not to discard these participants but to use what data we have. We could work out the mean score for these participants based on the items we have values or answers for.

- If we were working in terms of total scores rather than mean scores, then we could convert these mean scores into total scores by multiplying the mean score by the number of items for that scale.

37.1 What is computing new variables with some values missing?

When we collect data, some of it may be missing or it may not be clear what the data are. When we have a measure based on a number of values and some of those values are missing, then we have to decide what we are going to do in those circumstances. For example, we may be interested in measuring how quickly people respond. In order to obtain a reliable measure of their reaction time, we may obtain their reaction time to a signal on ten separate trials and take their mean time for those ten occasions. Now some people on some occasions may react before the signal has been given so that they have unrealistically fast reaction times. We would want to exclude these 'false starts' by coding these times as missing. If some people make many false starts, then we may feel that we have insufficient data on them to provide a reliable estimate of their reaction time and we may wish to exclude these individuals from our analysis. However, if individuals only make a few false starts, then we may be able to obtain a reasonable estimate of their reaction time. So we have to decide what our criterion is going to be for including or excluding people. We may decide that if people have more than 10% of false starts, we are going to exclude them. In other words, if they have a false start on more than one trial out of the ten then we are going to exclude them. If they make a false start on only one trial, then we will include them.

Another example is where we have a questionnaire scale consisting of a number of questions or items. We may have a questionnaire consisting of only four items where people are asked to respond to these items on a six-point Likert scale, where the answer 'Strongly disagree' receives a score of 1 and an answer of 'Strongly agree' a score of 6. In this case we may base our overall score for that scale if they have given clear answers to three or four items. If they have given clear answers to fewer than three items we will exclude their score on that scale. If the score for the scale is going to be based on a varying number of items, then we cannot score that scale by simply adding together or summing their scores for the items that they have answered as someone who has answered fewer items will generally obtain a lower score than someone who has answered more items. For example, if two people have answered 'Strongly agree' to all items, but one person answered all four items while the other person only answered three items, then the total score for the person answering all four items is 24 while the total score for the person only answering three items is 18. Yet both people may be similar in that they have answered 'Strongly agree' to all the items they have answered. What we have to do here is to take the mean score for the items they have answered. If we do this, then both people will have a mean score of 6 which indicates that they strongly agreed with all items. If the scale is generally interpreted in terms of a total score rather than a mean score, then we can convert this mean score into a total score by multiplying the mean score by the number of items in the scale. So, in this case, both people will have a total score of 24.

We will illustrate how to calculate a mean score based on having answered more than a certain number of items with the data in Table 37.1 (which are the same as those in Table 27.1). There are ten cases who have answered on a six-point Likert scale four questions that go to make up a particular index. To illustrate how this works, the first case will have missing data for the first item, the second case will have missing data for the first two items and the third case will have missing data for the first three items. Missing data are coded as zero. We would expect a mean score to be computed for the first case who has answered three items but not for the second and third cases who have not.

Table 37.1 Data for 10 cases from a four-item questionnaire

Cases	Item 1	Item 2	Item 3	Item 4
1	1	3	5	6
2	2	1	1	2
3	1	1	1	1
4	5	2	4	2
5	6	4	3	2
6	5	4	5	6
7	4	5	3	2
8	2	1	2	1
9	1	2	1	1
10	1	1	2	2

37.2 Computing a new variable with some values missing

Step 1:

Retrieve the data file from Chapter 27 and enter the missing values or enter the data anew.

	Item1	Item2	Item3	Item4
1	0	3	5	6
2	0	0	1	2
3	0	0	0	1
4	5	2	4	2
5	6	4	3	2
6	5	4	5	6
7	4	5	3	2
8	2	1	2	1
9	1	2	1	1
10	1	1	2	2
11	3	4	2	0
12	5	0	3	0
13	4	3	0	4

Step 2:

Code missing values for the first item as 0 by selecting 'Discrete missing values' and entering 0 in the box below.

Select 'OK'.

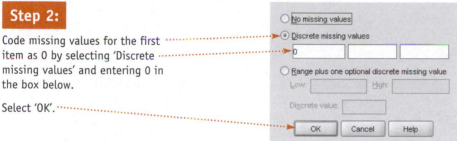

○ No missing values

● Discrete missing values

`0`

○ Range plus one optional discrete missing value

Low: ___   High: ___

Discrete value: ___

[OK] [Cancel] [Help]

Step 3:

Code the missing values of the other 3 variables as 0 by copying 0 in 'Missing', highlighting the 3 boxes below it and pasting in.

	Name	Type	Width	Decimals	Label	Values	Missing	
1	Item1	Numeric	8	0		None	0	
2	Item2	Numeric	8	0		None	0	
3	Item3	Numeric	8	0		None	0	
4	Item4	Numeric	8	0		None	0	

Step 4:

Select 'Transform' and 'Compute Variable ...'.

<u>T</u>ransform <u>A</u>nalyze <u>G</u>raphs <u>U</u>tilities Add-

Compute Variable...

x? Count Values within Cases...

Step 5:

Type a name for the new variable in the box under 'Target Variable:' (e.g. 'scale'). Either type in or select the terms of the expression in the 'Numeric Expression:' box. 'mean' is the keyword for computing a mean. '3' after the full stop indicates that this mean is based on 3 or more non-missing values.

Select 'OK'.

Select 'Paste' to save this procedure as a syntax command.

Target Variable:
`scale`

Numeric Expression:
`mean.3(Item1 to Item4)`

Type & Label...

Item1
Item2
Item3
Item4

Function group:
All
Arithmetic
CDF & Noncentral CDF
Conversion
Current Date/Time
Date Arithmetic

Functions and Special Variables:

If... (optional case selection condition)

[OK] [Paste] [Reset] [Cancel] [Help]

Step 6:

The new variable and its values are entered into the 'Data Editor'. Note that no mean score has been computed for the 2 cases that have more than 1 value missing. Save the file if you want to use it again.

	Item1	Item2	Item3	Item4	scale
1	0	3	5	6	4.67
2	0	0	1	2	.
3	0	0	0	1	.
4	5	2	4	2	3.25

Step 7:

If the new data are not immediately next to the original data, it may be better to select 'Analyze', 'Reports' and 'Case Summaries …'.

Step 8:

Select 'Item1' to 'Item4' and 'scale' and the ▶ button to put these 5 variables in the 'Variables:' box.
If you have a large sample, you could look at only, say, the first 10 rather than 100 cases by changing 100 to 10 in the 'Limit cases to first' box.

Select 'OK'.

The cases are listed in the 1st column according to their row number.

The 2nd to 5th column has the original values.

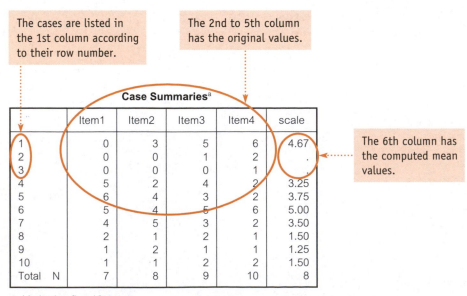

Case Summaries[a]

	Item1	Item2	Item3	Item4	scale
1	0	3	5	6	4.67
2	0	0	1	2	.
3	0	0	0	1	.
4	5	2	4	2	3.25
5	6	4	3	2	3.75
6	5	4	5	6	5.00
7	4	5	3	2	3.50
8	2	1	2	1	1.50
9	1	2	1	1	1.25
10	1	1	2	2	1.50
Total N	7	8	9	10	8

The 6th column has the computed mean values.

a. Limited to first 10 cases.

37.3 Saving the Compute procedure as a syntax file

To save this procedure as a syntax file, select 'Paste' in the main box. This syntax command appears in the Syntax window. (See Step 5.)

```
COMPUTE scale=mean.3(Item1 to Item4).
EXECUTE.
```

37.4 Adding some new data to Table 37.1

Add the values of these 3 new cases to this file.

10	1	1	2	2	1.50
11	3	4	2	0	.
12	5	0	3	0	.
13	4	3	0	4	.

37.5 Running the Compute syntax command

Step 1:

Select 'Run' and 'All' to run this syntax command. Alternatively, highlight the command and select the ▶ button.

```
COMPUTE scale=mean.3(Item1 to Item4).
EXECUTE.
```

Step 2:

Here are the computed values for the 3 new cases.

10	1	1	2	2	1.50
11	3	4	2	0	3.00
12	5	0	3	0	.
13	4	3	0	4	3.67

For further resources including data sets and questions, please refer to the CD accompanying this book.

38 Selecting cases

Overview

■ This chapter explains how to select a particular subgroup from your sample. For example, you may wish to analyse the data only for young people or for women.

■ It is possible to select subgroups for analysis based on multiple selection criteria such as age and gender (e.g. young women).

■ Sometimes the use of subgroups leads to a much clearer understanding of the trends in the data than would be possible if, for example, one used cross-tabulation by gender.

38.1 What is selecting cases?

Sometimes we may wish to carry out computations on subgroups in our sample. For example we may want to correlate musical and mathematical ability (a) in girls and boys separately, (b) in older and younger children separately and (c) in older and younger girls and boys separately. To do this, sex needs to be coded (e.g. 1 for girls and 2 for boys) and what age is the cutoff point for determining which children fall into the younger age group and which children fall into the older age group stipulated. We will use age 10 as the cutoff point, with children aged 9 or less falling into the younger age group and children aged 10 or more falling into the older age group. Then each of the groups of interest need to be selected in turn and the appropriate statistical analyses carried out. We will illustrate the selection of cases with the data in Table 38.1, which show the music and mathematics scores of ten children together with their code for sex and their age in years. (These values are the same as those previously presented in Table 34.1.)

Obviously the selection of cutoff points is important. You need to beware of inadvertently excluding some cases.

Table 38.1 Scores on musical ability and mathematical ability for 10 children with their sex and age

Music score	Mathematics score	Sex	Age
2	8	1	10
6	3	1	9
4	9	2	12
5	7	1	8
7	2	2	11
7	3	2	13
2	9	2	7
3	8	1	10
5	6	2	9
4	7	1	11

38.2   Entering the data

Step 1:

If you saved the data file for Chapter 34, select that file and define the new variables in 'Variable View' of the 'Data Editor'. Otherwise, define the 4 variables.

Remove the 2 decimal places.

	Name	Type	Width	Decimals
1	Music	Numeric	8	0
2	Maths	Numeric	8	0
3	Sex	Numeric	8	0
4	Age	Numeric	8	0

Step 2:

Enter the data in 'Data View' of the 'Data Editor'.

	Music	Maths	Sex	Age
1	2	8	1	10
2	6	3	1	9
3	4	9	2	12
4	5	7	1	8
5	7	2	2	11
6	7	3	2	13
7	2	9	2	7
8	3	8	1	10
9	5	6	2	9
10	4	7	1	11

38.3 Selecting cases

Step 1:

Select 'Data' and 'Select Cases …'.

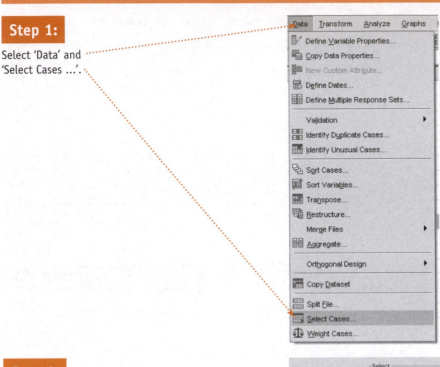

Step 2:

Select 'If condition is satisfied'.

Select 'If'.

Step 3a:

To select girls, select 'Sex' and the ▶ button.

Select '=' and '1'. Alternatively type in 'Sex = 1'.

Select 'Continue'.

Select 'OK' in the previous box.

Carry out the analysis you want (e.g. correlation).

Step 3b:

To select boys, select 'Data', 'Select Cases …' and 'If'.

Highlight '1' and replace it with '2'.

Select 'Continue' and 'OK'.

Conduct your analysis (e.g. correlation).

Step 3c:

To select girls 9 years or younger, select 'Data', 'Select Cases …' and 'If'.
Highlight '2' and replace it with '1'.

Select '&' (the ampersand), 'Age', the ▶ button, '<=' (the less than or equal sign) and '9'.
Alternatively type this in.

Select 'Continue' and 'OK'.

Conduct your analysis (e.g. correlation).

Step 3d:

To select girls older than 9 years, select 'Data', 'Select Cases …' and 'If'.

Highlight '<=' and replace it with '>' (the greater than sign). To see or remind you of what the signs mean, move the cursor to them and click on the right button of the mouse.

Select 'Continue' and 'OK'.

Conduct your analysis (e.g. correlation).

You can check that the correct sort of cases have been selected since those deselected are 'struck off' at the start of the appropriate rows of the data spreadsheet in Data View.

For further resources including data sets and questions, please refer to the CD accompanying this book.

39 Samples and populations
Generating a random sample

Overview

■ Random sampling is a key aspect of statistics. This chapter explains how random samples can be quickly generated. This is not a commonly used procedure in statistical analysis but can provide useful experience of the nature of random processes.

■ One can get a better 'feel' for inferential statistics and sampling by obtaining random samples from your data to explore the variability in outcomes of further statistical analyses on these random samples. The variation in the characteristics of samples is known as sampling error and is the basis of inferential statistics.

■ The procedure could be used to randomly assign participants to, say, an experimental and a control group.

■ Keep an eye on the dialog boxes as you work through this chapter. You will notice options which allow you to select samples based on other criteria such as the date when the participants were interviewed.

39.1 What is generating random samples?

In this chapter, the selection of random samples from a known set of scores is illustrated. The primary aim of this is to allow those learning statistics for the first time to try random sampling in order to get an understanding of sampling distributions. This should lead to a better appreciation of estimation in statistics and the frailty that may underlie seemingly hard-nosed mathematical procedures. We will illustrate the generation of a random sample from a set of data consisting of the extraversion scores of the 50 airline pilots shown in Table 4.1.

If one wished to randomly assign participants to the experimental or control group in an experiment prior to collecting the data, then simply create a variable in the SPSS spreadsheet and enter the numbers 1 to 50 (or whatever is the expected number of participants for the study) in separate rows of the spreadsheet. By selecting a random sample of 25 individuals, you can generate a list of participants who will be in the experimental group. So if the random sample is 3, 4, 7, 9, etc. then this means that the third, fourth, seventh, ninth, etc. participant recruited will be in the experimental group. The remainder would be the control group, for example.

You can find out more about sampling in Chapter 9 of Howitt, D. and Cramer, D. (2008) *Introduction to Statistics in Psychology*. Harlow: Pearson.

39.2 Selecting a random sample

Step 1:

If you saved the data, select the file. Otherwise enter the data again. Select 'Data' and 'Select Cases …'.

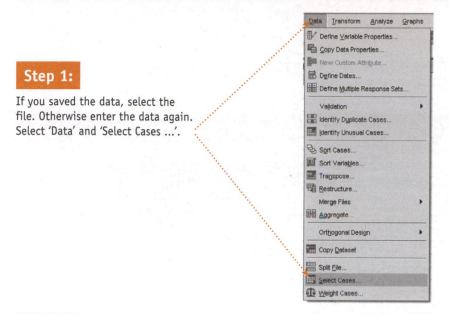

Step 2:

Select 'Random sample of cases'.

Select 'Sample'.

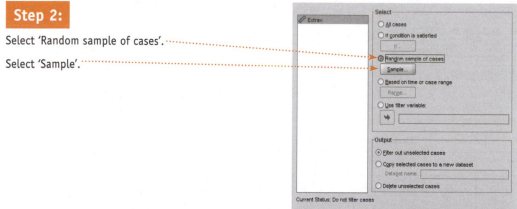

Step 3:

To select about 10% of all cases, enter '10' in the box beside 'Approximately'.

To select 5 cases exactly, select 'Exactly', enter '5' 'cases from the first' '50' 'cases'.

Select 'Continue'.

Select 'OK' in the previous box.

39.3 Interpreting the results

The cases that have been selected do not have a diagonal line across their case number and have a '1' in the new column created called 'filter_$'.

Cases that have not been selected have a diagonal across their case number and have a '0' in the new column called 'filter_$'.

39.4 Statistical analysis on a random sample

Step 1:

To analyse this sample, select 'Analyze' and the analysis desired such as 'Descriptive Statistics' and 'Descriptives ...'.

Step 2:

Select 'Extrav' and the ▶ button to put 'Extrav' in the 'Variable(s):' box.

Select 'OK'.

Descriptive Statistics

	N	Minimum	Maximum	Mean	Std. Deviation
Extrav	7	1	5	3.29	1.496
Valid N (listwise)	7				

Note that 7 cases were selected. If exactly 10% is required, then 5 from 50 cases should be specified in step 3 of section 39.2.

For further resources including data sets and questions, please refer to the CD accompanying this book.

40 Inputting a correlation matrix

Overview

- Some publications report a correlation matrix for their analysis that may also contain the means and standard deviations of the variables.

- SPSS allows you to do some further analyses on these matrices such as partial correlation, factor analysis and multiple regression.

- You need to use syntax commands to input the correlation matrix and to carry out the subsequent statistical analysis.

- The syntax commands for the statistical analysis are given first in the output when an analysis using menus and dialog boxes are run. Alternatively you can obtain these in the Syntax window by using the 'Paste' function in the main dialog box.

- We illustrate the inputting of and analysis of a correlation matrix for stepwise multiple regression with the data in Chapter 28.

- The exact way in which the matrix is referred to in the syntax command for the statistical analysis varies according to the statistical procedure. How this is done can be found by looking up the syntax command in the Help procedure.

40.1 What is inputting a correlation matrix?

If a correlation matrix has been published in a particular study, it is possible to enter this matrix into SPSS so that further analyses can be carried out. A table or matrix of correlations is sometimes presented in a publication to show the relation between the different variables. Having a matrix of correlations means that we can carry out some further statistical analyses such as partial correlation (Chapter 25), factor analysis (Chapter 26) and multiple regression (Chapters 28 and 29) which the study may not have reported. For example, we may wish to partial out a variable which the study has not mentioned or we may want to see what the higher order factors are in a factor analysis by carrying out a factor analysis on the correlations of the first factors. It is possible that the study contains means and standard deviations for the variables too.

We will illustrate how to input a correlation matrix together with the means and standard deviations of the variables with the data in Table 40.1 (which are the same as those in Table 28.1). The data in this table have been weighted so as to represent 120 rather than the six cases presented here. This has been done so that some of the relations between the variables will be statistically significant. Small correlations become significant in large samples.

Table 40.1   Data for producing a correlation matrix

Educational achievement	Intellectual ability	School motivation	Parental interest
1	2	1	2
2	2	3	1
2	2	3	3
3	4	3	2
3	3	4	3
4	3	2	2

The means, standard deviations and correlations for these variables are presented in Table 40.2. These can be computed from the data in Table 40.1 by carrying out correlations (Chapter 7) or a multiple regression (Chapter 28). They all have to be based on the same sample of cases. In other words, the listwise procedure for missing values needs to be used.

Table 40.2   Means, standard deviations and correlations of four variables

	Mean	SD	1	2	3
1 Achievement	2.50	0.961			
2 Ability	2.67	0.961	0.701		
3 Motivation	2.67	0.947	0.369	0.316	
4 Interest	2.17	0.690	0.127	0.108	0.343

$n = 120$

We will carry out the same stepwise multiple regression on this matrix as was carried out in Chapter 28 so you can see that the results are essentially the same. Any differences are due to the fact that the data for this analysis have been rounded to fewer decimal places than in the original analysis. The stepwise multiple regression has to be carried out using syntax commands. As this book does not describe these commands, they can be most readily generated by simulating the statistical procedure to be used and using the Paste function to produce the relevant syntax. We do this by creating a data file that has the relevant variables in it but does not have to have any data in it.

40.2 Syntax file for inputting a correlation matrix and running a stepwise multiple regression

Type in this syntax file. The regression syntax has been obtained by setting up a stepwise multiple regression and using Paste to enter its syntax into the syntax file. The syntax 'matrix=in(*)' needs to be entered after the 'REGRESSION' keyword to tell SPSS to use the correlation matrix above.

```
File  Edit  View  Data  Transform  Analyze  Graphs  Utilities  Run

matrix data variables=rowtype_ Achievement Ability Motivation Interest.
begin data.
mean 2.50 2.67 2.67 2.17
stddev .961 .748 .947 .690
n  120 120 120 120
corr 1.00
corr .701 1.00
corr .369 .316 1.00
corr .127 .108 .343 1.00
end data.
REGRESSION matrix=in(*)
  /DESCRIPTIVES MEAN STDDEV CORR SIG N
  /MISSING LISTWISE
  /STATISTICS COEFF OUTS R ANOVA CHANGE ZPP
  /CRITERIA=PIN(.05) POUT(.10)
  /NOORIGIN
  /DEPENDENT Achievement
  /METHOD=STEPWISE Ability Motivation Interest .
```

40.3 Running the syntax file

Select 'Run' and 'All' to run this syntax command.

Alternatively, highlight the command and select the ▶ button.

```
File  Edit  View  Data  Transform  Analyze  Graphs  Utilities  Run  Add-ons  Window

                                                          ▶  All
matrix data variables=rowtype_ Achievement Ability Motivation I  ▶  Selection
begin data.                                                  ▶  Current   Ctrl-R
mean 2.50 2.67 2.67 2.17
stddev .961 .748 .947 .690                                   ▶  To End
n  120 120 120 120
```

40.4 Part of the output

All the values in this table are the same as those in Chapter 28 apart for 'Std. Error' and the 'F Change'. This is due to rounding errors.

Model Summary

Model	R	R Square	Adjusted R Square	Std. Error of the Estimate	R Square Change	F Change	df1	df2	Sig. F Change
					Change Statistics				
1	.701[a]	.491	.487	.6882459	.491	114.010	1	118	.000
2	.718[b]	.516	.507	.6745614	.024	5.836	1	117	.017

a. Predictors: (Constant), Ability
b. Predictors: (Constant), Ability, Motivation

For further resources including data sets and questions, please refer to the CD accompanying this book.

41 Checking the accuracy of data input

Overview

■ It is essential to enter the data accurately into the Data Editor. With a small set of data it is most probably sufficient to check the inputted data against the original data. With a larger data set, this is more difficult to do.

■ One strategy is to enter the same data separately into two files and to compare the value of the same cells in the two files. This kind of procedure is available as part of SPSS Data Builder but this software is expensive and not readily available.

■ It is relatively easy to carry out this procedure in SPSS by combining the two files, using syntax commands to see if there is a difference between the same cells and to check and correct any differences.

■ This procedure assumes that it is unlikely that the same mistake will be made twice, particularly if different people enter the data.

41.1 What is checking the accuracy of data input?

Mistakes can occur when data are typed into the Data Editor of SPSS. When you have a small set of data, accuracy can be checked by simply comparing the Data Editor with the original data. If you find this difficult to do conscientiously or if you have a large data set, then it is better to use a procedure that is more systematic and accurate. This procedure involves entering the data twice and then comparing the two sets of data. It is better that different people are involved so that one person does not enter the data twice. Two different people are less likely to make the same mistake. The data are entered into two separate files so that data entry is independent. If there is a difference in the value of a cell between the two files, then both values cannot be correct and the original data have to be checked to see which value is correct. If there is no difference, then it is likely that the values are correct. Once all the values have been checked and corrections made as appropriate, one of the corrected files can be used for the data analysis.

We will illustrate this procedure with the data files in Tables 41.1, 41.2 and 41.3. Table 41.1 shows the correct data set of the values for the responses of six people to four questionnaire items answered on a four-point scale where 1 represents 'Strongly agree' and 4 'Strongly disagree'. A 0 represents an item that has not been answered or where the answer is not clear. As we are just checking the accuracy of data inputting it does not matter what the numbers represent. These values have been put into a table to make them easier to read but if we were entering the data then we would be most probably reading them off a questionnaire or some other form of record. We will assume that an optical scanner is not available or is not suitable for reading this information electronically.

Table 41.2 shows the data file for the first time the data are entered while Table 41.3 shows the data file for the second time that the data are entered.

We have introduced two mistakes in the first file in Table 41.2 and three mistakes in the second file in Table 41.3. For the second case in Table 41.2 the value for item 2 has been accidentally entered in the same cell as the value for item 1. The cell for item 2 has been left empty. For Table 41.3 the cell for item 3 for the third case has been left empty and the values of the cells for items 1 and 2 for the fourth case have been transposed.

Table 41.1 Correct data to be inputted

Item 1	Item 2	Item 3	Item 4
1	0	1	2
2	2	3	1
2	2	3	3
3	4	0	2
3	3	4	3
4	3	2	2

Table 41.2 First data file

Item 1	Item 2	Item 3	Item 4
1	0	1	2
22		3	1
2	2	3	3
3	4	0	2
3	3	4	3
4	3	2	2

Table 41.3 Second data file

Item 1	Item 2	Item 3	Item 4
1	0	1	2
2	2	3	1
2	2		3
4	3	0	2
3	3	4	3
4	3	2	2

41.2 Creating two data files

With a large number of variables it is better to carry out the following procedure, which is designed to minimise the amount of work involved.

1. Create the variable names in an SPSS file. At the end of each name add a character that cannot be easily confused with a character in the name. This character could be a hash sign (#). For example, the name of the first variable could be q1#. The reason for this will become apparent later on.

Enter the variable names in the 'Variable View' window. It is better to identify each case with an ·······> identification number ('idno'). Change the decimal places to '0'.

	Name	Type	Width	Decimals
1	idno	Numeric	8	0
2	q1#	Numeric	8	0
3	q2#	Numeric	8	0
4	q3#	Numeric	8	0
5	q4#	Numeric	8	1

You could specify other characteristics of the variables such as the names of categories if this is helpful for you or the person entering the data. However, you should not specify any missing values when comparing the files as you will be calculating the differences between the two values. If one of the values is missing, then a difference will not be computed for that pair of values.

2. Save this file with a name such as that of the person who is going to enter the data such as 'DC1'.

3. Save this file again with a different name such as 'DC2'.

4. Highlight the names of the variables in one of the files and paste them four times into a Word document and separated from one another.

5. Using the 'Replace' procedure, replace the hash sign (#) with an 'at' sign (@) for one set of variable names.

Select 'Edit' in Word ······· and 'Replace ...'.

Enter '#' in 'Find what:'
and '@' in 'Replace with:'.

6. Highlight these names ending in @ and paste them over the names in the second data file called 'DC2'. The names in the two data files for the same variable can now be easily distinguished.

7. Enter the data from Table 14.2 in the first file and the data from Table 14.3 in the second file.

41.3 Combining the two data files

When in one of the data files (say, DC1), carry out the following procedure.

Step 1:

Select 'Data',
'Merge Files' and
'Add Variables'.

Step 2:

Select 'DC2.sav' and
'Continue'.

Step 3:

Select 'OK'.

Step 4:

The variables of 'DC2.sav' have been put into 'DC1.sav'.

41.4 Creating a syntax file for computing the difference between the two entries for the same variables

We are going to subtract one entry of the variable (e.g. q1#) from the other (e.g. q1@) to create a difference score which we are going to call q1#@ using the following form of the syntax command for each of the four variables: compute q1# – q1@ = q1#@.

If you have a large number of such commands to make, it is easier to do this in Word copying and pasting the relevant terms into a table having seven columns and as many rows as variables. This table can then be copied and pasted into a syntax file. Add 'execute.' at the end of this file or select 'File' and 'Save' after running it.

compute	q1#@	=	q1#	-	q1@	.
compute	q2#@	=	q2#	-	q2@	.
compute	q3#@	=	q3#	-	q3@	.
compute	q4#@	=	q4#	-	q4@	.

With only 'DC1.sav' open, run this syntax file.

Step 1:

Select 'Run' and 'All' to run this syntax command. Alternatively, highlight the command and select the ▶ button.

Step 2:

The difference values are presented in 'Data View'. You need to check the original values where there is a difference or a full stop and to make the necessary changes. After you have done this you need to rerun the syntax file to check that all changes have been made.

Step 3:

If there are a large number of differences, select 'Analyze', 'Reports' and 'Case Summaries ...'.

Step 4

Select 'idno' 'q1#@' to 'q4#@' and the ▶ button to put these 5 variables in the 'Variables:' box.

If your sample is larger than 100, change the 'Limit cases to first' to the size of your sample (or greater).

Select 'OK'.

Case Summaries[a]

	idno	q1#@	q2#@	q3#@	q4#@
1	1	.00	.00	.00	.00
2	2	20.00	.	.00	.00
3	3	.00	.00	.	.00
4	4	−1.00	1.00	.00	.00
5	5	.00	.00	.00	.00
6	6	.00	.00	.00	.00
Total N	6	6	5	5	6

The variables and their values are listed in this table.

a. Limited to first 10 cases.

Step 5:

After correcting the values, run the syntax file again. There should be all '.00's for all the cells for variables ending in #@'. Save this file with a new name (e.g. 'DCc.sav').

Step 6:

Highlight the variables you want to delete (i.e.'q1@' to 'q4#@'). ·······

	Name	Type	Width	Decimals
1	idno	Numeric	8	0
2	q1#	Numeric	8	0
3	q2#	Numeric	8	0
4	q3#	Numeric	8	0
5	q4#	Numeric	8	0
6	q1@	Numeric	8	0
7	q2@	Numeric	8	0
8	q3@	Numeric	8	0
9	q4@	Numeric	8	0
10	q1#@	Numeric	8	2
11	q2#@	Numeric	8	2
12	q3#@	Numeric	8	2
13	q4#@	Numeric	8	2

Step 7:

Select 'Edit' and 'Clear' and save this file as 'DC1.sav'. Although this is not necessary you may like to delete the '#' at the end of each name. This is most easily done in the Word file by using 'Replace'.

If you have later data to check, then this is best done after all the data have been entered and checked.

For further resources including data sets and questions, please refer to the CD accompanying this book.

Appendix
Other statistics in SPSS

Other statistical methods provided by SPSS but not described in this book are shown below in terms of their options on the 'Analyze' menu, submenu and dialog box options.

Analyze menu	Analyze submenu	Dialog box
Descriptive Statistics	Crosstabs . . .	Lambda
		Uncertainty coefficient
		Gamma
		Somers' d
		Kendall's tau-b
		Kendall's tau-c
		Risk
		Eta
Correlate	Bivariate . . .	Kendall's tau-b
Regression	Curve Estimation . . .	
	Ordinal . . .	
	Probit . . .	
	Nonlinear . . .	
	Weight Estimation . . .	
	2-Stage Least Squares . . .	
	Optimal Scaling . . .	
Loglinear	Logit . . .	
Classify	TwoStep Cluster . . .	
	K-Means Cluster . . .	
	Hierarchical Cluster . . .	
	Discriminant . . .	
Data Reduction	Correspondence Analysis . . .	
	Optimal Scaling . . .	
Scale	Multidimensional Scaling . . .	
	Multidimensional Scaling[PROXSCAL] . . .	
	Multidimensional Scaling [ALSCAL]	

Analyze menu	Analyze submenu	Dialog box
Nonparametric Tests	Binomial . . .	
	Runs . . .	
	1-Sample K-S . . . (Kolmogorov–Smirnov)	
	2 Independent Samples . . .	Kolmogorov–Smirnov Z
		Wald–Wolfowitz runs
		Moses extreme reactions
	K Independent Samples . . .	Jonckheere–Terpstra
		Median
	2 Related Samples . . .	Marginal Homogeneity
	K Related Samples . . .	Kendall's W
		Cochran's Q
Time Series	Exponential Smoothing . . .	
	Autoregression . . .	
	ARIMA . . .	
	Seasonal Decomposition . . .	
Survival	Life Tables . . .	
	Kaplan–Meier . . .	
	Cox Regression . . .	
	Cox w/ Time-Dep Cov . . .	

Glossary

−2 log likelihood (ratio) test: Used in logistic regression, it is a form of chi-square test which compares the goodness of fit of two models where one model is a part of (i.e. nested or a subset of) the other model. The chi-square is the difference in the −2 log likelihood values for the two models.

A priori **test:** A test of the difference between two groups of scores when this comparison has been planned ignorant of the actual data. This contrasts with a post hoc test which is carried out after the data has been collected and which has no particularly strong expectations about the outcome.

Adjusted mean: A mean score when the influence of one or more covariates have been removed especially in analysis of covariance.

Alpha level: The level of risk that the researcher is prepared to mistakenly accept the hypothesis on the basis of the available data. Typically this is set at a maximum of 5% or 0.05 and is, of course, otherwise referred to as the level of significance.

Analysis of covariance (ANCOVA): A variant of the analysis of variance (ANOVA) in which scores on the dependent variable are adjusted to take into account (control) covariate(s). For example, differences between conditions of an experiment at pre-test can be controlled for.

Analysis of variance (ANOVA): An extensive group of tests of significance which compare means on a dependent variable. There may be one or more independent (grouping) variables or factors. ANOVA is essential in the analysis of most laboratory experiments.

Association: A relationship between two variables.

Bar chart: A picture in which frequencies are represented by the height of a set of bars. Actually it should be the areas of a set of bars but SPSS ignores this and settles for height.

Bartlett's test of sphericity: A test used in MANOVA of whether the correlations between the variables differ significantly from zero.

Beta level: The risk that we are prepared to accept of rejecting the null hypothesis when it is in fact true.

Beta weight: The standardised regression weight in multiple regression. It corresponds to the correlation coefficient in simple regression.

Between-groups design: Basically a design where different participants are allocated to different groups or conditions.

Between-subjects design: See between-groups design.

Bimodal: A frequency distribution with two modes.

Bivariate: Involving two variables as opposed to univariate which involves just one variable.

Bivariate correlation: A correlation between two variables.

Block: A subset of variables which will be analysed together in a sequence of blocks.

Bonferroni adjustment: A method of adjusting significance levels for the fact that many statistical analyses have been carried out on the data.

Boxplot: A diagram indicating the distribution of scores on a variable. It gives the median in a box the sides of which are the lower and upper values of the interquartile range. Lines at each side of the box identify the largest and smallest scores.

Box's *M*: A statistical test which partly establishes whether the data meet the requirements for a MANOVA analysis. It examines the extent to which the covariances of the dependent variables are similar for each of the groups in the analysis. Ideally, then, Box's *M* should not be significant. The test is used in MANOVA though its interpretation is complex.

Case: The basic unit of analysis on which data are collected such as individuals or organisations.

Categorical variable: A nominal or category variable.

Category variable: A variable which consists of categories rather than numerical scores. The categories have no particular quantitative order. However, usually on SPSS they will be coded as numbers.

Cell: The intersection of one category of a variable with another category of one or more other variables. So if a variable has categories A, B and C and the other variable has categories X, Y and Z, then the cells are A with X, A, with Y, A with Z, B with X, B with Y, etc. It is a term frequently used in ANOVA as well as with chi-square tables (i.e. cross-tabulation and contingency tables).

Chart: A graphical or pictorial representation of the characteristics of one's data.

Chart Editor window: In SPSS it is a window which can be opened up to refine a chart.

Chi-square distribution: A set of theoretical probability distributions which vary according to the degrees of freedom and which are used to determine the statistical significance of a chi-square test.

Chi-square test, Pearson's: A test of goodness-of-fit or association for frequency data. It compares the observed data with the estimated (or actual) population distribution (this is usually based on combining two or more samples).

Cluster analysis: A variety of techniques which identify the patterns of variables or cases which tend to be similar to each other. No cluster analysis techniques are dealt with in this book as they are uncommon in psychology. Often factor analysis, which is in this book, does a similar job.

Cochran's Q test: A test of whether the frequencies of a dichotomous variable differ significantly for more than two related samples or groups.

Coefficient of determination: The square of Pearson's correlation coefficient. So a correlation of 0.4 has a coefficient of determination of 0.16. It is useful especially since it gives a numerically more accurate representation of the relative importance of different correlation coefficients than the correlation coefficients themselves do.

Common variance: The variance that two or more variables share.

Communality: The variance that a particular variable in an analysis shares with other variables. It is distinct from error variance and specific variance (which is confined to a particular variable). It mainly appears in factor analysis.

Component matrix: A table showing the correlations between components and variables in factor analysis.

Compute: In SPSS, this procedure allows the researcher to derive new variables from the original variables. For example, it would be possible to sum the scores for each participant on several variables.

Condition: One of the groups in ANOVA or the t-test.

Confidence interval: A more realistic way of presenting the outcomes of statistical analysis than, for example, the mean or the standard deviation would be. It gives the range within which 95% or 99% of the most common means, standard deviations, etc. would lie. Thus instead of saying that the mean is 6.7 we would say that the 95% confidence interval for the mean is 5.2 to 8.2.

Confirmatory factor analysis: A test of whether a particular model or factor structure fits a set of data satisfactorily.

Confounding variable: Any variable which clouds the interpretation of a correlation or any other statistical relationship. Once the effects of the confounding variable are removed, the remaining relationship presents a truer picture of what is going on in reality.

Contingency table: A frequency table giving the frequencies in all of the categories of two or more nominal (category) variables tabulated together.

Correlation coefficient: An index which gives the extent and the direction of the linear association between two variables.

Correlation matrix: A matrix of the correlations of pairs of variables.

Count: The number of times (frequency) a particular observation (score or category, for example) occurs.

Counterbalancing: If some participants take part in condition A of a study first followed by condition B later, then to counterbalance any time or sequence effects other participants should take part in condition B first followed by condition A second.

Covariance: The variance which two or more score variables have in common (i.e. share). It is basically calculated like variance but instead of squaring each score's deviation from the mean the deviation of variable X from its mean is multiplied by the deviation of variable Y from its mean.

Covariate: A variable which correlates with the variables that are the researcher's main focus of interest. In the analysis of covariance it is the undesired influence of the covariate which is controlled for.

Cox and Snell's R^2: The amount of variance in the criterion variable accounted for by the predictor variables. It is used in logistic regression.

Cramer's V: Also known as Cramer's phi, this correlation coefficient is usually applied to a contingency or cross-tabulation table greater than two rows × two columns.

Critical value: Used when calculating statistical significance with statistical tables. It is the minimum value of the statistical calculation which is statistically significant (i.e. which rejects the null hypothesis).

Cronbach's alpha: A measure of the extent to which cases respond in a similar or consistent way on all the variables that go to make up a scale.

Data Editor Window: The data spreadsheet in which data are entered in SPSS.

Data handling: The various techniques to deal with data from a study excluding its statistical analysis. It would include data entry into the spreadsheet, the search for errors in data entry, recoding variables into new values, computing new variables and so on.

Data View: The window in SPSS which allows you to see the data spreadsheet.

Degrees of freedom: The number of components of the data that can vary while still yielding a given population value for characteristics such as mean scores. All other things being equal, the bigger the degrees of freedom the more likely it is that the research findings will be statistically significant.

Dependent variable: A variable which potentially may be affected or predicted by other variables in the analysis. It is sometimes known as the criterion or outcome variable.

Descriptive statistics: Indices which describe the major characteristics of variables or the relationships between variables. It includes measures of central tendency (mean, median and mode, for example) and measures of spread (range, variance, etc.).

Deviation: Usually the difference between a score and the mean of the set of scores.

Dialog box: A rectangular picture in SPSS which allows the user to select various procedures.

Dichotomous: A nominal (category) variable with just two categories. Gender (male/female) is an obvious example.

Direct oblimin: A rotation procedure for making factors in a factor analysis more meaningful or interpretable. Its essential characteristic is that the factors are not required to be uncorrelated (independent) of each other.

Discriminant (function) analysis: A statistical technique for score variables which maximises the difference(s) between two or more groups of participants on a set of variables. It generates a set of 'weights' which are applied to these variables.

Discriminant function: Found mainly in discriminant (function) analysis. A derived variable based on combining a set of variables in such a way that groups are as different as possible on the discriminant function. More than one discriminant function may emerge but each discriminant function is uncorrelated with the others.

Discriminant score: An individual's score on a discriminant function.

Dummy coding: Used when analysing nominal (category) data to allow such variables to be used analogously to scores. Each category of the nominal (category) variable is made into a separate dummy variable. If the nominal (category) variable has three categories A, B and C, then two new variables, say A versus not A and B versus not B, are created. The categories may be coded with the values 1 and 0. It would not be used where a variable has only two different categories.

Dummy variable: A variable created by dummy coding.

Effect size: A measure of the strength of the relationship between two variables. Most commonly used in meta-analysis. The Pearson correlation coefficient is a very familiar measure of effect size. Also commonly used is Cohen's d. The correlation coefficient is recommended as the most user-friendly measure of effect size as it is very familiar to most of us and easily understood.

Eigenvalue: The variance accounted for by a factor. It is simply the sum of the squared factor loadings. The concept is also used for discriminant functions.

Endogenous variable: Any variable in path analysis that can be explained on the basis of one or more variables in that analysis.

Eta: A measure of association for non-linear (curved) relationships.

Exact significance: The precise significance level at and beyond which a result is statistically significant.

Exogenous variable: A variable in path analysis which is not accounted for by any other variable in that analysis.

Exploratory factor analysis: The common form of factor analysis which finds the major dimensions of a correlation matrix using weighted combinations of the variables in the study. It identifies combinations of variables which can be described as one or more superordinate variables or factors.

Exponent or power: A number with an exponent or power superscript is multiplied by itself by that number of times. Thus 3^2 means 3×3 whereas 4^3 means $4 \times 4 \times 4$.

Extraction: The process of obtaining factors in factor analysis.

F ratio: The ratio of two variances. It can be used to test whether these two variances differ significantly using the F-distribution. It can be used on its own but is also part of the t-test and ANOVA.

Factor matrix: A table showing the correlations between factors and the variables.

Factor scores: Standardised scores for a factor. They provide a way of calculating an individual's score on a factor which precisely reflects that factor.

Factor, in analysis of variance: An independent or subject variable but is best regarded as a variable on which groups of participants are formed. The variances of these groups are then compared using ANOVA. A factor should consist of a nominal (category) variable with a small number of categories.

Factor, in factor analysis: A variable derived by combining other variables in a weighted combination. A factor seeks to synthesise the variance shared by variables into a more general variable to which the variables relate.

Factorial ANOVA: An analysis of variance with two or more independent or subject variables.

Family error rate: The probability or significance level for a finding when a family or number of tests or comparisons are being made on the same data.

Fisher test: Tests of significance (or association) for 2 × 2 and 2 × 3 contingency tables.

Frequency: The number of times a particular category occurs.

Frequency distribution: A table or diagram giving the frequencies of values of a variable.

Friedman's test: A non-parametric test for determining whether the mean ranks of three or more related samples or groups differ significantly.

Goodness of fit index: A measure of the extent to which a particular model (or pattern of variables) designed to describe a set of data actually matches the data.

Graph: A diagram for illustrating the values of one or more variables.

Grouping variable: A variable which forms the groups or conditions that are to be compared.

Harmonic mean: the number of scores, divided by the sum of the reciprocal ($1/x$) of each score.

Help: A facility in software with a graphical interface such as SPSS which provides information about its features.

Hierarchical agglomerative clustering: A form of cluster analysis, at each step of which a variable or cluster is paired with the most similar variable or cluster until one cluster remains.

Hierarchical or sequential entry: A variant of regression in which the order in which the independent (predictor) variables are entered into the analysis is decided by the analyst rather than mathematical criteria.

Hierarchical regression: see hierarchical or sequential entry.

Histogram: A chart which represents the frequency of particular scores or ranges of scores in terms of a set of bars. The height of the bar represents the frequency of this score or range of scores in the data.

Homogeneity of regression slope: The similarity of the regression slope of the covariate on the criterion variable in the different groups of the predictor variable.

Homogeneity of variance: The similarity of the variance of the scores in the groups of the predictor variable.

Homoscedasticity: The similarity of the scatter or spread of the data points around the regression line of best fit in different parts of that line.

Hypothesis: A statement expressing the expected or predicted relationship between two or more variables.

Icicle plot: A graphical representation of the results of a cluster analysis in which x's are used to indicate which variables or clusters are paired at which stage.

Identification: The extent to which the parameters of a structural equation model can be estimated from the original data.

Independence: Events or variables being unrelated to each other.

Independent groups design: A design in which different cases are assigned to different conditions or groups.

Independent *t*-test: A parametric test for determining whether the means of two unrelated or independent groups differ significantly.

Independent variable: A variable which may affect (predict) the values of another variable(s). It is a variable used to form the groups in experimental designs. But it is also used in regression for the variables used to predict the dependent variable.

Inferential statistics: Statistical techniques which help predict the population characteristics from the sample characteristics.

Interaction: This describes outcomes in research which cannot be accounted for on the basis of the separate influences of two or more variables. So, for example, an interaction occurs when two variables have a significant influence when combined.

Interaction graph: A graph showing the relationship of the means of three or more variables.

Interquartile range: The range of the middle 50% of a distribution. By ignoring the extreme quarter in each direction from the mean, the interquartile range is less affected by extreme scores.

Interval data: Data making up a scale in which the distance or interval between adjacent points is assumed to be the same or equal but where there is no meaningful zero point.

Just-identified model: A structural equation model in which the data are just sufficient to estimate its parameters.

Kaiser or Kaiser–Guttman criterion: A statistical criterion in factor analysis for determining the number of factors or components for consideration and possible rotation in which factors or components with eigenvalues of one or less are ignored.

Kendall's tau (τ): An index of the linear association between two ordinal variables. In other words, a correlation coefficient for non-parametric data.

Kolmogorov–Smirnov test for two samples: A non-parametric test for determining whether the distributions of scores on an ordinal variable differ significantly for two unrelated samples.

Kruskal–Wallis test: A non-parametric test for determining whether the mean ranked scores for three or more unrelated samples differ significantly.

Kurtosis: The extent to which the shape of a bell-shaped curve is flatter or more elongated than a normal distribution.

Latent variable: An unobserved variable that is measured by one or more manifest variables or indicators.

Level: Used in analysis of variance to describe the different conditions of an independent variable (or factor). The term has its origins in agricultural research where levels of treatment would correspond to, say, different amounts of fertilizer being applied to crops.

Levels of measurement: A four-fold hierarchical distinction proposed for measures comprising nominal, ordinal, equal interval and ratio.

Levene's test: An analysis of variance on absolute differences to determine whether the variances of two or more unrelated groups differ significantly.

Likelihood ratio chi-square test: A form of chi-square which involves natural logarithms. It is primarily associated with log-linear analysis.

Line graph: A diagram in which lines are used to indicate the frequency of a variable.

Linear association or relationship: This occurs when there is a straight line relationship between two sets of scores. The scattergram for these data will be represented best by a straight line rather than a curved line.

Linear model: A model which assumes a linear relationship between the variables.

LISREL: The name of a particular software designed to carry out linear structural relationship analysis also known as structural equation modelling.

Loading: An index of the size and direction of the association of a variable with a factor or discriminant function of which it is part. A loading is simply the correlation between a variable and the factor or discriminant function.

Log likelihood: An index based on the difference between the frequencies for a category variable(s) and what is predicted on the basis of the predictors (i.e.

the modelled data). The bigger the log likelihood the poorer the fit of the model to the data.

Logarithm: The amount to which a given base number (e.g. 10) has to be multiplied by itself to obtain a particular number. So in the expression 3^2, 2 would be the logarithm for the base 3 which makes 9. Sometimes it is recommended that scores are converted to their logarithms if this results in the data fitting the requirements of the statistical procedure better.

Logistic or logit regression: A version of multiple regression in which the dependent, criterion or outcome variable takes the form of a nominal (category) variable. Any mixture of scores and nominal (category) variables can act as predictors. The procedure uses dummy variables extensively.

Log-linear analysis: A statistical technique for nominal (category) data which is essentially an extension of chi-square where there are three or more independent variables.

Main effect: The effect of an independent or predictor variable on a dependent or criterion variable.

Manifest variable: A variable which directly reflects the measure used to assess it.

Mann–Whitney test: A non-parametric test for seeing whether the number of times scores from one sample are ranked significantly higher than scores from another unrelated sample.

Marginal totals: The marginal totals are the row and column total frequencies in cross-tabulation and contingency tables.

Matched-subjects design: A related design in which participants are matched in pairs on a covariate or where participants serve as their own control. In other words, a repeated or related measures design.

Matrix: A rectangular array of rows and columns of data.

Mauchly's test: A test for determining whether the assumption that the variance–covariance matrix in a repeated measures analysis of variance is spherical or circular.

Maximum likelihood method: A method for finding estimates of the population parameters of a model which are most likely to give rise to the pattern of observations in the sample data.

McNemar test: A test for assessing whether there has been a significant change in the frequencies of two categories on two occasions in the same or similar cases.

Mean: The everyday numerical average score. Thus the mean of 2 and 3 is 2.5.

Mean square: A term for variance estimate used in analysis of variance.

Measure of dispersion: A measure of the variation in the scores such as the variance, range, interquartile range and standard error.

Median: The score which is halfway in the scores ordered from smallest to largest.

Mixed ANOVA: An ANOVA in which at least one independent variable consists of related scores and at least one other variable consists of uncorrelated scores.

Mixed design: See Mixed ANOVA.

Mode: The most commonly occurring score or category.

Moderating or moderator effect: A relationship between two variables which differs according to a third variable. For example, the correlation between age and income may be moderated by a variable such as gender. In other words, the correlation for men and the correlation for women between age and income is different.

Multicollinearity: Two or more independent or predictor variables which are highly correlated.

Multimodal: A frequency distribution having three or more modes.

Multiple correlation or *R*: A form of correlation coefficient which correlates a single score (A) with two or more other scores (B + C) in combination. Used particularly in multiple regression to denote the correlation of a set of predictor variables with the dependent (or outcome) variable.

Multiple regression: A parametric test to determine what pattern of two or more predictor (independent) variables is associated with scores on the dependent variable. It takes into account the associations (correlations) between the predictor variables. If desired, interactions between predictor variables may be included.

Multivariate: Involving more than two variables.

Multivariate analysis of variance (MANOVA): A variant of analysis of variance in which there are two or more *dependent* variables combined. MANOVA identifies differences between groups in terms of the combined dependent variable.

Nagelkerke's *R*²: The amount of variance in the criterion variable accounted for by the predictor variables.

Natural or Napierian logarithm: The logarithms calculated using 2.718 as the base number.

Nested model: A model which is a simpler subset of another model and which can be derived from that model.

Non-parametric test: A statistical test of significance which requires fewer assumptions about the distribution of values in a sample than a parametric test.

Normal distribution: A mathematical distribution with very important characteristics. However, it is easier to regard it as a bell-shaped frequency curve. The tails of the curve should stretch to infinity in both directions but this, in the end, is of little practical importance.

Numeric variables: Variables for which the data are collected in the form of scores which indicate quantity.

Oblique factors: In factor analysis, oblique factors are ones which, during rotation, are allowed to correlate with each other. This may be more realistic than orthogonal rotations. One way of looking at this is to consider height and weight. These are distinct variables but they correlate to some degree. Oblique factors are distinct but they can correlate.

Odds: Obtained by dividing the probability of something occurring by the probability of it not occurring.

Odds ratio: The number by which the odds of something occurring must be multiplied for a one unit change in a predictor variable.

One-tailed test: A version of significance testing in which a strong prediction is made as to the direction of the relationship. This should be theoretically and empirically well founded on previous research. The prediction should be made prior to examination of the data.

Ordinal data: Numbers for which little can be said other than the numbers give the rank order of cases on the variable from smallest to largest.

Orthogonal: Essentially means at right angles.

Orthogonal factors: In factor analysis, orthogonal factors are factors which do not correlate with each other.

Outcome variable: A word used especially in medical statistics to denote the dependent variable. It is also the criterion variable. It is the variable which is expected to vary with variation in the independent variable(s).

Outlier: A score or data point which differs substantially from the other scores or data points. It is an extremely unusual or infrequent score or data point.

Output window: The window of computer software which displays the results of an analysis.

Over-identified model: A structural equation model in which the number of data points is greater than the number of parameters to be estimated, enabling the fit of the model to the data to be determined.

Paired comparisons: The process of comparing each variable mean with every (or most) other variable mean in pairs.

Parameter: A characteristic such as the mean or standard deviation which is based on the population of scores. In contrast, a statistic is a characteristic which is based on a sample of scores.

Parametric: To do with the characteristics of the population.

Parametric test: A statistical test which assumes that the scores used come from a population of scores which is normally distributed.

Part or semi-partial correlation: The correlation between a criterion and a predictor when the predictor's correlation with other predictors is partialled out.

Partial correlation: The correlation between a criterion and a predictor when the criterion's and the predictor's correlation with other predictors have been partialled out.

Participant: Someone who takes part in research. A more appropriate term than the archaic and misleading 'subject'.

Path diagram: A diagram in which the relationships (actual or hypothetical) between variables are presented.

Pathway: A line in a path diagram depicting a relationship between two variables.

Phi: A measure of association between two binomial or dichotomous variables.

Pivot table: A table in SPSS which can be edited.

Planned comparisons: Testing whether a difference between two groups is significant when there are strong grounds for expecting such a difference.

Point biserial correlation: A correlation between a score variable and a binomial (dichotomous) variable – i.e. one with two categories.

Population: All of the scores from which a sample is taken. It is erroneous in statistics to think of the population as people since it is the population of scores on a variable.

Post hoc test: A test to see whether two groups differ significantly when the researcher has no strong grounds for predicting or expecting that they will. Essentially they are unplanned tests which were not stipulated prior to the collection of data.

Power: In statistics the ability of a test to reject the null hypothesis when it is false.

Principal components analysis: Primarily a form of factor analysis in which the variance of each variable is set at the maximum value of 1 as no adjustment has been made for communalities. Probably best reserved for instances in which the correlation matrix tends to have high values which is not common in psychological research.

Probability distribution: The distribution of outcomes expected by chance.

Promax: A method of oblique rotation in factor analysis.

Quantitative research: Research which at the very least involves counting the frequency of categories in the main variable of interest.

Quartimax: A method of orthogonal rotation in factor analysis.

Randomisation: The assignment of cases to conditions using some method of assigning by chance.

Range: The difference between the largest and smallest score of a variable.

Ratio data: A measure for which it is possible to say that a score is a multiple of another score such as 20 being twice 10. Also there should be a zero point on the measure. This is a holy grail of statistical theory which psychologists will never find unless variables such as time and distance are considered.

Recode: Giving a value or set of values another value such as recoding age into ranges of age.

Regression coefficient: The weight which is applied to a predictor variable to give the value of the dependent variable.

Related design: A design in which participants provide data in more than one condition of the experiment. This is where participants serve as their own controls. More rarely, if samples are matched on a pairwise basis to be as similar as possible on a matching variable then this also constitutes a related design if the matching variable correlates with the dependent variable.

Related factorial design: A design in which there are two or more independent or predictor variables which have the same or similar cases in them.

Reliability: Internal reliability is the extent to which items which make up a scale or measure are internally consistent. It is usually calculated either using a form of split-half reliability in which the score for half the items is correlated with the score for the other half of the items (with an adjustment for the shortened length of the scale) or using Cronbach's alpha (which is the average of all possible split-half reliabilities). A distinct form of reliability is test–retest reliability which measures consistency over time.

Repeated-measures design: A design in which the groups of the independent variables have the same or similar cases in them.

Repeated-measures ANOVA: An analysis of variance which is based on one or more related factors having the same or similar cases in them.

Residual: The difference between an observed and expected score.

Residual sum of squares: The sum of squares that are left over after other sources of variance have been removed.

Rotation: see Rotation of factors.

Rotation of factors: This adjusts the factors (axes) of a factor analysis in order to make the factors more interpretable. To do so, the number of high and low factor loadings are maximised whereas the number of middle-sized factor loadings are made minimal. Originally it involved plotting the axes (factors) on graph paper and rotating them physically on the page leaving the factor loadings in the same points on the graph paper. As a consequence, the factor loadings change since these have not moved but the axes have.

Sample: A selection or subset of scores on a variable. Samples cannot be guaranteed to be representative of the population but if they are selected at random then there will be no systematic difference between the samples and the population.

Sampling distribution: The theoretical distribution of a particular size of sample which would result if samples of that size were repeatedly taken from that population.

Saturated model: A model (set of variables) which fully accounts for the data. It is a concept used in log-linear analysis.

Scattergram: see Scatterplot.

Scatterplot: A diagram or chart which shows the relationship between two score variables. It consists of a horizontal and a vertical axis which are used to plot the scores of each individual on both variables.

Scheffé test: A post hoc test used in analysis of variance to test whether two group means differ significantly from each other.

Score statistic: A measure of association in logistic regression.

Scree test: A graph of the eigenvalues of successive factors in a factor analysis. It is used to help determine the 'significant' number of factors prior to rotation. The point at which the curve becomes flat and 'straight' determines the number of 'significant' factors.

Select cases: The name of an SPSS procedure for selecting subsamples of cases based on one or more criteria such as the sex of participants.

Sign test: A non-parametric test which determines whether the number of positive and negative differences between the scores in two conditions with the same or similar cases differ significantly.

Significance level: The probability level at and below which an outcome is assumed to be unlikely due to chance.

Simple regression: A test for describing the size and direction of the association between a predictor variable and a criterion variable.

Skew: A description given to a frequency distribution in which the scores tend to be in one tail of the distribution. In other words, it is a lop-sided frequency distribution compared to a normal (bell-shaped) curve.

Sort cases: The name of an SPSS procedure for ordering cases in the data file according to the values of one or more variables.

Spearman's correlation coefficient: A measure of the size and direction of the association between two variables rank ordered in size.

Sphericity: Similarity of the correlations between the dependent variable in the different conditions.

Split-half reliability: The correlation between the two halves of a scale adjusted for the number of variables in each scale.

SPSS: A computer program which performs many important data analyses and statistical procedures. It can be regarded as the standard program worldwide.

Squared Euclidean distance: The sum of the squared differences between the scores on two variables for the sample.

Standard deviation: Conceptually the average amount by which the scores differ from the mean.

Standard error: Conceptually, the average amount by which the means of samples differ from the mean of the population.

Standard or direct entry: A form of multiple regression in which all of the predictor variables are entered into the analysis at the same time.

Standardised coefficients or weights: The coefficients or weights of the predictors in an equation are expressed in terms of their standardised scores.

Stepwise entry: A form of multiple regression in which variables are entered into the analysis one step at a time. In this way, the most predictive predictor is chosen first, then the second most predictive predictor is chosen second having dealt with the variance due to the first predictor, and so on.

Sum of squares: The total obtained by adding up the squared differences between each score and the mean of that set of scores. The 'average' of this is the variance.

Syntax: Statements or commands for carrying out various procedures in computer software.

Test–retest reliability: The correlation of a measure taken at one point in time with the same (or very similar) measure taken at a different point in time.

Transformation: Ways of adjusting the data to meet the requirements for the data for a particular statistical technique. For example, the data could be changed by taking the square root of each score, turning each score into a logarithm, and so on. Trial and error may be required to find an appropriate transformation.

Two-tailed test: A test which assesses the statistical significance of a relationship or difference in either direction.

Type I error: Accepting the hypothesis when it is actually false.

Type II error: Rejecting the hypothesis when it is actually true.

Under-identified model: A structural equation model in which there are not enough data points to estimate its parameters.

Unique variance: Variance of a variable which is not shared with other variables in the analysis.

Univariate: Involving one variable.

Unplanned comparisons: Comparisons between groups which were not stipulated before the data were collected but after its collection.

Unstandardised coefficients or weights: The coefficients or weights which are applied to scores (as opposed to standardised scores).

Value label: The name or label given to the value of a variable such as 'Female' for '1'.

Variable label: The name or label given to a variable.

Variable name: The name of a variable.

Variable View: The window in SPSS Data Editor which shows the names of variables and their specification.

Variance: The mean of the sum of the squared difference between each score and the mean of the set of scores. It constitutes a measure of the variability or dispersion of scores on a quantitative variable.

Variance–covariance matrix: A matrix containing the variance of the variables and the covariance between pairs of variables.

Variance estimate: The variance of the population of scores calculated from the variance of a sample of scores from that population.

Variance ratio: The ratio between two variances, commonly referred to in ANOVA (analysis of variance).

Varimax: In factor analysis, a procedure for rotating the factors to simplify understanding of the factors which maintains the zero correlation between all of the factors.

Wald statistic: The ratio of the beta coefficient to its standard error. Used in logistic regression.

Weights: An adjustment made to reflect the size of a variable or sample.

Wilcoxon signed-rank test: A non-parametric test for assessing whether the scores from two samples that come from the same or similar cases differ significantly.

Wilks' lambda: A measure, involving the ratio of the within-groups to the total sum of squares, used to determine if the means of variables differ significantly across groups.

Within-subjects design: A correlated or repeated-measures design.

Yates's continuity correction: An outmoded adjustment to a 2×2 chi-square test held to improve the fit of the test to the chi-square distribution.

z-score: A score expressed as the number of standard deviations a score is from the mean of the set of scores.

Index